IT Milestones

Englisch für Computer- und IT-Berufe

Veronica Leary
Klaus-Dieter Praglowski-Leary

in Zusammenarbeit mit
Georg Rempfer
Jörg Rempfer
Dietlind Al-Ishaki

Beratung:
Prof. Ralf Bär
Bereichsleiter Informations-, Elektro- und Medientechnik
Staatliches Seminar für Didaktik und Lehrerbildung (BS) Freiburg

Ernst Klett Schulbuchverlage
Stuttgart · Leipzig

IT Milestones
Englisch für Computer- und IT-Berufe

von Veronica Leary, Klaus-Dieter Praglowski-Leary
in Zusammenarbeit mit Georg Rempfer, Jörg Rempfer, Dietlind Al-Ishaki

Beratung: Prof. Ralf Bär

Werkübersicht

Schülerbuch	978-3-12-801049-6
Workbook	978-3-12-801051-9
Lehrerhandbuch mit Audio-CD	978-3-12-801050-2

1. Auflage 1 5 4 3 2 1 | 2011 2010 2009 2008 2007

Alle Drucke dieser Auflage sind unverändert (und können im Unterricht nebeneinander verwendet werden). Die letzte Zahl bezeichnet das Jahr des Druckes.

Internetadresse: www.klett.de

Redaktion: Volker Wendland, Astrid Keller
Gestaltungskonzept und Umschlaggestaltung: B2, Andreas Staiger, Stuttgart
Gestaltung: Ulrike Wollenberg
Reproduktion: Meyle + Müller GmbH + Co. KG, Pforzheim
Druck: Himmer AG, Augsburg
Printed in Germany.
ISBN 978-3-12-801049-6

9 783128 010496

Vorwort

Im Zuge der zunehmenden Globalisierung ist Englisch der Dreh- und Angelpunkt für viele Berufe geworden. Dies gilt insbesondere für die IT-Berufe. Ganz gleich, ob es sich um Schlüsselwörter von Programmiersprachen, das Erstellen von Dokumentationen oder das Versenden von E-Mails ins Ausland handelt, die Kommunikation läuft vielfach auf Englisch ab. Der Arbeitsmarkt braucht deshalb kompetente Fachkräfte, für die die englische Sprache ein vertrautes Kommunikationsmittel ist. Um diesem Anspruch gerecht zu werden, steigen auch die Anforderungen an das Unterrichtsfach Englisch in der beruflichen Aus- und Weiterbildung.

IT Milestones (das Lehrwerk ist eine Überarbeitung und Aktualisierung des bewährten Lehrwerks *Fachkurs Computer- und IT-Berufe*) setzt sich aktiv mit den wachsenden Anforderungen an den Fremdsprachenunterricht auseinander. Englische Grund- und Fachkenntnisse im Umfeld der Informatik und allgemeine kommunikative Kompetenzen in der Fremdsprache werden nicht isoliert dargeboten, sondern sind in realitätsnahe, für angehende Computerfachleute relevante Situationen eingeflochten. Auf diese Weise gewinnen die Lernenden Sicherheit im Umgang mit der Fremdsprache im Berufsalltag.

IT Milestones ist wie folgt aufgebaut:
Die erste Unit (Introduction) dient als Einstieg in die IT-Thematik und zugleich als Einführung in allgemeines Büroenglisch.
Die zehn Hauptunits sind thematisch gegliedert und orientieren sich an den Lernfeldern des Rahmenlehrplans. Die Zuordnung zu den einzelnen Lernfeldern ist im Inhaltsverzeichnis übersichtlich dargestellt. Themen, wie z. B. *Hardware*, *Peripheral Devices*, *System Software*, *Networking*, *Internet*, *Programming*, *System Administration*, *Security*, *Presentions* und *Jobs in Computing* werden von einem weiterführenden Text (Further reading) ergänzt. Alle Units (mit Ausnahme der einführenden Unit) schließen mit einem Unitteil *(Language and grammar)*, in dem sprachliche Aspekte (z. B. *False friends*, *Idioms*) und Themen aus der Grammatik im Vordergrund stehen.

Abwechslungsreiche Lesetexte, Übungen zum Hörverständnis, Partnerarbeit und Rollenspiel, Mediationsaufgaben sowie eine Auswahl an Schreibübungen bilden ein vielfältiges Angebot, um den Stoff intensiv zu trainieren.

IT Milestones orientiert sich am Europäischen Referenzrahmen und den dort beschriebenen Kompetenzen. Welche Kompetenzen in den einzelnen Aufgaben schwerpunktmäßig geübt werden, ist durch die deutliche Kennzeichnung der Aufgaben in allen Units (mit Ausnahme des Language and grammar-Teils) ersichtlich:
R (= Rezeption, mündlich wie schriftlich)
P (= Produktion, mündlich wie schriftlich)
I (= Interaktion)
M (= Mediation)

Hörverstehensübungen sind mit CD-Symbol ( ) gekennzeichnet. Einige Aufgaben zum Hörverständnis sind auch in der jeweiligen Unit abgedruckt und können ggf. auch als Leseübung verwendet werden.
Die Tapescripts zu den Hörverständnisaufgaben und die Lösungen und Zusatzinformationen für die Lehrkräfte befinden sich im Lehrerbuch.

IT Milestones ist für den Englischunterricht an gewerblich-technischen Berufsschulen, Berufsfachschulen, Fachschulen für IT, Berufskollegs und an Gymnasien des wirtschaftlichen oder technischen Zweigs geeignet. Daneben kann das Lehrwerk in allen IT-ausgerichteten Englischkursen eingesetzt werden. Das Lehrwerk deckt die Stufen B1 und B2 des Referenzrahmens des Europarats ab.

All-In-Ones

LINUX

Software Coming Soon

INTERNET CAFE

Introduction

Computer basics and office skills

1 Where are computers used?

P **a** **Draw a mind map showing places where computers are used.**

Example:

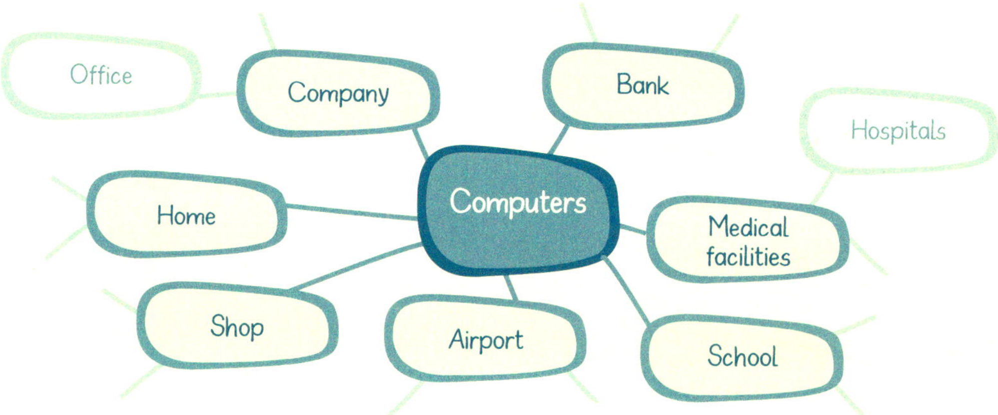

R **b** **The following sentences describe what people use computers for. Match them with possible places (see your mind map) where computers are used.**

Example: To teach not just programming, but a wide variety of subjects, as well as keeping a database of students, teachers and materials. → School

1. To save information about customers' money, to monitor cash machines and to execute financial transactions.
2. To send and receive e-mails, shopping, booking trips and entertainment.
3. To do the inventory, order goods, and administrate personnel data.
4. To provide information about gas, air pressure and oil and offer alternative routes.
5. To handle correspondence, make spreadsheets and presentations.
6. To make technical drawings and plans, program robots, and forecast production costs.
7. To monitor flight and reservation information and control air traffic.

1.1. Computer habits

R **a** **Listening for gist. You are going to hear five different people talking about how they use the computer. Listen and decide if the following statements are true or false.**

1 2 3 4 5

1. The first speaker works as the head of a car manufacturing firm.
2. The second speaker uses the computer more for private rather than work purposes.
3. The third speaker uses a computer for a variety of private and business reasons.
4. The fourth speaker has always used a computer at work.
5. The fifth speaker is the person in charge of all computer related problems at work.

R **b** **Listen again and and then answer the questions below.**

1. What does the first speaker's company make?
2. How does the first speaker feel about the amount of e-mails he receives daily?
3. What does the second speaker do with his computer?
4. What sorts of business related tasks does the third speaker use a computer for?
5. What do the members of the fourth speaker's family use the computer for?
6. Why doesn't the fifth speaker have a private computer?

I **c** **Interview your partner about his/her computer habits. Ask the following questions:**

Questions

Answers

1

Do you have a computer at home? How old is it? What kinds of peripheral devices (printer, scanner etc.) does it have?

Yes, I do. /No, I don't. It's … months/years old. I've got a …, but I haven't got …

2

Do you have access to a computer at work or school? What kind of computer is it?

Yes, I have. /No, I haven't. I'm not sure, but I think it's a …,

3

How often do you use a computer? How many hours a day/week …?

Well, I never/ seldom/sometimes/ usually/often/always use a computer when I'm at home.

4

What do you use the computer for?

I use it mainly for writing letters/ playing games/ designing …/…

5

Do you play games/surf/do online bank/send e-mails?

Yes, I do. /No, I don't.

6

What do you like/ dislike about working with a computer?

Well, what I like best about it is …, but I hate …

I/P **d** **Report back to the group about your partner's computer habits.**

Richard has got …

needs a computer to …

has access …

often uses …

spends up to …

1.2 What is a computer?

Computers have become an indispensable part of our modern world and play a role in almost every facet of our lives. There are built-in microprocessors in our home appliances, televisions and cars. MP3 players are specialized computers for processing music files, a GPS one for handling global positioning system signals and there are special computers, such as Nintendos, just for playing games.

But what exactly are computers? Mega machines? Data processors? Super calculators? Yes, they are all of these and more. But when people talk about computers they typically mean the personal computer, or PC.

A PC can be defined as a general purpose information processing tool, i.e. it can be used for a variety of tasks such as printing documents, sending e-mails, or programming. Basically the work of a computer can be divided into three basic steps. First, data or information is input or fed into the computer, either by a person via a keyboard or mouse, from a device such as a CD or through a network. The computer then processes or manipulates this data. The final step is to output the data, for example, by displaying it on the monitor, storing it, or sending it along a network.

Software is the term used for the data and programs, the "soft" or intangible elements of the system. Data refers to concrete information (numbers, words, images, etc.) while programs are the instructions on how to process this data. The "hard" or physical – mechanical and electronic – parts of a computer system are called hardware.

R **a** **Answer the following questions on the text.**

1. What are some different kinds of computers used in daily life?
2. What, in your opinion, is a good definition of a computer?
3. What are the three basic steps involved in computing?
4. What is software as opposed to hardware?

R **b** **Match the following brief definitions to some of the main software and hardware components a typical desktop computer system is made up of.**

1. RAM (Random Access Memory)
2. BIOS (Basic-Input-Output-System)
3. Motherboard
4. ROM (Read Only Memory)
5. OS (Operating System)
6. Hard Disk
7. CPU (Central Processing Unit)
8. Caching

a. The "brain" of the computer system which oversees all processes.
b. It is used to temporarily store current information.
c. A permanent type of memory storage.
d. A type of ROM for basic communication when the computer is turned on.
e. The storing of frequently used data in fast RAM directly linked to the CPU.
f. This is the main circuit board that the internal components connect to.
g. This is large-capacity permanent storage to hold programs and documents.
h. This is the basic software that lets the user interface with the computer.

1.3 Globalization and informatization

Even though the term globalization typically refers to economic relationships, it can also have broad social and cultural impact. Ideas, customs, and cultural movements all follow closely the trade of goods across national boundaries. Globalization as a *fact* refers to the real economic links, institutions, and facts, while globalization as a *value* aims to reinforce the integration of markets, pools of capital, and industries. Many people, however, seem to understand the term as referring not just to greater economic integration, but rather cultural and social integration.

Informatization refers to the process whereby information technologies, such as the world-wide web, have transformed economic and social relations and reduced cultural and economic barriers. There are, for example, now over one billion Internet users world-wide. It also refers to other related technologies that have to do with the transfer of information. These include more traditional media technologies, such as film, television, and telecommunications.

The two concepts, globalization and informatization, explain different concepts, but their social, political, economic, and cultural functions overlap. Although globalization ultimately refers to the integration of economic institutions, much of this integration occurs through the channels of technology. Although international trade is not a new phenomenon, the introduction of new communications technologies has sped up the pace and range of trade.

On the other hand, globalization allows the spread of information technologies, and creates a world wide market and clear strategic incentives for adopting information technologies.

Though globalization and informatization have clear advantages for human societies, there are many potential problems. On the positive side, globalization and informatization can empower individuals and societies to

participate and compete in the international arena for economic, political, and cultural resources. It allows for the greater flow of information, even from places and to people who have traditionally been cut off from global communication.
Moreover, there is a spread of information about lifestyles, religions, and culture. For example, the rise of the internet allows commerce to take place from anywhere, to anywhere, and is open to anyone. Consumers around the world can get access to information previously limited to the developed world. The telecommunications and computer networks also allow for unprecedented global activism. Nonprofit activist groups, for example, use technological means to recruit volunteers, teach about environmental and human rights activism, publicize events, and raise money.
Information technology can also be used to impart power and opportunities to communities living on the edge of the globe. Information technologies, including computing resources and telecommunications, as well as more low-tech media forms, are now more readily available for the purposes of national and local economic development. Some also argue that the new forces will help to democratize regimes that must either allow information or risk losing out on economic growth.
On the negative side, however, these two forces threaten to undermine centuries of tradition, local autonomy, and cultural integrity. The internet, for example, is overwhelmingly an English language medium. Anyone who wants to take active part in cyberspace has to have a working knowledge of English. Moreover, globalization establishes a global economic system in which those with the most capital are best able to profit from the global market.
Finally, one of the potentially most harmful effects of the forces of globalization and informatization is that a conflict is created between the new global economic order and the local interests. Though an individual might refuse to cooperate, the aggressive nature of the forces of globalization and informatization make it impossible for whole societies to stand against it and still prosper.

M **a** **Read the text and summarize the main points in German.**

R/P **b** **Read the text again and answer the following questions in your own words.**

1. What does globalization in general mean?
2. What is the difference between globalization as a fact and as a value?
3. What does the term informatization refer to?
4. What forms of media are encompassed by informatization?
5. How do globalization and informatization interact and impact on each other? Can you think of another example aside from the one given in the text?
6. What are some of the positive aspects of globalization and informatization? Are they all economic in nature?
7. What are some of the negative aspects of the twin forces of globalization and informatization?
8. What is your personal opinion? Do you view the two factors more positively or more critically? Why?

2 Office skills

2.1 Telephoning

I **a** **Complete the dialogue using a suitable form/tense of the marked verbs. Listen and check.**

Victoria: Hello.

John: Hello, this **be** John Stovers from Training Unlimited. I **like** to speak to Ms. Gonzales, please.

Victoria: **speak**.

John: Good morning, Ms. Gonzales. I **call** about the letter you **send** us enquiring whether there **be** currently any positions open for software trainers.

Victoria: That **be** right.

John: Well, I **be** afraid I **not have** any permanent position to offer you at the moment but we **look** always for qualified personnel. **consider** you also working on a freelance basis?

Victoria: That depends.

John: At the moment I **have** two evening courses – one in Windows and the other in Access that **start** soon. **be** you interested?

Victoria: Definitely. I **work** with both programs so I **be** sure I **not have** any problems.

John: Good. Perhaps we **meet** to discuss the details some time – let's say early next week. **have** you time on Monday at three?

Victoria: Monday at three? That **be** fine.

John: Good. I **show** you the computer classroom you **use** and **introduce** you to Jeff, our systems administrator.

Victoria: Great. I **look forward** to that.

John: **see** you on Monday at three, then.

Victoria: Till Monday.

I **b** **Work in pairs and make up dialogues using the phrases below.**

Phrases Telephoning

Incoming calls:
- ITSALES GmbH. Good morning. /Good afternoon.
- Who's calling?
- Hold the line, please. I'll put you through.
- I'm sorry, Mr/Ms … is not in /in his/her office.
- What is it about? Perhaps I can help you.
- Can I take a message?
- Thank you for calling.

Outgoing calls:
- I'd like to speak to Ms Summer.
- When will he/she be back?
- Can I leave a message?
- Can you tell Mr/Ms that …?
- I'll ring back later.
- I'm phoning about your order No. … of 1 June.
- I look forward to hearing from you.
- See you next week! (informal)

2.2 Making appointments on the phone

Setting up an appointment is usually done on the phone and can be a tricky business as you need to be able to understand names, dates, places and so on.

I **Study the phrases below, look at the following diaries (Student A: page 15, Student B: page 16) and practice making appointments with a partner.**

Example: Hi, Leo, this is Greg. Do you think we could get together sometime next week? I'll be in Ludwigsburg all day Wednesday but I would have time on … at …

Phrases Setting up a date/time

- I'd like to make an appointment with Mr /Ms …
- Would three-fifteen on Wednesday the 4th be convenient?
- We could meet on …
- I can (can't) manage Thursday at 10. (What about 10: 30?)
- I could fit you in on Friday at 11.

Positive response
(in descending order of formality/politeness)

- Three-fifteen on Wednesday? I'll look forward to that.
- That's fine. Three-fifteen on Wednesday, then.
- Thursday at ten is great.
- No problem. See you on …

Negative response
(in descending order of formality/politeness)

- I hate to inconvenience you but .... Would ... be possible instead?
- I'm afraid Wednesday at 3:15 is a bit difficult. Could we possibly meet on ... instead?
- Wednesday, did you say? That's a problem. How about Thursday at 10 instead?
- Thursday's no good. Make it Friday at two.

Confirming/Problems

- Sorry, I didn't catch that.
- Could you repeat that, please?
- Could you spell your name, please?
- Did you say thirteen or thirty?
- Could you speak up a bit?
- I'm afraid the line is busy.
- I'm afraid you've got the wrong number.

Student A

November

	3 Mon	4 Tue	5 Wed	6 Thu	7 Fri	8 Sat	9 Sun
08 am							Klaus' birthday
09 am	teleteaching	catch up e-mails?			Breakfast meeting with staff		
10 am		project group meeting		return from Ludwigsburg		tennis	
11 am	Video-conference/ Wagner et. al				Chinese visitors		
noon			Ludwigsburg				
01 am	Sales meeting			Prepare presentation/ Chinese visitors		shopping?	
02 am		Interview new TA candidates (3 or 4?)					
03 am							
04 am							
05 am							

Student B

November							
	3 Mon	**4** Tue	**5** Wed	**6** Thu	**7** Fri	**8** Sat	**9** Sun
08 am							
09 am	e-mail		Presentation for new IT trainees				
10 am	staff meeting						
11 am	Video-conference/ Wagner et. al						
noon				Lunch – Dr. Scheele	Seminar Fri–Sat in Düsseldorf		
01 am		Holzhausen/ Logistics					
02 am	project planning meeting			Videoconference re: sale of production line 3 to Czech plant			
03 am							
04 am							
05 am	Teleteaching						

2.3 Problems on the phone

R **a** Listen to the CD and write down the names, addresses and numbers you hear.

R **b** Listen again and check your notes.

I **c** Work in pairs and practise making appointments:

1. First each student makes a rough outline of their schedule for the coming week.
2. With your partner now try and find a convenient date for one or more of the following aktivities: a meeting/telephone conference/cinema date.
3. Move on to a new partner to make more appointments.

3 Conversational tools

3.1 Introductions and small talk

R **a** **Choose a suitable phrase from the boxes below to complete the dialogues. Then listen to the CD to check your answers.**

Dialogue 1

VB: Hello, may I … myself? My name is Victoria Boxer from Betasystems.
GH: Pleased to … you, Ms. Boxer. … Greg Demmer from Longman Incorporated. I don't think you've … my colleague Thomas Wight yet either. Thomas, … is Ms. Boxer from Betasystems.
TW: No, I haven't. How do you …, Ms. Baxter.
VB: Oh, call me Victoria, Ms. Baxter sounds so … .

formal • this • met • I'm • meet • introduce • do

Dialogue 2

A: I … you're from Aberdeen, is that right?
B: Yes, I am.
A: What's the weather … there at this time of the year? Rather rainy, I suppose.
B: Oh, not so bad. We had our share of … days in the past month but the … was shining when I left for the airport. And what's the … been like here?
A: A bit dry actually, not really good for my garden.
B: Oh, so you're a gardener. What do you go in for? Vegetables or more …?

flowers • weather • wet • hear • like • sun

Dialogue 3

A: Have you got a … ?
B: … but I'm a bit … at the moment. Could you get … to me in a few hours?
A: Sure, no … . I'll call you … .

problem • later • rushed • minute • so sorry • back

P/I **b** **Work in pairs. Make up dialogues based on the following scenarios. Use the phrases in the box below and on page 19. Listen and compare your dialogues with the examples.**

Scenario 1
You are out shopping with your brother/sister when you run into a new colleague of yours from France who only speaks English. Do the introductions.

Scenario 2
Your boss has requested you to meet a very important customer at the airport. Introduce yourself.

Scenario 3
You're lunching with a colleague from your company's joint venture in China. Make small talk about food/eating habits.

Scenario 4
You're with some key suppliers from South America and the World Football Championship is on. Talk football.

Scenario 5
You wanted to leave the office early and have a number of important calls to make. A colleague stops by to chat. Try to put him/her off politely.

Phrases Introducing

Introducing oneself

Less formal
Hi, my name's Katy.
Hello, I'm Katy/call me Katy.

More formal
Good morning, my name is Ms. Barth.
I'd like to take this opportunity to introduce myself. I'm Katherine Barth.
May I introduce myself? My name is Ms. Katherine Barth.

Introducing other people

Less formal
George, this is Susi. Susi, George here.
You two haven't met yet, have you? George, this is my sister Susi. Susi this is George, my new colleague.

More formal
George, may I introduce our sales representative in the Far East, Ms. Baxter? Ms. Baxter, this is George Simmons, head of the purchasing department.
Dr. Hendel? May I introduce you to my new administrative assistant, Ms. Wiener. Ms. Wiener, I'd like you to meet Dr. Hendel, our financial chief executive officer.

Phrases Small talk

Making small talk

It's been a beautiful/warm/wet/cold … day/evening/week/month … , hasn't it?
(for out-of-town visitors) So you're from Estonia/Indonesia/Athens … . What's it like there at this time of year?
I hear baseball/soccer/tennis/basketball … is big in (partner's city or country).
That's a nice/I like your bag/bracelet/jacket. Where did you get it?

Putting people off

I'm so sorry/I hate to put you off but I'm really rushed/busy right now.
Maybe we can discuss the matter next week/later/when I have more time.

Can you get back to me in … hours/days/weeks/months?
Can I get back to you in …?

Could we put this on hold for … hours/days/weeks/months?
Let's put this on hold for …

3.2 Politeness

M **a** **How would you translate the following German phrases into English? Match them to their English equivalents.**

1. Hätten Sie was dagegen, wenn ich …?	a. I hate to ask you, but …
2. Gern geschehen.	b. Why don't we …?
3. Können wir nicht …?	c. I'd prefer/I'd rather …
4. Mir wäre es lieber/Ich würde lieber …	d. Do you mind/Would you mind if I …?
5. Es tut mir Leid, aber …	e. My pleasure.
6. Es kommt darauf an.	f. I'm afraid that's not …
7. Ich frage mich, ob …	g. I'm sorry, but …
8. Übrigens, …	h. That all depends.
9. Prima Idee!	i. I was wondering if …
10. Ich fürchte, das ist nicht …	j. By the way, …
11. Ich weiß, Sie haben zu tun, aber …	k. Great idea!
12. Ich frage ungern, aber …	l. Speaking of which/Talking of …
13. Danke für den Vorschlag.	m. Could you do me a favour?
14. Könnten Sie mir einen Gefallen tun?	n. Thanks for the suggestion.
15. Da wir gerade davon sprechen …	o. I know you're busy, but …

P/I **b** **Politeness is more than a matter of simply mouthing "please" and "thank you"; showing genuine consideration and knowing when and how to change the topic as well as "softening" strategies when requesting, rejecting and complaining are also important.**
Make mini-dialogues using the phrases below.

Phrases Politeness

Changing the topic
Talking of/speaking of families, books, politics …
That reminds me of the time …
By the way, have you ever …

Softening strategies
Could you possibly/by any chance lend me your mobile?
I was wondering if you …
I'm awfully sorry but …
Actually, the position has already been filled, I'm afraid.

P/I **c** **Study the following phrases and practice making requests and suggestions.**

Phrases Requests

	Request	Response +	Response –
least formal	I need help (quick!)	What's wrong? I'm on my way.	
	Could you do me a favour, please? Could you lend/give/help me …?	Of course/Sure/No problem!	That all depends.
	Do you mind lending/giving …	Of course not.	I'm sorry, but …
	I know you're busy but … I hate to ask …	Not at all.	Don't be silly.
Most formal	Would you be so kind as to …	If I can be of service. Certainly, my pleasure.	I'm afraid I can't … /I'm sorry but … (always give a reason)

Phrases Suggestions

	Suggestion	Positive reaction	Negative reaction
informal	Let's …	Yeah, great.	No way.
formal	You/we could … Why don't you … Shall we …	Sure. Why not? That's a good idea! Thanks for the suggestion.	Let's … instead. I'd rather … I'd prefer to … I'm afraid I can't …

3.3 Talking about your job and your company

Interview your partner. Ask them about their training, job duties and place of work. Present your partner to the group. Make use of the phrases in the box below to answer your partner's questions.

Questions:

- What are you training as?
- What are your job duties/ responsibilities?
- Who's in charge of …/Who's responsible for …?
- What products or services does …?
- Who do you report to?
- What kind of company …?

Phrases **Training, jobs, companies**

Jobs, responsibilities

- I'm an IT trainee.
- I'm training to become a(n) management assistant in informatics / management assistent in IT-systems / IT specialist/assistant manager for office communication/IT assistant sales manager.
- I attend vocational training school/take part in workshops for …
- I work at Techno Ltd./for a small software house/in the networking field.
- My responsibilites/duties include …
- I'm responsible for …
- I often/sometimes/always have to work overtime/travel/meet with colleagues/talk to customers/install software/troubleshoot problems.

Your company

- My company produces/manufactures/offers/specializes in …
- The headquarters of our company are located in …
- There are … departments …
- We have branches in …
- Our subsidiaries are located in …
- The company employs …
- The staff consists of …

Organigram

- Mr/Ms is the managing director.
- Mr/Ms … is the head of the marketing/accounts/human resources/ research and development department.
- He/She reports to Mr/Ms …
- He/She is assistant to Ms Winter.

4 Written correspondence

4.1 Types of business correspondence

R **Identify the following phrases as being appropriate for which of the following types of business correspondence:**

Example: Please find the enclosed cheque for € … (Payment)

Enquiry • Order • Invitation • Complaint • Payment • Offer • Delivery

1. We saw an advertisement for your digital cameras in PC WORLD.
2. We are placing the following order: (detail re price, quantity etc.)
3. Your service has been very dissatisfactory of late.
4. We can quote a 10 percent discount for orders over 200.
5. Please send us the catalogue and price list of your latest drivers.
6. Please send the items listed on the enclosed order form.
7. Delivery is essential by Monday the 24th of July.
8. You are cordially invited to attend our Open House on …
9. I expect to receive full and immediate reimbursement for the faulty software.
10. As agreed, payment is to be made by cheque/bankers draft/postal order on receipt of your invoice/the goods.
11. Come and visit us at our booth in Hall J at CEBIT – Oct. 10-14th.
12. Thank you for your letter of 15 June enquiring about our new range of DVD drives.
13. Please send us details about your terms of delivery.
14. Please find the enclosed cheque for € …

4.2. E-mail and fax

Though letter writing is still an important business skill, faxes and, above all, e-mails have all but replaced formal letters for the day-to-day communication within and between companies. Understandably there is a certain amount of insecurity about what is considered acceptable when faxing or e-mailing within a business environment, and opinions can differ.

R/I a **Read the following statements on e-mails and decide if you agree or disagree. Discuss the statements in pairs or the group at large.**

1. It's okay to leave out a formal salutation such as "Dear Sir" in an e-mail.
2. The proper form of address in an e-mail is "Hi" or "Hello".
3. You don't have to bother to correct any misspellings or typos in an e-mail – speed is what counts.
4. The writing style of faxes and e-mails is generally more informal than that of business letters.
5. Nobody cares whether you are polite or friendly when e-mailing or faxing.
6. Passing on someone's e-mail address to a third party without their permission is perfectly acceptable.

R **b** **Match the following elements of an e-mail message header.**

1. Subject:	a. Tue, 18 Oct 200_ 15:35:36 - (EST)
2. Cc: (copy)	b. Martine Fäustl bvv@vhs-bayern.de
3. Date and Time:	c. European Language Conference
4. From: (sender)	d. bluestreak@elbe.de
5. Bcc: (further copy)	e. icc_europe@aol.com
6. To: (recipient)	f. monika@vhs-regensdorf.de

P **c** **After reading the following e-mail you decide that it is too informal for business purposes. Rewrite the mail using more formal language.**

To: "Klaus Blass" klaus.blass@thorenterprises.com
From: "Henry Zeiss" henry.zeiss@seeway.com
Subject: Confirmation of Order

Hi Martin!

Just wanted to drop a line to let ya know that we got your order DRF# 20918 – cool! You can figure on the stuff getting there by Friday. Like you wanted, we are sending it along asap. By the way, we're happy to let you know that we can also knock 10 % off the price. How about that!?

See you around.

Regards,
Henry

P **d** **Look back to "Making appointments on the phone" on pages 14-16. Assume you haven't been able to reach your partner on the phone to make an appointment. You decide to send a fax instead. Adopt either Student A's or Student B's schedule and send a fax giving a brief outline of your week's appointments and suggesting a date.**

P **e** **Look at the dialogue on page 13. Assume you are John Stovers and have not been able to reach Victoria Gonzales on the phone. Send her an e-mail instead with information about the courses in question and suggesting an appointment.**

R **f** **Listen to the following recording of numbers and dates. Write and punctuate them the way an English speaker would.**

4.3 The form of a business letter

R **a** **Identify the following parts of a letter.**

Example: [1] = company logo

Model business letter

[1] ITSOFT GmbH

[2] Samensstraße 14
93045 Regensburg

Telephone: 0941-202-3156
Fax number: 0941-202-3859
e-mail: rainer.schmidt@itsoft.de

[3] Susan Webster
Sales Manager
Softi Sells
2309 Hollywood Boulevard
Los Angeles, California
USA 31860

[4] October 11, 200…

[5] *Raid* – Anti-virus software

[6] Dear Ms Webster

[7] In reference to our telephone conversation on October 5th I would like to confirm my company's interest in your new anti-virus software *Raid*, order No. 10736589. We have received and tested the demonstration version you sent us and are very satisfied with the results.
A retail price of $29.95 per package is listed in the product description you enclosed. I would like to know what percent discount you offer for orders of fifty or more. Could you please send me your offer for fifty packages, including shipping and packaging costs?
Our company would also be interested in your selection of adventure game software. Please send us any relevant material in the way of brochures, price lists and possible demo versions.
I am looking forward to hearing from you. Please note my e-mail address above.

[8] Yours sincerely

[9] Rainer Schmidt
Purchasing Department

date • company logo • recipient's name and address • sender's name and department • complimentary close • opening salutation • subject line • body of the letter • company address

P **b** **Write an answer to the model letter above. Make up details as required. See the Info Box on page 26 for help.**

4.4 Letter of complaint

R **a** **Complete the following letter with the words in the box below.**

receiving • extension • disconnected • futile • ignored • claimed • delivery • placed • recent • results • enclosed • considerable

Dear Dr De Rosso,

On several occasions I have ordered software from your firm with satisfactory 1 . My once positive opinion has been severely shaken, however, due to the gross incompetence and downright rudeness in my most 2 dealings with SOFTSALES.
On February 5th of this year I 3 an online order for the following software products:

15 xDebian GNU/Linux
10 xPAC Back-up UPS 400
2 xpost-it software notes 2.0 Office

Although your database 4 that all of the above products were in stock and available for immediate 5 , this was not the case. Only 5 of the 15 Debian GNU/Linux ordered were 6 although we were billed for all 15. (See enclosed copy of our credit card bill for February 20th). E-mails sent on March 5th, March 21st and April 5th pointing out the error and requesting reimbursement were completely 7 .
Dialing your hotline has been equally 8 . Twice I've found myself in a call queue only to be abruptly 9 . On the one occasion I did manage to get through I was very rudely treated by a member of your technical staff. He rang off without either forwarding my call or giving me the 10 number.
As the systems administrator for a small but growing organization I am responsible for the purchase of a 11 amount of software yearly. Your firm's range of software is attractive but if the current deplorable state of affairs with regard to service persists, I have no other option than to transfer our custom elsewhere.
I expect to receive full and immediate reimbursement for the money overcharged us which amounts to 375.21 pounds.
Thank you and I look forward to 12 your check by June 1st.

Yours sincerely,

Jane Howards

P **b** **Write a letter of complaint based on the following guidelines. (Suggested topics: defective hardware/bug-laden software/non-delivery of goods ordered/non-payment for services/poor or rude services)**

Letter of complaint (Guidelines)
Dear Mr/Ms ... comment: Be polite but personal – direct your letter by name to a high ranking person.
I find it absolutely unacceptable/I was appalled/very shocked to learn/dissatisfied ... comment: Take a firm stance right from the start.
The software is bug-ridden/the locking device is faulty/the noise is deafening comment: Back up your complaint with hard facts and relevant details.
I talked to your head office but .../I was put in a call queue/ignored/wrote to a number of ... comment: Include the steps you have already undertaken to no avail.
Our company buys .../I was planning ... comment: Hint that they risk losing your business which is well worth having.
I look forward to hearing from you by .../I hope at the latest .../If not I will be forced ... comment: Firmly place the ball in their court with a deadline or even threat.

INFO BOX How to write a business letter

1. Include a heading.
2. You should plan what you want to write in advance and make an outline.
3. Your sentences should be short and to the point.
4. You should structure each new point in a separate paragraph. In a memo it's a good idea to number your paragraphs.
5. Use simple, direct language. Avoid flowery phrases and circumlocution.
6. Your layout should be attractive and straight-forward, not cluttered.
7. Always go over your text checking for grammar, punctuation and spelling mistakes.
8. Make your letter as direct and to the point as possible. Avoid unnecessary phrases and asides.
9. Include all the necessary information such as dates, account numbers and names.
10. Courtesies such as an opening salutation, a complimentary close and polite phrases are important.

Unit 1

Hardware, bits and codes

The term "hardware" refers to the physical parts of a computer and its peripherals as opposed to "software" that executes within the hardware.

1 The motherboard

R/P **a** **Complete the following introductory text with the correct words from the box on the right.**

The motherboard

The motherboard is a printed 1 board (PCB) that contains and controls the components responsible for 2 data. These include the CPU, memory, and basic 3 for the system. It also has a Real-time 4 (RTC), ROM, BIOS, CMOS RAM, RAM sockets, 5 for attaching devices to a bus, CPU sockets or slots, cache RAM slot or sockets, jumpers, keyboard controller, interrupts, 6 connectors, and external connectors.

Decisive for a computer's performance are the 7 of the bus and its components. A "bare bones" system refers to the ribbon cables, 8 supply, CPU, and RAM of the motherboard. The systems clock 9 the operation of the bus and other components while the 10 allow a user to set different clock rates to work with the CPU, among other things.

power • internal • processing • synchronizes • jumpers • architecture • bus slots • circuit • controllers • clock

R **b** **Match the elements of the motherboard below to their correct definitions.**

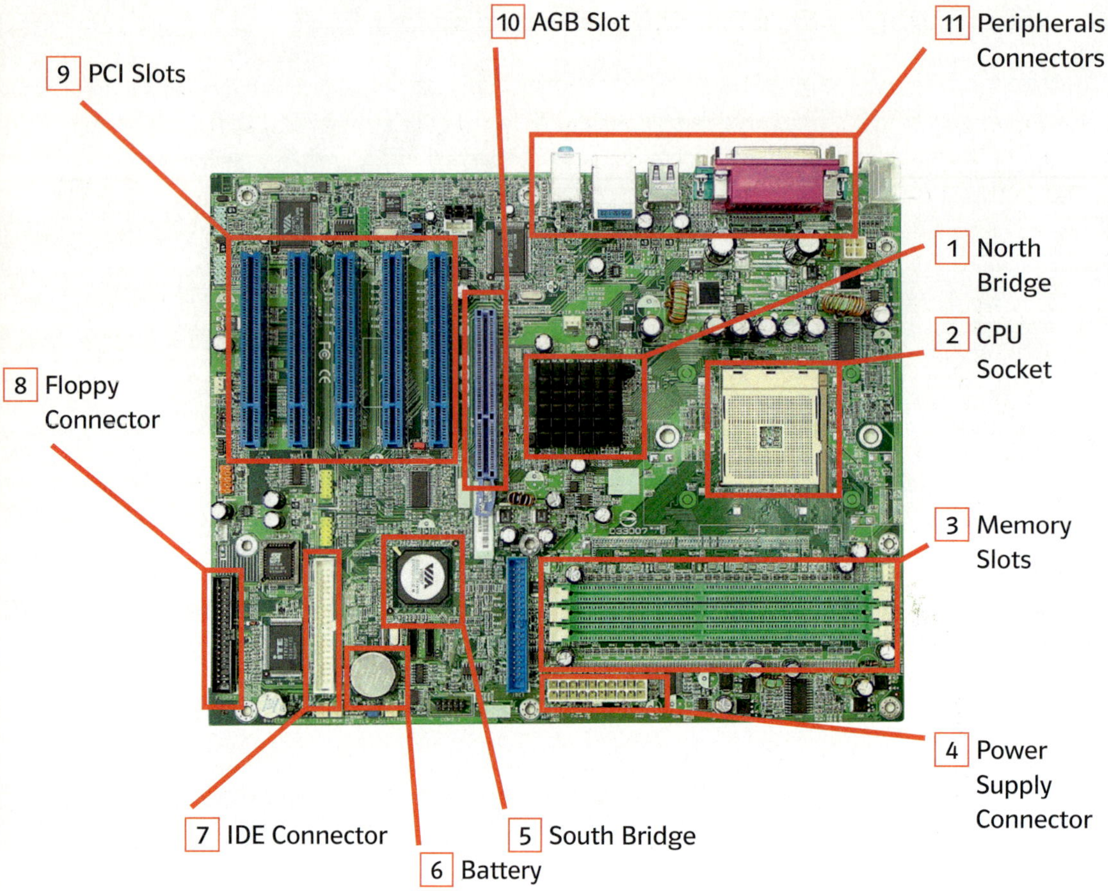

A They hold the memory which stores the executable commands and the data, which are being processed.

B A sort of "mediator" chip, which controls the flow of data between the CPU and other parts of the computer as well as its peripherals. (See also: "North Bridge")

C It is based on PCI, but is designed especially for the throughput demands of 3-D graphics.

D The electrical power source is plugged in there.

E It holds the computing part of the computer, also called the "processor".

F All external devices are attached here. The one shown is the LPT. The ones next to it are for network connection, keyboard, mouse etc.

G This is an interface for mass storage devices such as hard disks, CD-ROMs. One port can hold up to two devices.

H During the time the computer is switched off, this provides the electrical power necessary for the clock and the basic settings of the motherboard.

I The mediator chip or chipset, controlling all internal data flow between the CPU and other parts of the motherboard, such as RAM and AGP / PCI.

J These are standard interfaces for additional hardware components such as TV-cards. Faster versions are called PCI-Express.

K A portable storage device can be plugged in there.

R/P **c** **You want to print a text file. You do this by clicking on the file in the context menu and then clicking on the print button to get a printout of the file. But what happens inside the computer? Put the following steps into the correct order.**

1. After being executed by the CPU, the text processing software transfers the text file via the IDE interface – South Bridge – North Bridge – CPU – North Bridge into RAM.

2. The operating system registers the mouse click on the printer icon. This initiates the transfer of the word processing software from the hard disk to the RAM so that the CPU can run its code.

3. Finally, the word processing software creates a bitmap image of the page and transfers this to the Printer Port for sending to the printer. Data path: RAM-CPU-North Bridge-South Bridge-Printer Port-Printer.

4. The blocks of data are thereby passed through the IDE interface-South Bridge-North Bridge and arrive at the CPU which transfers them to RAM, again via the North Bridge. There it is finally stored to wait for its execution by the CPU.

5. The word processing software causes the OS to open a new window, showing the characters of the text file in it. The OS then creates the image of this window as a bitmap. This bitmap is then stored in the video buffer of the graphics card. Data path: CPU-North Bridge-AGP slot-Graphics Card-VGA Interface-Monitor.

2 The CPU

What is a CPU?

As its name implies, the Central Processing Unit (CPU) plays a central role and is often referred to as the "brain" of the computer. It executes the program instructions and also coordinates all the other activities of the system. It consists of three main parts: the control unit, the arithmetic logic unit (ALU) and the registers.

The control unit examines and interprets a given program's instructions, activating the execution of various functions. The ALU performs mathematical calculations and logical operations while registers are high-speed memory units to store and control data. The program counter (PC) registers the next instruction to be executed in the main memory and instruction registers (IR) contain the current instruction.

A CPU that is manufactured as a single integrated circuit is usually known as a microprocessor. Beginning in the mid-1970s, microprocessors of ever-increasing complexity and power gradually supplanted other designs, and today the term "CPU" is usually applied to some type of microprocessor.

R **a** **Read the text above and answer the questions below.**

1. What is the CPU?
2. What are its three main parts?
3. What is the function of the control unit?
4. What is the job of the ALU?
5. What are registers?
6. What is the function of the PC versus that of the IR?

R **b** **Architecture of a modern CPU**

Study the following diagram and match the 10 elements of the CPU with their correct definition.

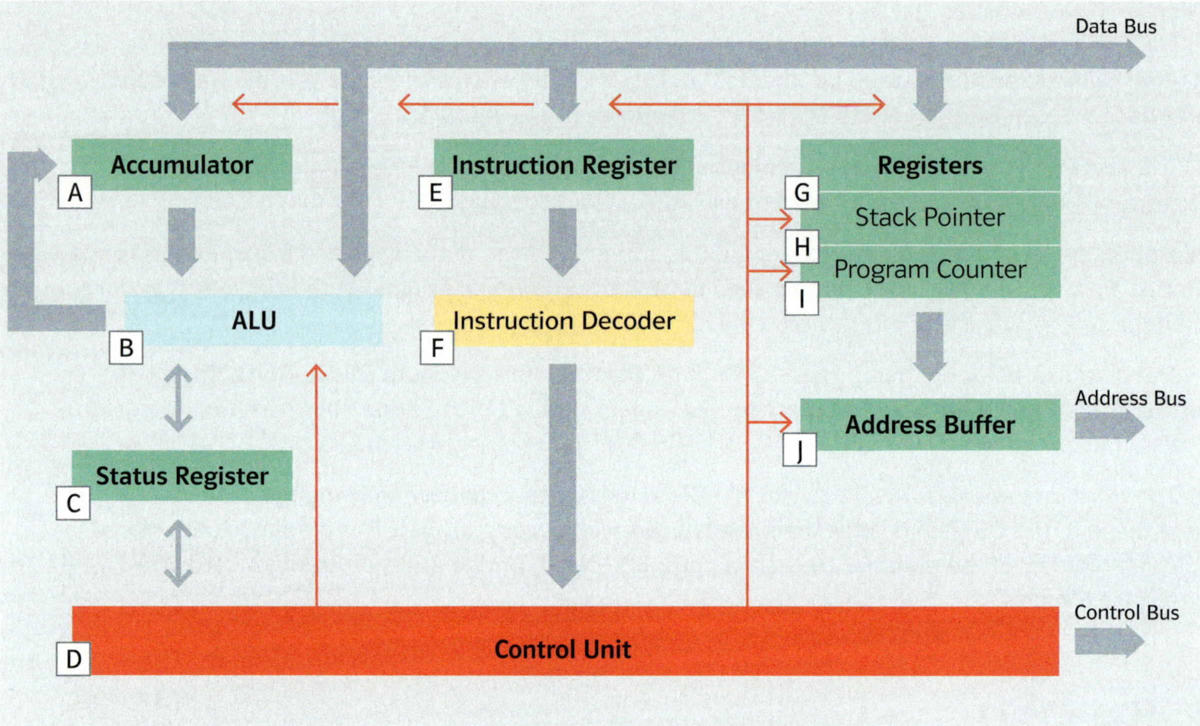

1. It controls all data traffic on the CPU. It opens and closes gates. It requests data from external devices. It sets switches and readies everything for data transfer. (See red arrows.)
2. It holds the instructions currently being processed.
3. It reads the instructions and decides which numbers can be forwarded directly to the Control Unit or whether data has to be added from external devices.
4. This high-speed circuit does the calculations and comparisons. Numbers are transferred from memory into it for calculation, and the results are sent back to memory.
5. It stores data to be fed into the ALU, as well as ALU output for later processing.
6. It holds additional information provided by the ALU, e.g. whether a result is negative or positive.
7. It holds the external memory addresses when an instruction is executed which requires access to external data.
8. If the CPU has to leave a given sequence to call a sub-program, this element ensures that the CPU can return to where it left off by storing the correct address.
9. It stores the number of the instruction which is currently being executed.
10. They are used to hold external data and interim results.

R/P **c** **The von Neumann architecture**

Von Neumann architecture is the term for a computer design model that uses a single storage structure to hold both instructions and data. The von Neumann Cycle refers to the steps the CPU takes when executing a program.
Put the steps of the cycle in the correct order.

1. If necessary get more data from memory.
2. Increase program counter by 1.
3. Get data and/or instructions from memory.
4. Perform instruction.
5. Start with step 1 all over again.
6. Interpret instruction according to instruction list.

INFO BOX John von Neumann

John von Neumann (Neumann János) (December 28, 1903 – February 8, 1957) was a Hungarian mathematician and polymath who made important contributions in quantum physics, functional analysis, set theory, economics, computer science, numerical analysis, hydrodynamics (of explosions), statistics and many other mathematical fields.

3 Computer advertisements

R/P **a** Read the following statements taken from advertisements. Decide which are opinions and which are facts.

1 **Compuprint is a world leader in the field of automatic identification systems.**

2 **Innovative communication technology transfers key information in seconds.**

3 **The NUKA 5000 Connector is so small you can put it in your pocket and carry it everywhere.**

4 **Courage is the driving force of progress.**

5 **Day trading is a brutal world.**

6 **Keeping in touch with colleagues, family and friends is important.**

7 **EBAY connects buyers and sellers on the internet.**

8 **Nothing should be taken at face value when it comes to government assurances.**

9 **New software can block ads from appearing on the screen.**

I **b** **Discuss in groups which statements you agree with most, which ones you disagree with. Give reasons. Choose one member of your group to report back.**

Our group agrees with …

Most of us don't agree that …

It's true that …

We disagree that …

We think it's true that …

P **c** **Look at the following words and find matching pairs with similar meanings and pairs of opposites.**

Example: practical = handy

communicative • time-saving • expensive • compact • indifferent • fascinating • intelligent • frustrating • helpful • complex • reliable • multi-functional • exciting • creative • dependable • elegant • practical • old-fashioned • advantageous • efficient • dynamic • flexible • global • handy • harmful • inspiring • logical • boring • maddening • popular • portable • precise • progressive • innovative • revolutionary • successful • timeless • up-to-date • valuable • user-friendly • useless

INFO BOX Match and mix when learning new words

Match: Learn two words for the price of one; find a partner for your new word, a word with the same or similar meaning, a synonym.
Example: global = world-wide
Mix: Find the opposite, an antonym, or a word you can associate with the new vocabulary item.
Example: potent – weak, black – white

R/P **d** **Now look at the collection of computer adverts on page 33. Make two lists. Decide which statements are facts and which are opinions. Note the technical terms and words conveying factual information and data as opposed to expressions with a highly emotive impact.**

INFO BOX Facts and opinions

Facts are the answers to "what-questions" concerning concrete, objective information.
Example: Unauthorized persons are denied access.
Opinions are the answers to "how-questions" concerning subjective thoughts and feelings.
Example: Get the whole world for the price of a PC.

ADVANCED Notebooks and Computers

Home | Products | Order | Contact

HAL Compaq Notebook

~~899 €~~

Packed full of the latest technology and mobile office features, this notebook provides low-cost business computing without compromising on performance. State-of-the-art security devices ensure that unauthorized persons are denied access.

➤ Visit us at hal.com/uk to find out more about our cashback offer valid through 31st January.

SALE 849 €

➤ 🛒

Get the whole World for the Price of a PC

Nuka 1000 Connector

1599 €

The Nuka 1000 Connector is the ultimate notebook experience with cutting edge design & features. Nothing else is needed to get and stay in contact: phoning, faxing, sending messages, Internet, organising. All incorporated in one handy device. Advanced technology for the ultimate portable multimedia or gaming experience. Superior functionality for high-end, mobile entertainment. Specially trained XPS service & support teams

And the Nuka 1000 Connector is so small you can slip it into your pocket or handbag and take it anywhere, anytime.

➤ 🛒

Anytime – Anywhere

Ideal Home and Office-PC

629 €

The Saleo high-performance PC is ideal for home and office use. The new Saleo boasts a new compact and funky design, features advanced digital connectivity including FireWire and WLAN and offers all the power and performance you need for editing photos and movies, as well as fast Internet and home office applications.

- Reliability: with leading edge technology suppliers for latest technologies and fast and reliable delivery
- Tailor-made: proactive on different customer requirements and variety of technology platforms
- Connectivity: front side interfaces for convenience, connectivity through modem, LAN and WLAN
- Flexibility: new created design in silver with blue LED, fits to all your and your family needs.

➤ 🛒

The perfect balance between advanced multimedia, style and affordability

Desktop Dream from Fujirama

1399 €

Features genuine

- Windows Vista Media Center Edition for complete digital entertainment
- a digital or analogue TV tuner for live TV
- personal video recorder (only with TV Tuner)
- electronic programme guides for schedule information
- two hard disc drives to store a wealth of digital media.

High-end PC performance and digital entertainment are combined with great graphics, powerful audio, a 9-in-1 Digital Media Reader, enhanced DVD burning with LightScribe Labelling on selected models and 802.11 WLAN.

Bright colours and clean lines make this PC a contemporary addition to your home. An impressive two tone, design extends to the keyboard, mouse and monitors. It is echoed in Desktop Dream's latest printers for a complete system and effortless style.

➤ 🛒

M **e** **Read the advertisements on page 33 again and find the English equivalents of the following German words:**

1. Zuverlässigkeit
2. Zugang, Zugriff
3. sich rühmen
4. hochmodern
5. aufweisen, ausgestattet sein mit
6. Leistung
7. überlegene Technologie
8. maßgeschneidert
9. Kundenwünsche
10. flippig, „abgefahren"
11. luxuriös, edel
12. echt
13. eine Fülle von
14. verbessert
15. zeitgemäß
16. klare Linien
17. Merkmal, Besonderheit
18. ausgewählt

4 Bits and bytes

R **a** **Match the following adjectives with the numbers in the lists below.**

standard • astronomical • tiny • mean • full-scale • infinitesimal

Small	Medium	Large
1	average	5
microscopic	middle-sized	sizeable
minute	3	huge
miniature	4	giant
2	intermediate	6

R **b** **Find the prefixes with the following meaning in the word square below.**

Example: one million = MEGA

1. one 2. two 3. ten 4. one thousand 5. one million
6. one thousand million 7. small 8. very small 9. many

M	I	N	I	M	K
U	L	M	M	I	G
L	K	D	E	C	I
T	I	W	G	R	G
I	L	G	A	O	A
M	O	N	O	B	I

P **c** **Make a list of words with these prefixes.**

Example: megabyte

R/P **d** **Complete the following text with the words in the box.**

pebibyte • decimal • gibibyte • bit • tebibyte • value • calculations • coded • mebibyte • tiny • abbreviations • byte • unit

A computer is basically an enormous collection of 1 electronic circuits that are either ON or OFF – current is either flowing through the wires or it isn't. A binary digit or 2 with "1" representing the ON state and "0" the OFF state is simply the smallest unit or bit of information in the binary system. A 3 consists of eight bits arranged in eight-digit codes. They are used to represent the letters, numbers and symbols of the keyboard. A string of letters – really a number of differently 4 bytes – are grouped into words which are arranged into sentences that add up to so many pages of text and so on. The table in the Info Box below shows the two separate 5 systems for measuring the storage capacity of computers. The left-hand side represents the 6 related system and the right-hand side the binary related system. The decimal system was originally adopted to simplify the 7 and comparisons of storage capacities. As computers and storage mediums grew astronomically the gap between the real values, i.e. the binary values, and the decimal values in general use also widened drastically. In reality, however, a computer's memory size has a binary 8 and we use the units kibibyte (2^{10} bytes), 9 (2^{10} kibibytes), and 10 (2^{10} mebibytes), 11 (2^{10} gibibytes) and 12 (2^{10} tebibytes) to measure its capacity. We generally refer to these measurements by their 13 : KB, MB, GB,TB, PB.

INFO BOX Gigabyte – Gibibyte

In 1999, the prefixes *kibi-*, *mebi-*, *gibi-*, etc., and the symbols Ki, Mi, Gi, etc. were introduced by the International Electrotechnical Commission in order to specify binary multiples of a quantity.
They have since been officially adopted by many other organizations. However, they have not yet been widely adopted by manufacturers and individuals; many continue to use the SI prefixes in a binary sense, despite the lack of support from official bodies. As a result, there is no unambiguous notation for decimal multiples of bits and bytes.

SI-UNITS (decimal) (international standard)	**IT-UNITS (binary) (international standard)**
bit	bit
byte = 8 bit	byte = 8 bit
kilobyte = 10^3 byte = 1000 byte	kibibyte = 2^{10} byte = 1024 byte
megabyte = 10^6 byte = 1000 kilobyte	mebibyte = 2^{20} byte = 1024 kibibyte
gigabyte = 10^9 byte = 1000 megabyte	gibibyte = 2^{30} byte = 1024 mebibyte
terabyte = 10^{12} byte = 1000 gigabyte	tebibyte = 2^{40} byte = 1024 gibibyte
petabyte = 10^{15} byte = 1000 terabyte	pebibyte = 2^{50} byte = 1024 tebibyte

R/P **e** **Are the following statements true or false? Correct the false statements.**

1. One **Gigabyte** is more than one **Gibibyte**.
2. One **Kibibyte** equals 8000 **BIT**.
3. 1024 **Kilobyte** equals 1 **Mebibyte**.
4. 210 **Mebibyte** equals 1 **Gibibyte**.
5. 1 **Terabyte** equals 1000 **Gigabyte**.

5 Codes and pixels

5.1 ASCII Code

M/P **a** **Read the following text and write a short summary in German, comparing ASCII to Unicode.**

ASCII (American Standard Code for Information Interchange), generally pronounced “ask-key” and based on the English alphabet, was for many years one of the most widespread codes for representing text in computers. It was first published in 1967 and was last updated in 1986. Strictly speaking, it is a seven-bit code and only defines a relationship between specific characters and bit sequences. ASCII reserves the first 32 codes for control characters, such as the keyboard functions Tab and Return. The codes 33–126 represent the ten digits, pronunciation marks, the letters of the alphabet and other common symbols, the so-called printable characters.

There are also a wide variety of other codes for depicting the characters and letters of other languages, but they all have the disadvantage of being limited in size and incompatible with other language environments.
Starting in 1991, though, the 8-bit, respectively the 16-bit Unicode Standard with a much wider array of characters has come to replace more and more existing encoding schemes.
Unicode is designed to allow the representation of text and symbols from all of the writing systems of the world. It provides a unique code point, i.e. a number, not a glyph – for each character and has been adopted by many industry leaders.
Incorporating Unicode into client-server or multi-tiered applications and websites offers significant savings over the use of legacy character sets. It enables a single software product or a single website to be targeted across multiple platforms, languages and countries without re-engineering. Data can be transported through many different systems without corruption.

M/P **b** **Translate the last paragraph of the text above into German. Take special note of the terms “multi-tiered”, “legacy”, “targeted”, “platform”, “re-engineering” and “corruption”.**

5.2 Pixels – Monochrome and colour

What you get to see on a computer screen – the graphics and characters – are actually made up by combining large numbers of single, tiny dots known as pixels. In a bit-mapped display these pixels or dots correspond to bits which are stored in the graphics card. The bits are stored in groups representing the horizontal and vertical position of the pixels on the screen. They also represent whether the pixels are on (black) or off (white). In a monchrome system a bit value, for example 1, corresponds to a pixel on the screen and is seen as being "on" (black).

A specific combination of the three primary colours, red, green and blue makes up the pixel in a colour system. The colour palette is the range or number of colours that can be displayed on the screen and depends on the graphics adapter. This is a device for converting bits into visual signals, whereby the more bits per primary colour the wider the range of colours.

R **Read the text above and answer the questions below.**

1. How are the visual elements represented on a computer screen?
2. What are pixels?
3. Where are the bits which correspond to the pixels stored?
4. What do the bits represent?
5. What is the difference between a monochrome and a colour system?
6. What is a colour palette?
7. What is a graphics adapter?
8. What determines the range of colours?

6 Further reading: The great e-waste recycling debate

The high tech boom has brought with it a new type of waste – electronic waste, a category of refuse that barely existed 20 years ago. Now e-waste represents the biggest and fastest growing manufacturing waste problem. The black and white TVs have given way to colour sets, the basic mobile phones now need to come equipped with a camera, personal organizer and music, and who wants last year's computer when it can't handle the latest software? As we continually update and invent new products, the lifespan of the old ones is becoming more and more short-lived all the time. As in the case of shipbreaking, e-waste recycling involves the major producers and users shipping the obsolete products to Asia, Eastern Europe, and Africa. Instead of being ecology-minded we are exporting waste containers full of problems to people who have to choose between poverty or poison.

A story of e-waste – the computer

On average a computer is made of 23% plastic, 32% ferrous metals, 18% non-ferrous metals (lead, cadmium, antimony, beryllium, chromium and mercury), 12% electronic boards (gold, palladium, silver and platinum) and 15% glass (see pie chart). Only about 50% of the computer is recycled, the rest is dumped. The toxicity of the waste is due, by and large, to the lead, mercury and cadmium – nonrecyclable components of a single computer may contain almost 2 kilograms of lead. Much of the plastic used contains flame retardants,which makes it difficult to recycle.

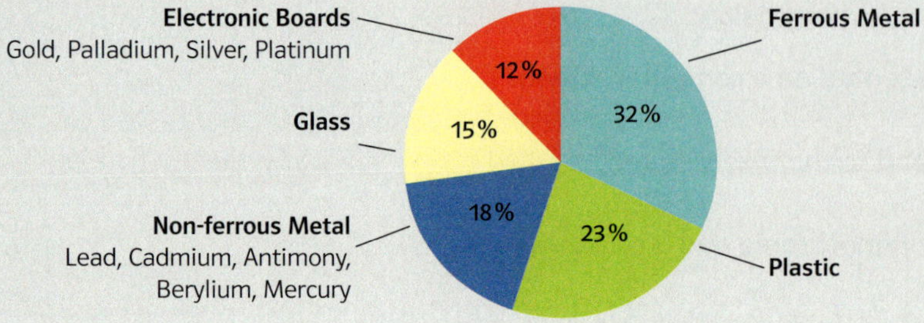

How is a computer recycled? In a number of countries entire communities, including the children, earn their livelihoods by scavenging metals, glass and plastic from old computers. To extract the small quantity of gold, capacitors are melted down over a charcoal fire. The plastic on the electrical cords is burnt in barrels to expose the copper wires. All in all each computer yields about US $6 worth of material (Basel Action Network). Not very much when you consider that burning the plastic emits dioxin and other toxic gases into the air. Large volumes of worthless parts are also dumped nearby, allowing the remaining heavy metals to contaminate the area.

Let me give you a computer

Communities in West Africa receive used computers from donors in developed countries. What was intended as a useful gift, however, quickly becomes a waste product. When things go wrong, as they often do with old computers, they end up on the scrap heap due to the lack of technical support. It is estimated that there are over a billion personal computers in the world at present. In developed countries these have an average lifespan of only 2 years. In the United States alone there are over 300 million obsolete computers. (US National Safety Council). The Basel Convention has before it an amendment pending which would ban the export of hazardous waste for disposal to developing countries. Some countries, among them those of the European Union, have already implemented this proposed amendment. In addition, countries like China have banned the importation of e-waste, although significant volumes are still entering the country illegally.

R/M **a** **Skim the article and summarize the key information in German.**

I **b** **Discussion:**
Refer to the text above and discuss in small groups how computers could be recycled in a more efficient, state-of-the-art way, and without contaminating the area.

P **c** **Online Task:**
Find businesses which specialize in recycling e-waste (no export of e-waste, no adding to landfill, no use of prison labour).
Present your findings to the class.

R **d** **Within a text synonyms are often used to add variety. Find matching pairs of synonyms in the text above.**

Example: waste = refuse

7 Language and grammar

7.1 Have got

a **Conduct a survey to find out who has what. Interview as many people as you can in the time given.**

Example: Have you got a scanner? How many … have you got?

colour printer • MP3 player • digital camera • USB stick • DVD drive • CDs • scanner • Internet connection • mobile phone

LANGUAGE AND GRAMMAR BOX Have got

"Have got/has got" with the built-in "got" is a fixed element and corresponds to the German "haben". We use it to indicate ownership or that something is available.
Examples: I've got a new printer. Have you got a minute?
In everyday speech we do sometimes drop the "got" but generally only in positive statements. So be careful!
Example: I have time now.

b **Report back to the class.**

Example: Sven has got a new laptop. Yvonne hasn't got a mobile phone but she does have an answering machine.

7.2 Daily work routine: Adverbs of frequency

a **Interview your partner about his/her daily routine. Ask questions such as the following:**

Phrases Asking questions

How do you get to work/school?

When do you …?

What do you do first?

Do you use the internet/make calls/write letters, memos/consult with colleagues?

How often do you …?

Do you sometimes …?

b **When answering your partner's questions use the following adverbs of frequency to indicate how often or seldom you perform tasks:**

never • rarely • seldom • occasionally • sometimes • generally • usually • often • frequently • always

Example: I often make calls.

C **Report back to the class about your partner's work routine. Include the adverbs of frequency on page 40.**

Example: Sally often receives e-mails and writes memos but she rarely faxes anything.

7.3 S-Genitive, S-Plural, S-Short form, S-Third Person Singular

Complete the following text with the correct form: s, es, 's, or s'. Is it s-plural, s-genitive, s-short form of is/has or s-3rd person singular?

Keyboard

Of all the input device 1 the classic keyboard 2 still one of the most common one 3 . A PC compatible keyboard include 4 alphanumeric key 5 , function key 6 and editing key 7 . It 8 numeric keyboard 9 on the right-hand side and function 10 as both a set of numeric and editing key 11 , using the NUM LOCK key to switch from number 12 to editing task 13 . The user 14 need to issue command 15 or to produce alternative character 16 is fulfilled by special key 17 . The ALT GR key 18 most common application, for example, is to produce the @ in internet address 19 .

7.4 Prepositions

Complete the following sentences using the correct prepositions from the box on the right.

out of • through • to • down • on • at • of • with

1. Have a look ___ my new compact phone.
2. If you want to turn it ___, press this red button.
3. It can scroll ___ the whole menu and even dial the phone book ___ only one touch.
4. The recording function lets you keep up ___ 20 seconds ___ conversation.
5. You can flip ___ the antenna when you want it ___ the way. It's great!

7.5 False friends

Complete the sentences choosing the correct word in.

1. Miracle Computers is launching an all out action/campaign to win over new customers.
2. The factual/actual problem with ASCII is that it is no longer actual, up-to-date .
3. My boss/chief is brave/nice and never makes me visit/attend any boring meetings.
4. I know you don't like critic/criticism but this outline/concept is full of typing mistakes.
5. The CU controls/checks all data traffic on the CPU and the status register controls/checks whether a result is negative or positive.

1

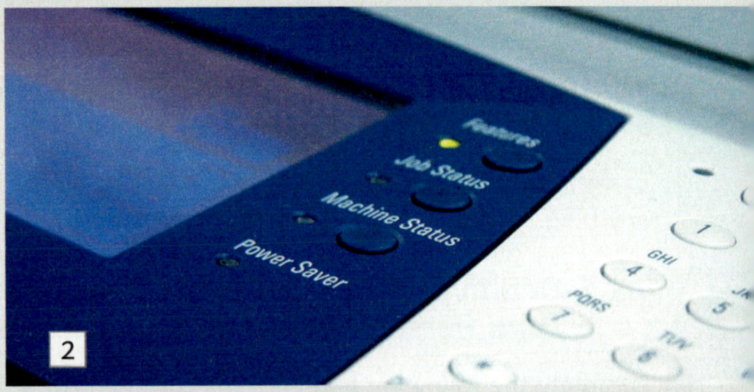

2

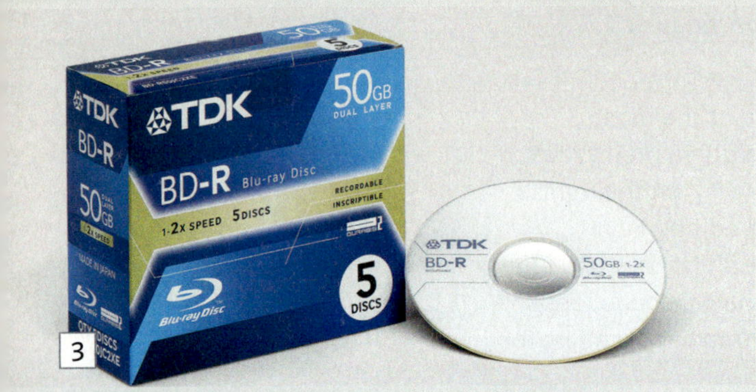

3

4

Unit 2

Input, output and storage devices

A peripheral is any computer device that is connected to a host computer in order to expand its abilities. The term is used to describe optional devices, as opposed to hardware that is always required. Peripherals can be mounted in the same case with the main part of the computer or outside the computer case.

Complete the following mind map on a separate sheet of paper. How many peripheral devices were you able to come up with?

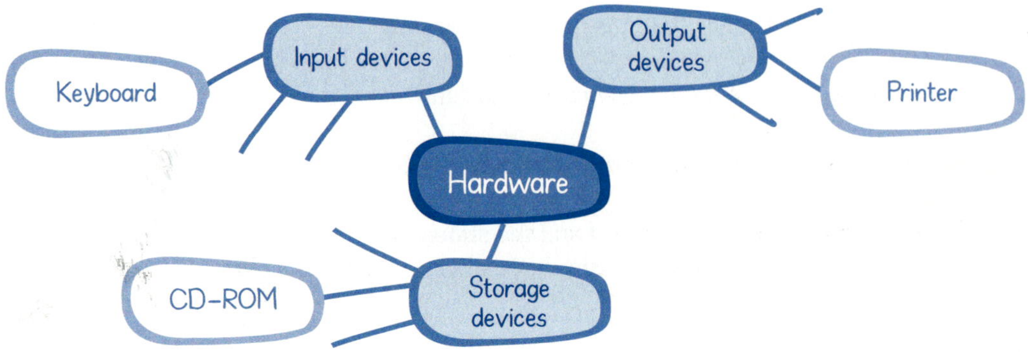

1 Input devices

R **a** **Match the following descriptions to the depicted input devices. (Note: Two of the devices described below are not depicted.)**

1. Ergonomically designed, allows you to place your hands, wrists and forearms in a natural position for greater comfort while typing.
2. Easy scrolling, simply roll the wheel forward or backwards, fast scroll automatically with a single click, two buttons.
3. USB interface enables you to connect with wide variety of peripheral devices. You can also print simultaneously. Extremely fast speed, a full page preview takes only 3.33 seconds, 48 Bit, 3200 dpi optical resolution.
4. This high resolution state-of-the-art device is outfitted with a 9 MP sensor and 32 MB of internal memory.
5. Perfect for flight simulator games, and much more. It comes with turbo switch and has two buttons.
6. An ergonomic alternative to a traditional mouse or trackball, this pen-like vertical mouse is held like a pen so that you can move the mouse keys with your index finger and scroll with your middle finger. Specially developed for notebook users as it requires less space than a mouse.
7. An innovative, multi-purpose gaming device that combines a keyboard with a gaming pad

A

B

C

D

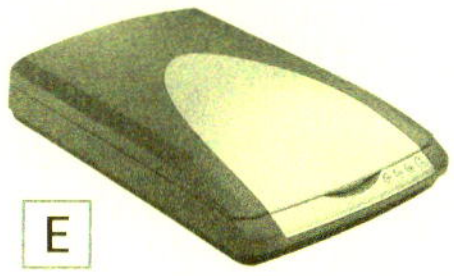
E

R **b** **Match the definitions to the words in the box. Note: There are two definitions per device: its regular meaning and its special computer meaning.**

1. an examination instrument, for example radar
2. a small mammal, rodent
3. an input device with keys for letters, numbers and special functions
4. the control stick in an airplane
5. an input device that "reads" images as a series of dots
6. a musical instrument
7. a device made to fit over the ears to receive radio messages
8. a small handheld input device that is rolled, causing the cursor to move around the screen
9. an instrument for receiving sound waves and relaying them into the computers memory
10. an input device used in computer games to move the cursor around the screen

mouse • scanner • joystick • head-set • keyboard

R **c Complete the following sentences using the input devices from the box on the right.**

1. A ___ is an input device and works like an upside down mouse. It controls the movement of the cursor on the screen.
2. With a ___ the screen itself is the positioning reference. You can choose options by pointing directly with your finger to the position on the screen.
3. With a ___ system the user speaks into a microphone. The computer converts the sound waves generated into digital form. It then compares the digitized sound waves to stored patterns of sound and identifies them.
4. A(n) ___ device uses a camera equipped system. The computer then converts the light waves (as compared to the sound waves of a voice recognition device) into digital form. The computer then compares the digitized light waves to its stored patterns of light waves and identifies them.
5. With a ___ the user moves his/her finger over a surface which is equipped with capacitive sensors. This causes the cursor to move on the screen relative to the motion of the user's fingers.
6. Shaped like a pen but inkless, the ___ is used instead of a finger for inputting on touch-screen enabled devices such as PDAs and graphic tablets.

touchpad • image recognition • stylus • trackball • virtual touch screen • voice recognition

P **d Compare and summarize: In what ways are voice and image recognition similar? Briefly list the steps involved in voice, respectively, image recognition.**

R **e Which input device is best suited for the following applications? Match the applications (1.–7.) with the information on the input devices below (a.–g.).**

1. For a magazine article with illustrations for later editing ...
2. For precise architectural design drawing ...
3. For independent learning by pre-school children of the basic concepts of colors, shapes and numbers ...
4. For motor-impaired users with coordination problems who cannot use a keyboard or mouse ...
5. For an information kiosk at an international airport ...
6. For interactive foreign language training ...
7. For writing an e-mail letter ...

a. I would use a virtual touchscreen because it is easy to use for those who are unfamiliar with computers.
b. I would use the mouse to click options , a keyboard to input text and a head-set to listen to texts and to practice your own pronunciation.
c. I would use a trackball because it requires less coordination skills than the other devices
d. I would use a touchscreen or trackball because they require less coordination than either a keyboard or mouse, for heavily handicapped persons who have little or no control over their limbs, a voice recognition device is the better option.
e. I would use a scanner because it lets you change and edit a text with the least amount of effort.
f. I would use a graphics tablet because it is the most accurate of the input devices and lets you input drawings and sketches with more ease.
g. I would use a keyboard because it is quick, especially if you are familiar with it.

P/I **f** **Discuss and report:**
Which input device do you prefer/often use and for what reasons?

R **g** **The keyboard**
Match the different types of keys to their descriptions below.

1. function keys 2. special keys 3. numeric keypad 4. alphanumeric keys 5. editing keys	a. These keys are for issuing commands or making alternative characters using key combinations such as *Alt Gr + q* = @. b. In word processing these keys are used to move the cursor within the document or to insert or delete text. c. This is a set of numeric or editing keys. The key in the upper left-hand corner of the pad is used to switch from numbers to editing functions. d. These keys instruct the computer, depending on the program in operation, to perform certain tasks. e. These are the keys with the letters and numbers arranged as on a typewriter.

h **What are the following keys (① – ⑦) used for? What are they called in German?**

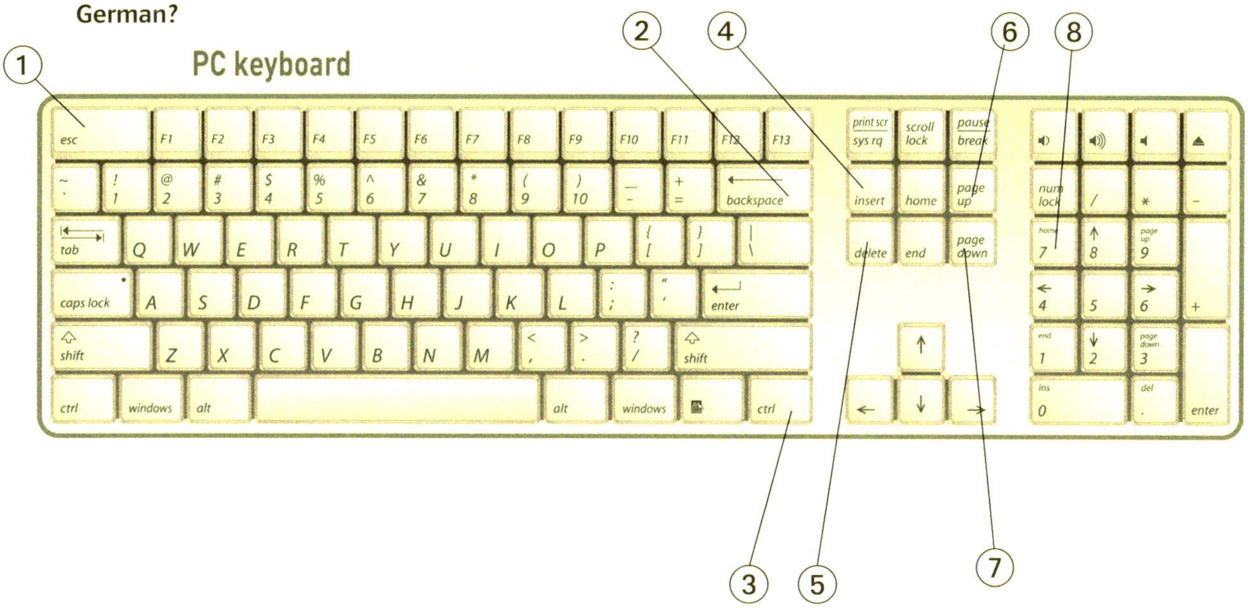

2 Output devices: Printers

R **a** **Compare the advertisements on page 47 and answer the following questions.**

1. Which of the laser printers makes it easier to work with other systems?
2. Which of the ink jet printers is the cheaper one?
3. Which printer has the most functions?
4. Which printers offer the highest resolution?
5. Which printer is the most flexible?
6. Which printer has the most memory?
7. Which printer has the largest paper input capacity?

R/P **b** **Which of the printers in the advertisements is best suited for which of the following applications? Give reasons for your choices.**

1. An events management firm with a high volume of snail mail sendings, as well as the need to print advertising flyers and larger-sized placards.
2. A high school student on a low budget who needs to print assignments, some correspondence and private photos for fun.
3. A small translation service business which is run out of the home. Bills are usually faxed and some copying and scanning has to be done from time to time.
4. The main printer for the design office of a precision equipment manufacturer which has to serve the high-end printing needs of a number of workstations and the laptops of the sales force.

P/M **c** **Read the advertisements again and find the acronyms for the following technical specifications. What English words do the letters stand for?**

1. Punkte pro Zoll
2. optische Zeichenerkennung
3. Seiten pro Minute
4. Drucker-Steuerungssprache
5. Universeller serieller Bus
6. Protokoll für die Postzustellung
7. Mehrwertsteuer

ADVANCED Printers

Home | Products | Order | Contact

Business Inkjet 2700 Commercial printer

€255.64

Easy printing with optional photo colour. Ideal for printing letters, budgets, book reports and résumés. Black up to 30ppm and dazzling colour at up to 20ppm. Resolution 4800 dpi colour printing on premium photo paper. Easy setup and hassle-free operation make printing a dream. Lifelike colours with original Color Layering Technology.

➤ Price: €255.64 (Excluding: VAT)

➤

PRO21 Postscript Printer

€699

22ppm-up to 1200 dpi laser printer. Automatic emulation and interface switching. Network boards, platform flexibility. Postscript printing. 3 trays, up to 850 sheet paper cassette. 288MB Memory, optional duplexing.

Price: €699.00 (Excluding: VAT)

➤

Photoprint All-in-One

€305

Multi-function colour printer, scanner, copier and fax. Breakthrough print and copy speeds of up to 32 ppm black and 31 ppm color; photos as fast as 14 seconds. Unique six individual inks are designed for high-volume printing. Up to 4800 dpi color when printing from a computer and 1200-input dpi. Superior scanning on an oversized 8.5 x 12-inch glass with 4800 dpi optical resolution, 48-bit color. Built-in OCR software for colour scanning.

➤ Price: €305.00 (Excluding: VAT)

➤

QX Laser Printer

€599

This high specification bin laser printer prints black up to 20 ppm and colour up to 4 ppm.
Compatible: PCL 6, Postscript 2 Emulation, Epson, IBM. Expandable to 96 MB memory, 264 Mhz processor.
Envelope or poster print option.
Intelligent sleep mode.
Semi automatic duplex mode.
USB and parallel.
Automatic document feeder: 2 x 200 sheet paper input .
Auto e-mail printing (Pop 3 Network)

Price: €599.00 (Excluding: VAT)

➤

R **d** **Complete the following text with the words in the box on the right. Then listen and check.**

A guide for choosing the right printer for your special needs

Good quality output is naturally the first criteria to keep in mind when choosing a printer. A good indicator of a printer's ability to capture details is its **1** . 1200 dpi (dots per inch) generally produces a razor sharp text and decent photographic **2** . For high-resolution pictures and **3** you might want 4800 dpi or more. With colour print-outs dynamic range, resolution and accurate colours are what you're looking for.

Another key factor is **4** which is measured in pages per minute with top-of-the-line printers claiming to churn out up to 30 or more ppm. Heavy formatting, graphics, photographs and, of course, colour slow down the printer's work considerably. Along with prices ranging from practically pennies to a small fortune, these are the most obvious criteria.

A factor which is sometimes overlooked though important for high resolution is **5** ; at least 8 MB for mono and in the range of 192 MB for colour is required.

features • resolution • images • needs • graphics • maintenance costs • speed • scanner • plotters • memory • colour print-outs • user-friendliness • drivers • dot-matrix • ink-jet printers

In the area of ergonomics factors such as installation, noise, maintenance and 6 count: How do I install a new toner cartridge? (And what does it cost?) Will I wake the whole family if I start printing at midnight? What about repairs and upkeep? Can I bypass options and just press a button or two if I'm in a hurry?

What other features such as 7 for running the relevant software and interfacing for networking options and expansion are included? Paper handling is also an issue: Does the printer come equipped with more than one tray? What is the sheet capacity? When checking out the documentation have a critical look at the technical data, glossary, index and error messages. Aside from a guarantee, in the service area there's the question of a hotline and driver updates via internet.

Basically we can distinguish between impact – contact is made between paper and pins, pens or characters – and non-impact printing. The old 8 printers, relatively slow, loud and with poor resolution, use pins to print dots on the paper. No longer popular on the PC market, they still maintain a niche in applications where impact printing is an advantage, for example in issuing carbon copies of invoices. 9 are special impact printers which use ink and fine pens held in a carriage to draw very detailed designs for construction plans and illustrations.

Non-impact printers, though, now dominate the market with ink-jet printers predominant in the home and laser printers playing a larger role in offices. As the name implies 10 project tiny droplets of ink onto the paper. They're quiet, fast, can achieve high resolutions and are not necessarily expensive. They're quite popular because they can deliver 11 of high quality. The drawback is the relatively high 12 as the colour cartridges are expensive and need to be replaced quite frequently.

For reasons of speed, image quality and flexibility laser printers are preferred by experts. A laser beam scans the image and transfers it to paper with a special ink powder.

Multi-function printers have become very popular recently. These are laser or inkjet printers that also operate as a photo-copier, fax machine, and 13 . Multi-function printers are ideal for saving space and costs when operating a small business.

When choosing a printer keep in mind your personal or your company's specific 14 . Decide on your priorities, which options are essential and which 15 you can dispense with.

P **e** **Summarize the text using approximately 100 words.**

3 Storage devices

P **a** **What do these abbreviations stand for?**

MT • HD • FD • DVD • CD-ROM • USB • BD

Example: MT = Magnetic Tape

R **b** **Read the following statements dealing with the storage devices above. Decide which statements are true of which devices. Hint: A statement might be true of more than one device.**

Example:
They are sensitive to magnetic fields and high temperatures. → MT and FD

1. They are re-writable.
2. You must format them before you can record information.
3. People use them to store back-up files in archives.
4. They can hold vast amounts of information – more than 650 MB.
5. They have the smallest access time values (2.8 –20 ms).
6. We use them to store personal data and files that are subject to frequent change.
8. They are a good way to store or distribute large amounts of information such as images, sound, applications and so on.
9.They use optical technology to record and read information.
10. They allow sequential access only and are slower than hard drives.
11. It is a high density optical storage medium with up to 50 GB, double-sided, 2 layered storage capacity.
12. It's a good way to store films and multi-media applications.

R **c** **Match the descriptions with the storage devices.**

1. It has a small, handy format, used as easily removable storage media for portable devices.	a. hard discs
2. Very fast, more capacity than other discs, but also more expensive. Most discs are not portable.	b. optical discs
3. A laser is used to read and write data. Very large storage capacity but not as fast as some other discs.	c. tapes
4. Relatively inexpensive, large storage capacities possible, no random access of data.	d. memory sticks

d **Read the following text and list the differences and similarities between CD-ROM, DVD and Blu-ray Discs.**

Example:

	CD ROM	DVD	Blu-ray Disc
Shape	disc shaped	disc shaped	disc shaped
Track pitch	1.6 micron	0.74 micron	0.32 micron

CD versus DVD versus Blu-ray Disc

As far as looks go, a DVD disc, CD and Blu-ray disc (= BD) could be triplets. Relying on lasers to read data stored in pits in a spiral track, all three are plastic discs 120 mm in diameter and 1.2 mm thick. Thus, BD products are backwards compatible with CD and DVD, i.e. a seamless transition from one technology to the other is possible. While there are considerable differences in the storage capacity of CDs, DVDs and BDs, the increases are due, by and large, to a fine tuning of the same basic system.

Nonetheless, there are a number of essential differences. On DVDs and BDs the track pitch (distance between each) is tighter, i.e. the tracks are placed much closer together, than on a CD. They are 0.32 micron apart on a Blu-ray disc and 0.74 micron on a DVD or less than a fifth, respectively, half of the CD's 1.6 micron. The pits where the data is stored are also much smaller on DVDs and BDs allowing more pits per track. The minimum pit length for a Blu-ray disc is 0.15 micron versus a single layer DVD's minimum pit length of 0.4 micron and 0.834 micron for a CD. The reduced track pitch and smaller pit size contribute to giving Blu-ray discs almost 40 times and DVD-ROM discs seven times the storage capacity of CDs.

Smaller pits require that the laser produce a smaller spot which is the real technological innovation. The DVD achieves this by reducing the laser's wavelength from the 780 nm (nanometers) infrared light of a standard CD, to 635 nm or 650 nm red light. Simply by changing the focus of the read laser, the DVD specification also allows information to be scanned from more than one layer of a DVD, almost doubling capacity with a single disc delivering 8.5 GB of data.

The wavelength of a Blu-ray Disc is only 405 nm. As the name implies, the Blu-ray uses a blue instead of a red laser. Along with improved lens specifications, this allows for a much smaller focus laser beam making it possible to record smaller and higher density pits on the disc.

Information is always stored first near the hub of the disc. With DVDs, though, the discs' second data layer can contain data recorded 'backwards', or in a reverse spiral track. This means it takes only an instant to refocus a lens from one reflective layer to another. A single-layer CD which stores all the data in a single spiral track naturally takes longer to relocate the optical pickup to another location on the same surface. On a Blu-ray Disc the data layer is much "closer" to the laser lens than in a DVD resulting in less distortion and improved tolerances for more precision and ultra high storage densities. ▶

CD

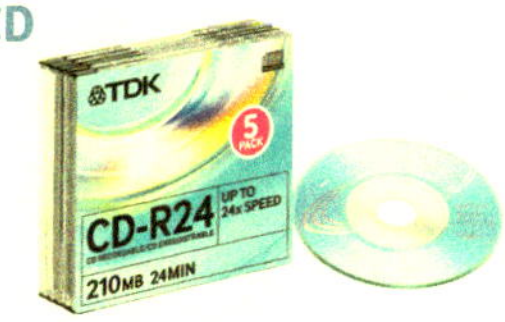

DVD

Blu-ray Disc

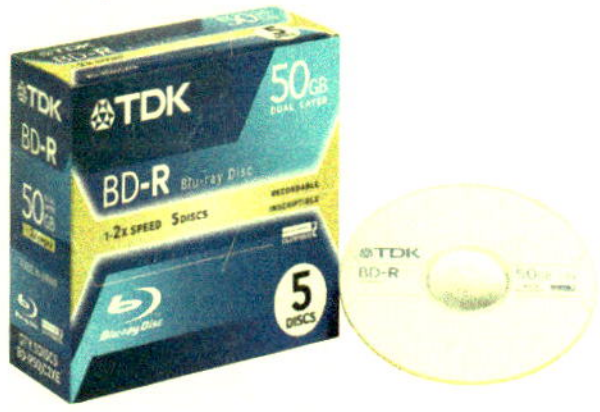

DVDs are also double-sided discs. To help focus the laser on the smaller pits and reduce the depth of the layer of plastic the laser has to travel through to reach the pits, manufacturers needed a thinner plastic substrate than that used by a CD-ROM. However, the resulting discs – 0.6 mm or half as thick as a CD-ROM – were too thin to remain flat and withstand handling. Consequently manufacturers bonded two discs back-to-back – resulting in discs that are 1.2 mm thick, effectively doubling the potential storage capacity of a disc.

The Blu-ray Disc is manufactured as a single layer disc comparable to a CD. Unlike a DVD, though, the production process does not require bonding two substrates, resulting in less material, a shorter production time and thus lower production costs per disc.

The structure of the data on DVDs and BDs is also more efficient. The early development of CDs required some heavy-duty and relatively crude error correction systems to guarantee the discs would play. This error detection uses bits which cannot then be used to carry useful data. The more efficient and effective error correction code (ECC) of the newer technologies leaves more room for data.

J/P **e** **Smart Cards may look and be the size of an ordinary credit card but are really small electronic storage devices which often have an embedded integrated circuit. They are used for a wide variety of purposes. Discuss the following questions with your partner and then report back to the class:**

1. Which of the cards pictured do you already possess?
2. Would you prefer an all-in-one smart card? What information would it need to contain to be able to replace all your other cards?
3. Can you think of other uses for smart cards?
4. Would there be any disadvantages to a smart card?

M **f** **Study the adverts for disc drives and a memory stick on page 53. What are the English equivalents for the following German terms?**

1. Sicherheitseinrichtungen
2. Stromausfall
3. Lademechanismus
4. durchschnittliche Suchzeit
5. Datenübertragungsrate
6. wieder beschreibbar
7. mehrfach segmentierter Puffer
8. räumliche Dichte

ADVANCED Storage devices

Home	Products	Order	Contact

320 GB UDMA 133

€70

Futurama Hard disc drive: 320 GB UDMA 133, 133 MB/sec* burst data transfer rate, average seek time 4.16 ms and 16 MB multi-segmented buffer with rotation speeds of 7200 rpm. New perpendicular recording technology enables higher areal density, fewer moving parts and increased dependability. Offers consistent read/write performance from the beginning to the end of your computing workload. Clean Sweep automatically calibrates your drive.

➤ Price: €70.22 (Excluding: VAT)

➤

PX 700

€39

The PX-700 DVD±R/RW CD-R/RW internal ATAPI drive from Sany offers all the advantages of our renowned CD-RW drives with slot-in loading mechanism and horizontal or veritical mounting. Additional features are the the digital servo mechanism and speedy 16X CAV technology to keep the drive on track. The drive burns an 8.5 GB Double Layer DVD in less than ten minutes.

➤ Price: €39.00

➤

Sundance Mobile Memory Stick

€25
4 GB

Features

- Greater storage capacities (256 MB, 512 MB, 1 GB, 2 GB and 4 GB) than standard Memory Sticks
- A high-speed data transfer rate of 15 Mbps for DVD-quality video in real time
- Quick transfer rates prevent data loss by power cut-offs or accidental removal of media
- Advanced security functions and technology

➤ Price: €25.00 (excluding VAT)

➤

R **g** **The race is on between the different storage mediums! Listen to the "sports" broadcast and answer the following questions.**

1. Who's the winner of the race?
2. Who comes in second?
3. Who's third?
4. Fourth?
5. Last?
6. What does this order show? Which storage medium has more capacity, is faster?

P **h** **HD DVD and Blu-ray Discs are not mentioned. Where would you place them in the race?**

R **i** **The following instructions for setting default document properties are in mixed order. Put them in the correct sequence.**

To set default document properties

1. From the Printer menu, choose *Properties*. Or choose the *Properties* button on the toolbar.
2. In the Printer Details dialogue box, choose the *Job Defaults* button.
3. In the Document Properties dialogue box, choose the *Options* button.
4. Set *advanced options* in the Advanced Document Properties dialogue box.
5. In Print Manager, select the printer's *icon* or *window*.
6. In the Printer Properties dialogue box, choose the *Details* button.

4 Buying hardware

R **a** **Read the following review of a new notebook (Compro Prestige 3000) and decide if the statements below are true or false.**

1. Innovative technological devices tend to be exclusive at first.
2. The new Prestige 3000 weighs more than competitive products in the same price class.
3. The Prestige 3000 is thinner than other similar products.
4. Compro's new notebook product is cheaper than those of Sun's and Tokio's.
5. The external CD-ROM and DVD-ROM drives cost extra.
6. There is an extra charge of $99 for pre-installed office software.
7. The Prestige 3000 has a smaller screen size but is cheaper than competitive products.
8. The Prestige 3000 is just as small as the PROFI edition notebook.
9. You can run just about any kind of application on the Prestige 3000.
10. The reviewer sees a number of serious drawbacks in the Prestige 3000.

Compro Prestige 3000 Review

More and Less for your Money

The history of portable technology is the history of executive status symbols eventually becoming mainstream consumer products. This is true of the first laptop computers, mobile phones and PDAs. Compro is making it happen again with their line of "thin and light" notebooks.

Weighing just 2.1 pounds and less than 1/2 inch thick, the new Prestige 3000 is lighter and just as thin as most of the competition's products. What makes it more attractive than competitive products, though, is its rock bottom price of only $1,099. It comes with a 3500 MHz Pentium IV processor, 3 GB of memory, and a 300 GB hard disc. An added attraction is that the external CD and DVD writer do not cost extra.

For a pre-installed Microsoft Big Business Edition instead of Microsoft Works there is an added charge of $99 but we took a pass.

Since frequent fliers first fell for Sun's ultrathin Zombie and Tokio's Portage notebooks, those vendors haven't made their products much cheaper. The Prestige 3000 has a 12. 2-inch, TFT screen and costs about as much as the Zombie Z16 with a 10.3-inch or Portage 21 with a 11.3-inch display. The Compro device comes with a built-in modem. It even boasts a gigabit Ethernet interface and an IEEE 1394 port which lets you store data at a higher speed.

More important than the lower cost is the increased convenience of having a notebook that is no bigger than last year's top of the range PROFI edition notebook. It is a computer that is equally comfortable using in our lap as on a desk or lounging with our feet up. While it isn't powerful enough for heavy-duty CAD or graphics applications, it is more than adequate for office tasks and even DVDs or games. The lack of parallel and PS/2 ports means you have to use the USB route to connect a printer, mouse, or full-sized keyboard but we can live with that.

Dislikes? Yes, unfortunately. Laptops tend to have lightweight batteries but Compro's lithium-ion cell is quite puny. While we don't expect the ten hours or so of a desktop replacement, our Prestige 3000 repeatedly faded after a few short hours. That's more than weak and the sole reason for our award of four and not five stars.

R **b** **Listen to Judy and George discuss their purchasing plans and answer the following questions.**

1. What is Judy planning on buying?
2. What is she going to use it for?
3. When are the stress management workshops taking place?
4. What advise does George give her?
5. Is Judy planning an immediate purchase?

I **c** **Discuss with your partner your own computer purchasing plans in the near or far future. Ask each other questions such as the following:**

Why are you going to buy a new …?

What are you planning on buying?

How much are you planning on spending?

Where are you going to buy it?

P **d** **Report back to the class.**

5 Further reading: Hard discs

Data is recorded on hard discs by magnetizing a magnetic material in a pattern corresponding to the data. The data can be read back by detecting this magnetization. Hard discs usually have a spindle which holds one or more flat circular discs called platters for recording data. To make the platters a non-magnetic material, usually glass or aluminum, is coated with a thin layer of magnetic material.

Information is written to a platter as it spins at high speeds past mechanisms called read-and-write heads. While flying very close over the magnetic surface, the head detects and modifies the magnetization of the material immediately under it. Each magnetic platter surface on the spindle has one head which is mounted on a common arm. The arm moves the heads in an arc (roughly radially) across the spinning platters, allowing each head to access the whole surface of the platter.

The magnetic surface of each platter is separated into numerous tiny sub-micrometre-sized magnetic regions. Each region is composed of a few hundred magnetic grains and used to encode a single binary unit of information. They each form a magnetic dipole which is a closed circulation of electric current. This dipole generates a nearby highly localised magnetic field. The write head magnetizes a magnetic region by creating a strong local magnetic field nearby. The read and write head are separate mechanisms, but are on the same actuator arm.

The hard disc's read-write heads fly on a cushion of air only nanometers above the disc surface, i.e. there is only a sub-microscopic gap between the heads and disc. The disc's internal environment must therefore be kept absolutely free of contamination such as fingerprints, hair, dust, and particles. That is why, to prevent any damage, hard discs are almost completely sealed.

The use of rigid platters and sealing on hard discs give them much tighter tolerances than in floppy discs. As a result, hard discs can store more data and access and transmit it faster. A hard disc (2007) can store between 80 GB and 750 GB of data, rotate at 7,200 to 15,000 RPM and have a sequential media transfer rate of over 80MB/s. The hard discs of laptops are generally smaller and slower, spinning at between 5,400 RPM and 7,200 RPM.

R/P **Read the text about hard discs above and answer the questions below in full sentences in English.**

1. What are the physical components of a hard disc and what are they made of?
2. What is the basic technology employed for recording data on a hard disc? What other storage device(s) employ this technology?
3. What device is used to change and read the data onto the platter? How does it function?
4. How are the heads able to access nearly the entire platter surface?
5. How and why is the platter surface partioned?

6 Language and grammar

6.1 Tenses: Present continuous or present simple?

R **Match the questions on the left with the answers on the right.**

1. What are you doing?	a. This year? Hawaii, I believe.
2. What do you do?	b. Yes, every year.
3. Does it scan colour photos?	c. I'm trying to connect the printer.
4. Is it scanning the colour photos?	d. Of course, and the range is pretty decent, too.
5. Does the CEBIT take place in November?	e. As soon as I finish my training.
6. Is CEBIT taking place in November?	f. I'm a programmer.
7. When do you start work?	g. Of course, just look at the monitor.
8. When are you starting work?	h. I'm pretty sure it is, but I can check it out for you.
9. Where's he going on vacation?	i. Oh, his family has a cottage on Martha's Vineyard.
10. Where does he go on vacation?	j. I have flexi-time but generally between 8 and 9.

LANGUAGE AND GRAMMAR BOX Present continuous

The following groups of verbs do not normally form a continuous tense:

Verbs expressing feelings or desires (like, hate, fear, want etc.)

Verbs of perception (see, hear, feel, taste)
Exception: when we use to see to mean to meet with, or feel to mean state of health.
Examples: I am seeing him today (= meeting).
She's feeling out of sorts (= in poor health).

Verbs expressing opinions (think, feel, believe, expect
Exception: when we use think to mean a mental activity, expect to mean to await.
Examples: Let me concentrate – I'm thinking.
We're expecting (= await) the guests to arrive at any moment.

Verbs of possession (have, belong to, own, possess etc.)
Exception: when we use have in one of its special meanings (= eat, drink, celebrate etc.)
Examples: We're having a party on Saturday (= celebrating).
What are you having (= like to drink)?

6.2 Preposition and gerund

Finish the following sentences using the correct preposition and the gerund form of an appropriate verb.

Example: We look forward (hear) from you soon → We look forward to hearing from you soon.

1. He's used (work) long hours.
2. Are you interested (buy) a new notebook?
3. They finally succeeded (connect) the printer properly.
4. The customer insisted (pay) the scanner by cheque.
5. The computer hotline had difficulty (find) the error.

LANGUAGE AND GRAMMAR BOX The gerund

The gerund should not be confused with the continuous form of the verb though they both end in "ing". The gerund usually emphasizes an activity and is really a verbal noun.

Example:

Smoking is bad for your health. Smoking is a gerund (Das Rauchen).

He is now smoking more than a pack a day. Smoking here is part of the continuous form of the verb. In German: *Er raucht zur Zeit mehr als eine Packung pro Tag.*

6.3 Comparative and superlative

Comparing and describing hardware

Put the adjectives in brackets into the comparative or superlative form.

Example:

DVDs have a (high) density than CD-ROMS.

DVDs have a higher density than CD-ROMS.

1. Generally speaking, the (high) the resolution of the monitor, the (accurate) and (intensive) are the colours.
2. This information on the two memory sticks is actually (detailed) than I need it to be: (little) is sometimes (much).
3. For (far) information on our hardware consult our website at www.ptmag.con
4. The (simple) an explanation is in a manual, the (good).
5. Clearly one of the (important) features of the new laser printer is its enormous speed.
6. Blu-ray discs are the (great) advancement in optical media since the DVD.

Unit 3
Operating systems and software

1 Operating systems

P **a** **Look at the illustration. What do you think the function of the operating system is? Why is the OS so important?**

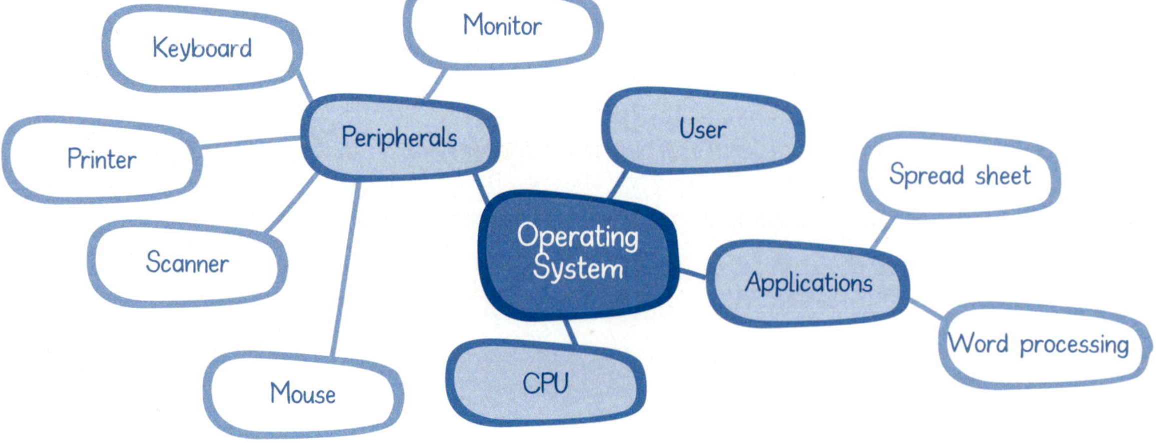

R **b** **Complete the following text with the words in the box below.**

> operating • software • execute • resources • application • word processing • files • system • translating • interpreters

After concentrating on the hardware aspects of computing we are now going to focus on the information provided by programs and data, also known as 1 . Programs vary in complexity but are basically sets of instructions or commands. They cause the computer to 2 certain operations and jobs. Generally we distinguish between two main types: system and 3 software. 4 programs and spreadsheets are examples of application programs. These are programs developed for specific purposes to perform certain tasks.
We call the programs which control the basic functions of a computer and keep the system running system software. They include 5 utilities which are small programs designed to improve a system's performance such as file search or backup programs. There are also language translators, for example, compilers for 6 instructions into machine code as well as 7 .
The 8 system governs the hardware and software 9 of a system. Communicating directly with the computer it consists of a set of programs and 10 which control all the elements the average user sees.

P **c** **Go back and read over the text again. Define and, if possible, give examples for the following terms:**

1. software
2. system software
3. application software
4. operating system

R/P **d** **Susan Graham, a computer trainer, is talking about different operating systems. Read the text or listen to the text and complete the sentences on page 62 on a separate sheet of paper using your own words.**

Susan Graham: "As you probably know already the operating system is often supplied by the manufacturer and comes with your system when you buy a computer. You need an operating system, of course, to control the hardware and software resources of your system. It's an essential element that can make or break your system.
MS-DOS is an older, text based operating system. It lets you communicate with the computer by typing in commands on the keyboard. Of course, this means the user has to either learn the instructions by heart or keep looking them up. A typical command is COPY which does just that – it will copy a file or files from your disk.
Allowing multi-tasking is the user-friendlier OS/2. This system contains hundreds of routines which are sequences of instructions. With these routines the user can start up the computer, transfer data from disks to peripherals and control the RAM space.

Windows 95 and its followup Windows 98 from Microsoft Company were operating systems in their own right, though not authentically multi-tasking. Like OS/2, the systems are not text based but use an attractive graphical interface. Though they look very similar to their predecessor, Windows Millenium, Windows XP and the newer Windows VISTA operating systems are authentically multi-tasking. They're more stable and less prone to crash which is a big plus naturally. Designed for professional purposes the Windows VISTA allows you to set up a server for work stations.

Conceived from the first as a multi-tasking system, UNIX from Bell Company is written in C, a high-level programming language. Most computers today are capable of running some version of UNIX. An offshoot of the commercial UNIX system is Linux."

1. The companies which make computers usually …
2. You need an operating system to …
3. When using MS-DOS operating system you communicate with the computer …
4. The COPY command …
5. The OS/2 has …
6. You use different routines to …
7. Windows 95 and Windows 98 are not really …
8. Windows Vista is …
9. With Windows Vista you can …
10. UNIX is written …

P **e** **Make a list of all operating systems you can think of. What do they have in common? What applications are they used for?**

M/R **f** **Accounting is an important aspect of running a computer system. It is the process of keeping track of a user's activity while accessing the system's resources, including the amount of time spent logged into the system, the services accessed and the amount of disk space used either during the session or an a regular basis. Accounting data is used for trend analysis, capacity planning, billing, auditing and cost allocation.**

Answer the following questions about systems accounting in German.

1. Was ist Systemabrechnung?
2. Was umfasst Systemabrechnung?
3. Wozu wird Systemabrechnung eingesetzt?

R **g** **Match the following accounting facilities of a UNIX operating system to the correct description.**

1. last	a. Turns system accounting on or off.
2. lastcomm	b. Indicates last logins of users and terminals.
3. acct	c. Generally maintains system accounting files.
4. ac	d. Enables and disables process accounting.
5. accton	e. Login accounting.
6. sa	f. Shows in reverse order the last commands executed.

2 BIOS – Basic input output system

BIOS

BIOS stands for basic input output system and is a term which refers specifically to the initial code run by a personal computer. Operating between the hardware and higher software levels, its primary function is to prepare the PC so that other programs can be booted, i.e. loaded and executed. It is embedded on a chip that works directly with the hardware and peripheral devices of a system and deals with quite elementary operations such as writing individual bytes onto the monitor or a disk.

BIOS routines used to be stored in ROM and were unalterable. Nowadays the BIOS are usually held on EEPROM or flash memory devices which offer the advantage of being "electronically erasable", i.e. they can easily be updated by the user. The downside, however, is that an improperly configured BIOS can cause the system to crash.

To counteract such problems some motherboards have a backup or so-called Dual BIOS. Most BIOS also have a "boot block" which is a section of the ROM which runs first and cannot be changed. This code checks whether the rest of the BIOS is in order before proceeding further.

Initially BIOS executed most of the input-output tasks but more modern operating systems took over such jobs, leaving the BIOS to simply initialize the setup and bootstrap. More recently, though, BIOS has taken on more complicated functions such as power management, hotplug and thermal management. As a result, BIOS code has become more complex and interfacing with the operating systems a matter of high priority.

R **a** **Read the text above and decide if the statements below are true or false.**

1. BIOS is a hardware device.
2. BIOS is the term used for the initial code for all types of computer systems.
3. BIOS performs very basic tasks.
4. The main job of BIOS is to load and execute software programs.
5. The advantage of more recent BIOS is that all the routines can be changed.
6. If you install a BIOS update improperly, it can make the computer unusable.

R **b** **Match the words on the left (1.–13.) with their equivalents on the right (a.–m.).**

1. inspecting	8. logging	a. to pass over	h. to work on
2. entering	9. forwarding	b. to understand	I. to be
3. terminating	10. running	c. to examine	j. to write down
4. existing	11. processing	d. to register	k. to pass on
5. skipping	12. mounting	e. to work	l. to make modern
6. reading	13. using	f. to employ	
7. updating		g. to end	m. to start

3 Utility software

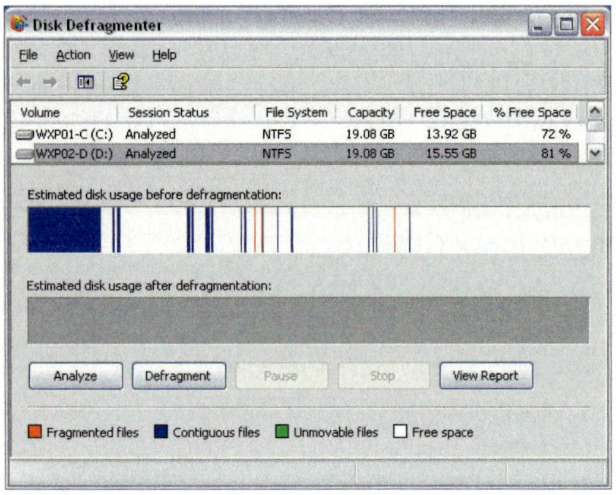

Utility software

Utility software, known also as system utilities or tools, is designed to help manage and tune the elements of your system-hardware, operating system or software. They are small programs for performing a single task or a small range of tasks. Although a selection of utilities are integrated into most major operating systems, you can take advantage of a computer's potential and improve its performance by upgrading your system with optional tools.

There are a variety of disk management tools, for example, to save space and reduce access time to data on the hard disk. Among them are tools like Microsoft's disk defragmenters (shown above) which locate disjointed file fragments and piece them back together to increase efficiency, while disk checkers hunt down and eliminate corrupt files and spot damaged areas on the hard disk. Disk cleaners help track down superfluous or space hogging files and disk compression software compresses the data so that more storage space is available on the hard disk.

Other tools include system profilers which give details about installed software and connected hardware and backup software which makes a copy of the stored data at regular intervals so that it can be restored in the event, for example, of a disk failure or the accidental deletion of information.

Virus scanners scan files and folders for viruses, text editor utilities are used to change the text or data of a file without WYSIWYG, for example, when changing a configuration file or the source code of a program. Compression utilities are used to compress data, i.e. output a shorter stream or smaller file and encryption utilities produce encoded data using a specific algorithm.

R/M **a Read the text above and answer the questions below.**

1. What is a definition for system utilities?
2. What is the main purpose of system utilities in general?
3. Do you need to install utilities to keep your system running? Why or why not?
4. Briefly outline in German the job of the ten utilities described in the above text.

P **b** **Study the selection of free system utility downloads below and then answer the questions below.**

1. Which utilities would you choose to provide more security when surfing?
2. Which utilities can help you speed up your online activities?
3. Your computer is slow to boot. Which utility do you need?
4. Which utility do you want to win more space on your disk?
5. Which utilities help to control your driver?
6. What utility provides you with a date reminder?
7. Which utility is relevant for a better management of your GUI?
8. Which utilities involve optimizing tasks?
9. Which utility can you use to make security copies of your data?

System utilities

1. **Snapshot** makes it easy to capture your desktop or a window and e-mail it.
2. **Driver Health** monitors the health of your hard drives locally and across a network.
3. **Stream Detective** helps you find and manipulate hidden data streams.
4. **Diskspy** allows you to monitor the processes accessing your drives and the files they are accessing.
5. **PhotoCU** turns your PC into a digital image viewer for local photos and RSS feeds.
6. **Betterbrowser** allows you to preview Web links without clicking them.
7. **Buttonup** lets you organize and group your task bar buttons the way you want.
8. **Taskmaster** lets you schedule over 40 different types of tasks for enhanced productivity.
9. **Duplex** tracks down duplicate files and recover valuable disk space.
10. **Taskcontroller** monitors and controls apps, tasks, services, and drivers.
11. **Replay** takes the hassle out of backing up and protecting critical files and folders.
12. **Surfer** lets you measure and compare your web surfing speed.
13. **Starter** cleans up your startup for faster and smarter launch.
14. **Cookiecop** weeds out bad cookies, pop-ups, Flash, and ActiveX.
15. **Matchmaker** compares and synches the files of two folders, wherever they are.
16. **Snoopy** previews and "snoops" information about files before you open them.
17. **Scout** provides web guide for topics like iPods, Digital Cameras, and HDTV.
18. **Profiler** streamlines Website log-ons, fills out forms, and protects your identity.
19. **Bookmarker** provides quick and easy management of favorite sites.
20. **Postman** notifies Windows when you change the location of a program.
21. **Postit** uses colorful notes to remind you of upcoming events.
22. **Linklock** keeps your private links private.

4 Linux and the "open source movement"

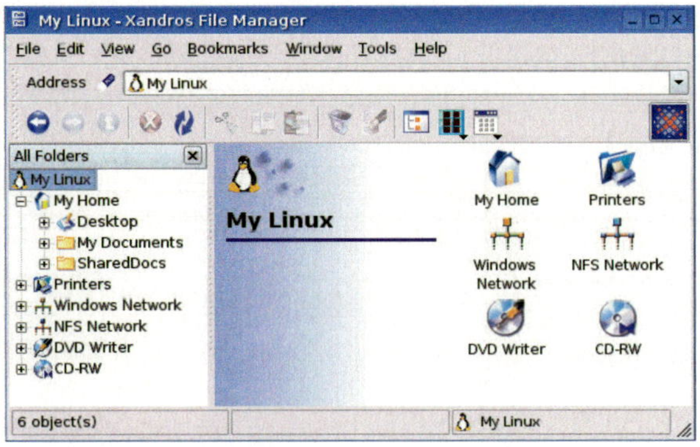

Linux: Love It or Leave It

Linux is a computer operatings system family with close links to Unix. It was initiated by Linus Torvalds from Helisinki University. In his now famous e-mail he extended an open invitation to give him input on a free operating system he was developing: "Hello everybody out there ..." The response was overwhelming. Originally developed and used by private computer enthusiasts, Linux now enjoys the support of any number of major corporations and government agencies, as well as fans all over the world and has a reputation for being more stabile and secure than other operating systems.

Linux is free software and of open source development. It is free because it is not restricted by a property code, i.e. no company or individual owns Linux. Anyone is free to make copies and redistribute it.

Open source means the source code of Linux can be changed to suit one's own needs. The only stipulation is that you make the modified code available to everyone else. Source code modifications and related works are licensed under the GPL (= General Public License), referred to sometimes as a "share and share-alike" system.

New users generally get a general purpose distribution of Linux with the basic operating system as well as some enhanced programs. Downloadable versions of distributions are available online or you can buy sets of pre-loaded CDs with printed manuals at a shop or directly from the distribution's publisher.

So where's the catch? There's no denying the fact that Linux is basically the technically challenging UNIX operating system: It is complex and has a steep learning curve. New users have to get used to another GUI with a different concept which irritates some. It is also very helpful, if not absolutely necessary, to be able to understand written English because most help texts and even some error messages are in English. But one can always count on help for the Linux community is nothing if not accomodating.

Linux is also not an alternative for those who need to have the latest in game software or apps since it is not as widespread among private users and there are often no Linux versions for such software. It is also rare for a company to sell their computers pre-loaded with Linux.

P **a** **Explain the *Open Source Movement* in your own words.**

R/P **b** **Read the text on page 66 and then answer these questions.**

1 Why is Linux called free?
2. Who is responsible for programming Linux?
3. What is meant by an *open source* software?
4. How can I get Linux?
5. Briefly outline some of the major advantages and disadvantages of Linux.

P **c** **Rewrite the reading text below as a step-by-step procedure summarizing the five main points.**

First resize …
On most used systems, the hard drive is already dedicated to partitions for other operating systems. You'll need to resize these partitions in order to make space for Linux. If you're going to run dual-boot system, it's strongly recommended that you read one or more mini-HOWTOS, which describe different dual-boot configurations.
Newer Linuxes start by running a screen-oriented installation programme which tries to interactively walk you through these steps, giving lots of help.

You will probably get the option to try and configure X right away so that the installation programme can go graphical. If you choose this route, the installation programme will quiz you about your mouse and monitor type before getting to the installation proper. Once you get your production Linux installed, these settings will be saved for you. You will be able to tune your monitor's performance later, so at this stage it makes sense to settle for a basic 640x480 SVGA mode.
Just follow the prompts in the programme. It will take you through the steps necessary to prepare your disk, create initial user accounts and install software packages off the CD-ROM.

P/M **d** **Study the system utility example and answer the questions in German.**

userdel
userdel removes a user and, optionally, a user's home directory and any subdirectories from the system.
userdel -r
Files in the user's home directory will be removed along with the home directory itself. Files located in other file systems will have to be searched for and deleted manually.
userdel will not allow you to remove an account if the user is currently logged in. You must kill any running processes which belong to an account that you are deleting. You may not remove any NIS attributes on a NIS client. This must be performed on the NIS server.

1. Zu welchem Zweck wird userdel eingesetzt?
2. Was passiert bei Eingabe von userdel -r?
3. Können Sie auch Dateien in anderen Systemen entfernen? Wie?
4. Unter welchen Umständen funktioniert userdel nicht?
5. Wie können Sie ein aktives Benutzerkonto entfernen?

5 Graphical User Interface (GUI)

R **a** **Match the following icons displayed on the lower menu bar with their functions.**

1. home directory
2. KDE online browser
3. lets you write small notes
4. utilities
5. mail client
6. sound control
7. find utility
8. text editor
9. calculator

R **b** **Read the description of the snapshot of the GUI on page 69 and complete the text with the words in the box.**

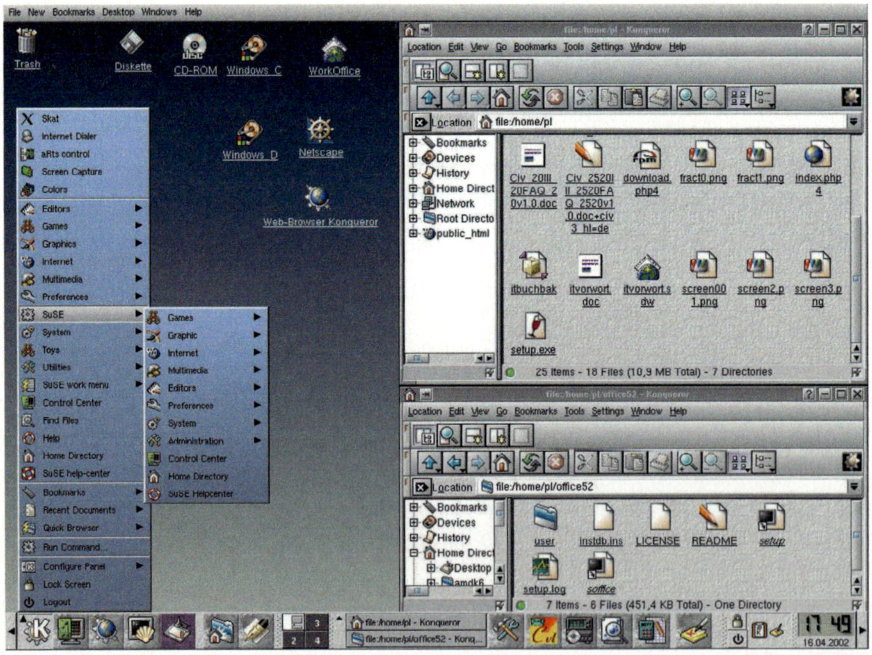

Graphical User Interface

applications • software • scroll bars • file • square • X • date • menu • mouse • icons • options • hardware

A graphical user interface is an operating environment based on graphics. By simply pointing and clicking with your mouse the user can activate the different features of a computer system.

In the upper left hand side of the screen there is a collection of labelled 1 . They represent various 2 devices such as the printer or floppy disk drive, 3 such as Open Office or Internet Browser as well as other options. You can activate them by clicking with your 4 .

On the right hand side of the picture you can see two windows, one just above the other. They allow the user to work on a number of documents or 5 simultaneously. Across the top are menu bars with a selection of 6 , file, edit, view and so on.

Along the right hand side are the 7 which allow you to scan up and down, viewing the contents of the currently active 8 . Clicking one of the three symbols in the very upper right hand directly manipulates the window. Clicking the dot minimizes the window but it's still active. Clicking the 9 enlarges the size of the window to encompass the whole screen and the 10 closes that window.

Along the left hand side of the screen there are two pull-down menus displaying various options. Clicking on the K in the very lower left hand corner of the screen activates the first 11 . The arrows along the right indicate subdirectories that the user activates by moving the pointer in the direction indicated.

Back to the bottom: Moving from the left to the right along the lower ... , let's have a look at some further features. You can switch desktops by either choosing the folder to its right or one of the four numbered bars a little further along. The folder with the little house represents the user's home directory. Activating the lower icon of the two to its right lets you lock your display while the top icon lets you log out. Making a jump to the far right, you'll see the time and 12 on display.

C Answer the following questions concerning the GUI.

1. What does the abbreviation GUI stand for?
2. Name at least four features of a typical GUI (hint: the acronym WIMP gives you clues).
3. What is the purpose of icons? Are they always labelled?
4. Explain how to enlarge, close and minimize a window.
5. Name at least three options that can be found in an internet sub-directory.
6. Is there sometimes more than one way to activate a feature? Give an example.

6 Further reading: European launch for long-awaited Windows Vista

The Microsoft boss, Bill Gates, promised that the long-awaited version of the Windows operating system would revolutionise everything from making phone calls to watching television as he launched it in Europe today.

Unveiling the consumer version of the successor to Windows XP at the British Library in London, Mr Gates predicted a world in which television was personalised and students worked without paper textbooks.

"We're just at the beginning of that. We've just begun to see what we can do," he said.

Windows Vista – which has been more than five years in the making – was released alongside a new version of Microsoft's flagship Office business suite, which includes Word, Excel and PowerPoint.

Journalists and invited guests, some blogging from the launch, packed a British Library conference theatre for the event, which included a performance by the British band The Feeling.

Mr Gates introduced the new operating system by reminding the audience that it was 24 years since Microsoft had produced the first version of Windows.

"Now, in Windows Vista, we have the foundation to take things to a whole new level," he said.

The Microsoft chairman said Windows Vista would revolutionise television by letting people watch personalised shows, for example containing longer news items on subjects they were interested in.

Even television advertising would be targeted to the individual viewer, he said.

However, concerns have already been voiced that Windows Vista's new features to protect computer users against viruses and identity theft are insufficient.

Mr Gates said extensive testing – including the help of 5m volunteers who downloaded early versions of the software – meant Windows Vista and 2007 Microsoft Office were the “highest quality products we’ve ever released”.

He was joined on stage by the British Library chief executive, Lynne Brindley, to announce that two rare Leonardo Da Vinci notebooks had been made freely accessible online for the first time.

The so-called Codex Leicester, part of Mr Gates’s personal collection, can now be viewed alongside the Codex Arundel on the British Library’s website.

Ms Brindley said the “electronic reunification” of the Da Vinci manuscripts for the first time in 500 years would be the first use of the library’s version of its Turning the Pages digitisation software.

Windows Vista’s improved graphics handling makes digitising books and manuscripts much quicker, and means viewing them online is much smoother and more realistic, Mr Gates said.

The British Library is also working with Microsoft to finish copying 25m pages of its 19th century books into digital format this year.

Mr Gates hosted the worldwide launch of Vista in Times Square, New York, yesterday, supported by the punk band Angels and Airwaves, who played a version of Louis Armstrong’s What a Wonderful World.

January 30, 2007 Guardian Unlimited

a Scan the text to find the following values:

1. years to develop Windows Vista
2. years since first Windows launch
3. number of volunteer testers
4. number of digitalized Da Vinci notebooks
5. age of the Da Vinci notebooks

R **b Answer the following questions on the text above in full sentences in English.**

1. When, where and by whom was the new Windows Vista first launched?
2. What changes does Bill Gates foresee in connection with television viewing and Vista?
3. What is OFFICE and the generic terms for its main elements – Word, Excel and PowerPoint?
4. What venue was used for the European launch of Vista and was the event well attended?
5. Have any criticism been expressed with regard to Vista and, if so, what?
6. According to Bill Gates how does Vista compare to other Windows products ? Why is this so?

M/P **c Write a brief summary of the text in German (~ 70–85 words).**

I **d Search the internet and find out about the pros and cons of Windows Vista today. Discuss your results in class.**

7 Language and grammar

7.1 Tenses: The future

a Rewrite the following plans using the "going-to future".

Example: John plans on moving to Tulsa in November.
John is going to move to Tulsa in November for his new job.

1. They're scheduled to launch the latest Linux distribution in November.
2. The boss intends to install new anti-virus software.
3. What do you intend to do about the trouble with our new operating system?
4. The company's plan is to take over the software industry.
5. Where do they plan to set up the new support center?

b Match the sentences on the left with those on the right closest in meaning.

1. I'll help you install the new compression software.	a. I'm offering to help right now.
2. I'm going to help you install the new compression software.	b. I would like to know if you plan to talk to him.
3. I'm sure she'll come.	c. I know because she told me she plans to.
4. She's going to come.	d. I think they are careless and might regret it some day.
5. Are you going to talk to him about the new operating system?	e. If you ask her she should say yes.
6. Will you talk to him about the new operating system?	f. I intend to help when the time comes.
7. They'll get into trouble one of these days if they don't encrypt their sensitive data.	g. I am sure they are going to have problems if they are not more careful.
8. They're going to get into trouble one of these days if they don't encrypt their sensitive data.	h. I would like you to talk to him.

c Choose the correct future form of the verb.

Will infinitive • will continuous • present continuous • present simple • going-to

1. Classes **start** next month on the third.
2. I **start** a computer crash course next month on the third.
3. I **take** a computer course next semester.
4. Perhaps I **take** a computer course next semester.
5. I **must take** a computer course some day.
6. I **take** at least three computer courses next semester.
7. Okay, since you insist, I **take** the computer course with you.
8. I think we **get off** to a good start. *(before actually starting)*
9. I think we **get off** to a good start. *(after actually starting)*

Unit 4
Application software

Application software

Application software, often called apps, can be defined as a sub-category of software which allow users to perform specific tasks, as opposed to system software employed for coordinating a system's resources. Application suites refer to a number of applications bundled together as a package. Such suites might come pre-installed with the computer hardware but most often have to be bought separately.
Typical applications include business software, educational software, medical software and computer games.

R **Read the brief introduction to application software above and then answer the questions below.**

1. What is the difference between application and system software?
2. What are application suites?
3. Are applications always included when you purchase a computer?
4. Aside from business software, what other forms of applications are there? What are they used for?

1 Word processing

R **a** **Complete the following text with the terms in the box on the right. Listen and check.**

Word processing provides a flexible way of creating, editing and printing your documents and text files and is the most common computer application. With a 1, the generic term for the relevant software, you can not only create and store documents, but also modify them in any number of ways, making such programs powerful performance tools.

Though word processors vary, they all support a row of basic features. Probably the most useful one is their ability to 2 not just characters or words, but also lines, paragraphs or even whole sections of a text. If you make a typo, you just back up the cursor, either with special arrow keys or the mouse, and correct it. 3 allows you to cut out or remove part of the text from one place in the document and insert or paste it in where you want to have it. Of course, you can also 4 a section of the text by simply highlighting it with your mouse or you can use the printer to make 5.

You can also determine different 6 with the word processor automatically changing the text so that it fits. 7 is another useful feature that has the software look through the whole text for a certain word or phrase to either delete it or replace it.

8 means that the word processor automatically moves from one line to the next as they are filled with text. In order to give your document a neat, professional appearance, though, word processors also generally feature automatic hyphenation and justification. Using a comprehensive dictionary, the automatic 9 constantly monitors and checks words as you input them. If a word is too long when you come to the end of a line, this feature automatically kicks in, splits the word, adds a hyphen and places the rest of the word on the next line. 10 spaces your words evenly across a line so that the text is flush with the margin.

These are just the basic features of so-called text editors but full- featured word processors have a number of very useful, additional features.

hyphenation • search and replace • page sizes and margins • word wrap • copy • delete or insert • justification • cut and paste • hardcopies • word processor

R **b** **Match the features to their descriptions.**

1. file management	a. allows the automatic numbering and placement of references
2. font specifications	b. helps you find synonyms, i.e. words with the same or similar meaning
3. graphics	c. is a word or character which replaces certain, frequently used combination of keystrokes
4. macros	d. different margins and paragraph indentations can be specified within a document
5. merges	e. lets you work on two documents simultaneously
6. spell checkers	f. allows you to insert or even create your own illustrations
7. footnotes and cross references	g. a useful tool that highlights any misspelt words and offers alternative suggestions
8. headers and footers	h. can be created based on special codes that are embedded directly into the document
9. page numbering	i. lets you change the size, appearance (e.g. bold, italics) and typeface (e.g. Arial) of letters and characters.
10. thesaurus	j. lets you insert text from one file into another file which is useful when you have multiple files with the same format but different data
11. windows	k. the document is previewed on the screen as it will look printed (what you see is what you get)
12. WYSIWYG	l. lets you create, delete, move and search for files
13. table of contents and indexes	m. automatically keeps track so that the correct one appears on each page
14. word completion	n. you can tailor your document so that a special line of text, word or illustration always appears at the bottom and/or top of the page
15. layout	o. automatically finishes a, usually longer, word once you have typed in the first few letters

I/P **c** **Take turns describing your favourite word processor features. Have the others guess which one you are talking about.**

M **d** **Find the English equivalents in the text on page 74 for the following German word processing terms:**

1. automatischer Zeilenumbruch
2. Rechtschreibprüfung
3. Synonymwörterbuch
4. Seitennummerierung
5. Verzeichnisse
6. Gestaltung
7. Seitenrand
8. Suchen und ersetzen
9. Silbentrennung
10. Schriftart

R **e** **Find the matching squares for the word processing terms.**

Example: A tab = J moves the cursor to a preset position

A tab	B the horizontal position of text: left, center, right	C cursor	D automatic movement of text from the end of one line to the beginning	E header
F blank space along the edges of a document	G line-spacing	H where your fingers "live" on the keyboard	I scrolling	J moves the cursor to a preset position
K keys used to move the insertion point up, down, left or right	L insertion point	M arrow keys	N moving through the document from top to bottom, left to right	O home keys
P word-wrap	Q used to adjust the space between line (usually single or double)	R alignment	S information that appears at the top of every page	T margin

M **f** **Match the following terms to their German equivalents.**

1. cut and paste	a. Rechtschreibprüfung
2. save as	b. Ansicht
3. spelling	c. Einfügen
4. insert	d. Sonderzeichen
5. redo	e. Ausschneiden und einfügen
6. view	f. Absatz
7. paragraph settings	g. Speichern als
8. special characters	h. Neu anfangen

M **g** Jack, an English speaking visitor wants to use Ute's computer to do some layout work. Unfortunately, she only has German version software. Complete the following dialogue with the correct translation or explanation.

Jack: Oh no, this is all in German – I don't understand a word!
Ute: No reason to panic. We'll manage this together. It is not so difficult. Now, first you want to, uh, feed the words in, right?
Jack: Well yeah, I need this menu on the left – how do you pronounce it, *Datei*?
Ute: Correct – what you call 1 ?
Jack: Right. Okay now I'll just click the top one – *neu* – that's 2 I know. And now, oh ...! *Textdokument* and *Präsentation* I can guess are 3 and 4 but what about this one, *Zei..., Zeich...*
Ute: *Zeichnung* – that's 5 , *Nachrichten* is 6 and *Bild* is, you know, 7 .
Jack: Not so fast – I have to write this down. Now what do I do if I want to close or print a document?
Ute: *Close* is 8 and *Print* is 9 .
Jack: Okay. Now, what's this *Bearbeiten* menu?
Ute: I don't know the name in English but you use it to 10 the text or parts.
Jack: You mean *Edit*?
Ute: Yes, that's it.
Jack: So which one is *Cut*?
Ute: That's 11
Jack: And *Kopieren* is 12 I suppose. But what in the world is *Einfügen*?
Ute: Oh je, I don't know the English but after you cut the text you want to put it back together.
Jack: Oh – that's 13 . But here's *Einfügen* again as a menu.
Ute: Then it is your 14 . Let's click it on. See, there's *Kopfzeile* for the top of the text.
Jack: The 15 , okay. And the footer is ...
Ute: It's 16 .
Jack: Boy, this sure gets complicated.
Ute: One more thing you'll want the 17 here.
Jack: What we often call *Tools*, I suppose.
Ute: Maybe. But this is important, the first one, *Rechtschreibung*.
Jack: That must be 18 and below is the thesaurus. I think I've got the hang of things now. Thanks a million, Ute, you've been a great help!
Ute: My pleasure.

R **h** **Now listen to the dialogue and check your answers.**

I/R **i** **Work in pairs. Using the clues in the box below take turns describing the WORDS. Can your partner guess the right WORD?**

Example: It's written in plain text bold and underlined. Number 4? That's right.

1. <u>word</u>	enlarged
2. *word*	<u>underlined</u>
3. **"word"**	*italics*
4. **<u>word</u>**	**bold**
5. [word]	CAPITALS
6. (WORD)	"quotation marks"
7. **<u>WORD</u>**	highlighting
8. ["word"]	(parenthesis)
9. **(WORD)**	[brackets]
10. word	plain text

2 Spreadsheets and diagrams

R **a** **Look at the spreadsheet and answer the following questions.**

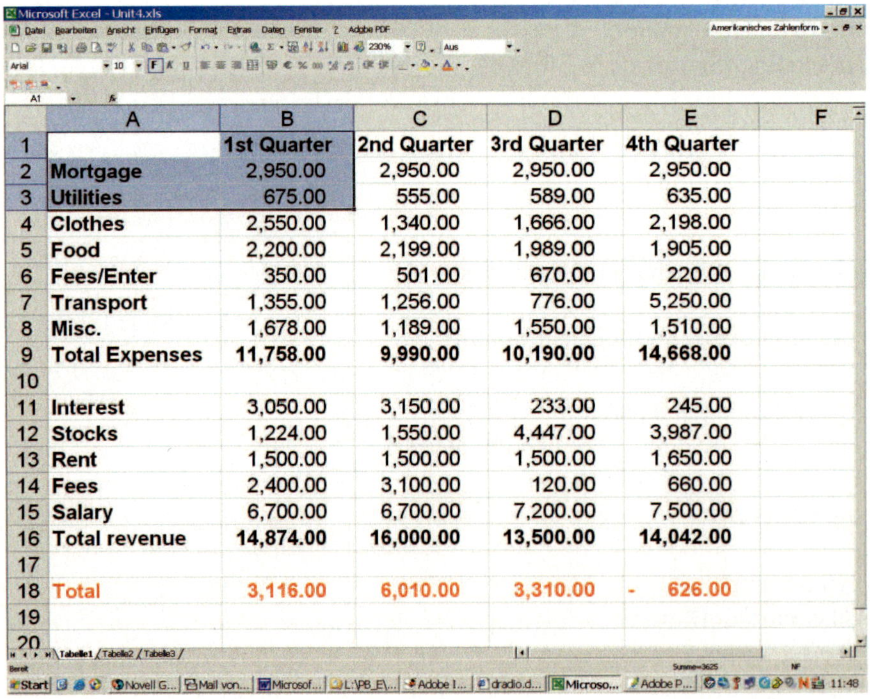

	A	B	C	D	E	F
1		1st Quarter	2nd Quarter	3rd Quarter	4th Quarter	
2	Mortgage	2,950.00	2,950.00	2,950.00	2,950.00	
3	Utilities	675.00	555.00	589.00	635.00	
4	Clothes	2,550.00	1,340.00	1,666.00	2,198.00	
5	Food	2,200.00	2,199.00	1,989.00	1,905.00	
6	Fees/Enter	350.00	501.00	670.00	220.00	
7	Transport	1,355.00	1,256.00	776.00	5,250.00	
8	Misc.	1,678.00	1,189.00	1,550.00	1,510.00	
9	Total Expenses	11,758.00	9,990.00	10,190.00	14,668.00	
10						
11	Interest	3,050.00	3,150.00	233.00	245.00	
12	Stocks	1,224.00	1,550.00	4,447.00	3,987.00	
13	Rent	1,500.00	1,500.00	1,500.00	1,650.00	
14	Fees	2,400.00	3,100.00	120.00	660.00	
15	Salary	6,700.00	6,700.00	7,200.00	7,500.00	
16	Total revenue	14,874.00	16,000.00	13,500.00	14,042.00	
17						
18	Total	3,116.00	6,010.00	3,310.00	- 626.00	
19						
20						

1. What does this spreadsheet provide information about?
2. What are the three basic elements of a spreadsheet called?
3. How many rows are there altogether?
4. How many months does a column represent?
5. What does the cell at the intersection of the fourth column and the fifth row tell you?
6. When do you think a number of new shares were bought? What makes you think so? Where did the money come from?
7. Is there any quarter in which expenses exceeded earnings?
8. Are there any seasonal fluctuations in expenditures? Can you think of any explanations?
9. You have just received delayed payment for a consulting job completed in December. Which cell(s) will be affected?
10. What formula do you need to compare quarterly earnings and expenses?

M **b Find the English equivalents for the following German words in the spreadsheet on page 78.**

1. Nebenkosten
2. Hypothek
3. Zins
4. Aktien
5. Ausgaben
6. Einnahmen
7. Honorar
8. Sonstiges

R **c Match the diagrams to their labels.**

1. bar chart
2. flow chart
3. line graph
4. grid
5. matrix
6. organigram
7. pie chart
8. table

A

Month	Jan	Feb	Mar
Rainfall	17	20	15
Sunny days	16	11	20
Average temp.	5	10	12

B

Twin Cities	Airport	Art gallery	Underground
Regensburg		•	
Odessa		•	
Aberdeen	•	•	•

C

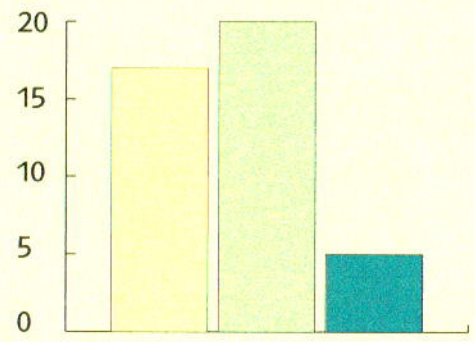

D

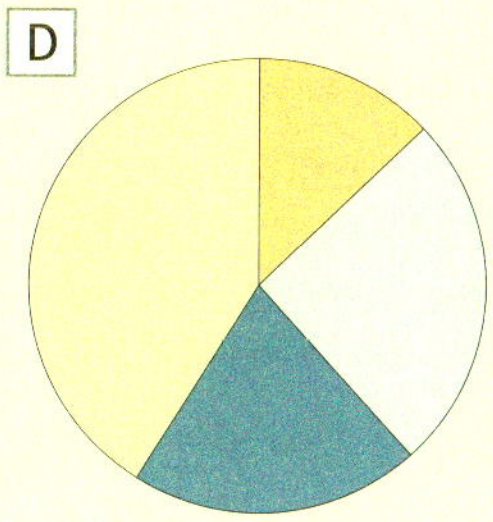

E

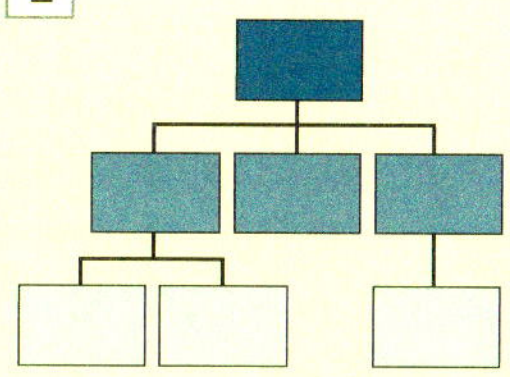

F

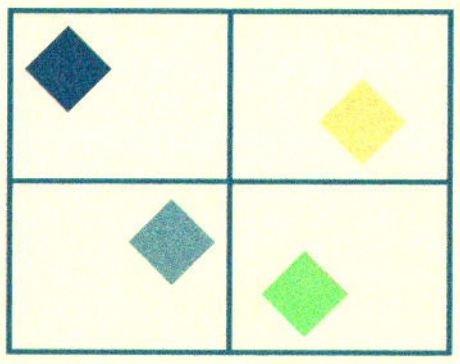

G

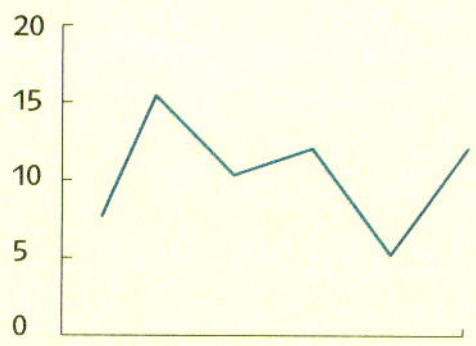

H

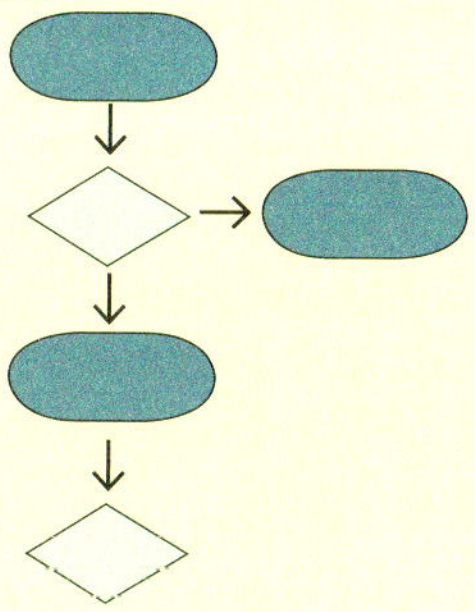

d **Match the diagrams on page 79 to their definitions below.**

1. They are used to show steps in a process such as a computer program.
2. A development over time is represented by lines, especially suitable for fluctuations in totals or percentages.
3. Totals are displayed as vertical or horizontal blocks, especially suitable for comparisons.
4. Two scalable variables of a number of items are shown by positioning them in one of four quadrants.
5. Items and their corresponding characteristics are presented vertically and horizontally.
6. A total is divided into segments of a round disc.
7. Items and their corresponding figures are exhibited in columns.
8. The structure of a hierarchy or conglomerate is illustrated.

P **e** **The contents of the following texts have to be diagrammed. Decide which model (see page 79) is best suited for displaying the various information. Ideally the results of your analysis should be presented in the form of a sketch of the respective diagrams.**

1. The volume of sales for our firewall software during the first half of the year was a series of ups and downs. Sales were less than 6% of the market share in early January, and then rose sharply to almost 9% in less than two months, only to drop sharply below the 6% level towards the end of March. A more gradual rise then took them up to their peak of just under 10% by late June. A slight dip and then a sharper drop led to a rate of 7% by late summer. The trend continued in the early fall with sales reaching their lowest point in October at just over 5%. November saw a renewed climb to more than 7% by the end of the month, but then they dipped back to achieve their former share of 6%.

2. Almost every American household has at least one TV, while some 85% own VCRs and more than 70% DVD players. More than 50% of households come equipped with a telephone answering machine and cordless phones – 56% for the former and 51% for the latter. Not quite 50% of American households own a CD player and 35% a MP3 player, though only 33% can boast of having a PC. Not surprisingly, practically every household owns one or more cellular phones – 91%.

3. When calling a meeting, decide who should attend, clarify your aims and write an agenda. Arrange date time and venue and notify the participants. At the meeting itself first welcome everyone and make any necessary introductions. Then present and briefly go through the agenda. As chairperson it's your job to make sure everyone has a chance to express their views. Try to reach a consensus and don't forget to summarize important discussion points and decisions made. Before closing the meeting, again summarize the main points, set deadlines for who's to do what. Thank your team!

4. You can get a PC for nothing, or next to nothing, nowadays but the deals naturally have their drawbacks. The Enchilada, for example, only costs $399. It comes with a 1 Ghz RAD K6-111 system, stereo speakers and three years of internet access. The drawback is that you have to pay for tech support, the monitor and warranty separately.
You can also win a Cyrix with free internet access from Free-Pac (www.free-pac.com) but you have to use the system for at least 10 hours per month and 40% of its display is plastered with advertising.
For only $29.95 a month you can also get a 800 Mhz Celeron-based PC with internet access from Interpod (www. Interpod.com). The trouble is you have to commit to 30 months and either pay in advance or submit to a credit card check.
Our freePC.com (www.ourfreepc.com) provides you with a low-end PC with internet access for $ 26.79 per month. The catch is you have to commit to 19 months and pay up front.

I **f Discuss the advantages or possible drawbacks of the different forms of graphical representation. Consider the various types of information and data you deal with in your daily work life. Which diagram is best suited for presenting which type of material?**

3 Presentation software

Presentation software is used to display information, usually as a slide show. They include an editor to insert and format text, a tool to insert and manipulate graphics and a slide-show system to display the content.

P/I **a Discuss with a partner the optimal order for the following steps involved in creating a presentation. Give reasons for your choices.**

- Insert a new slide by choosing **insert** > **slide** from the menu bar
- Add animations and transitions to slide shows
- Choose the type of presentation you want, usually a "Blank Presentation" to start.
- Save your work regularly right from the start
- Create a title slide by typing in your title and subtitle
- Print out handouts or transparencies
- Open the presentation software
- Add text and images to slides
- Change presentation attributes
- Choose a new slide layout. To start with select the "Title Slide" layout.
- Choose view options

P **b The symbols on the right represent graphic functions that you can use in creating presentations. Write sentences about what they are used to do.**

Example: Symbol number 8 lets you display the code.

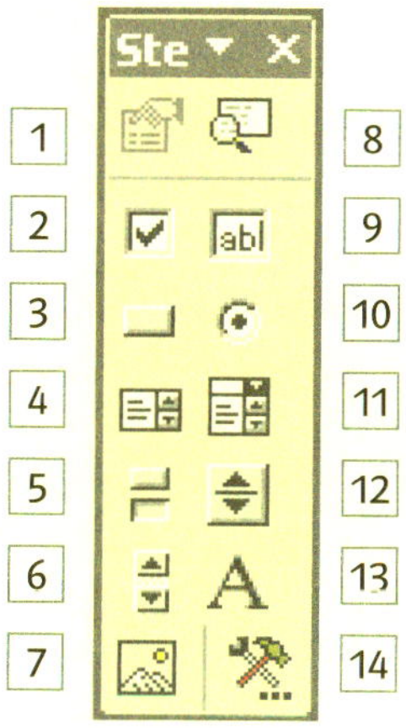

M **C** **Give a summary of the following text in German.**

Creating presentations

There are a number of basic rules to keep in mind for creating effective software presentations with impact. First of all, you have to think about the background, with contrast and consistency being two most important criteria in this connection. For presentations on paper a dark text on a light background is recommended but for slide projection a light text on a semi-dark background is the better alternative as the eye is attracted to light. Simple, textured backgrounds work well but complicated ones make the text difficult to read. Another point is to be consistent and stick to just a single background as it sets the stage for your presentation and you shouldn't constantly be changing the backdrop in the middle of the act.
It is also generally recommended to align the points on the left margin of the slide, one above the other. This gives the text a neat appearance and makes the bullet points easier to read and a focal point.
Graphics and other visuals can add interest to your presentation but caution should be exercised. Firstly, they should be kept as simple as possible and not be just for the sake of decoration but well matched to the message. The placement of graphics is also important. Putting your graphics in the middle of the slide is not advised as this leaves little room for the text. As a rule they should be placed off center, generally on the left for better balance and to provide more room. Left placement also leads the eye to the text.
You should avoid writing all caps because such text is very hard to read and gives the impression that you are shouting. Generally, most people capitalize the first word of a bullet point and leave it at that. Exceptions are, of course, proper nouns or if you want a more formal style of presentation, in which case you might then capitalize the first letter of every word in your titles but not in the bullet points.

▶

As far as fonts go, one, at the most two, per slide are considered adequate and they should be straightforward and legible and large – at least 14pt. Also avoid using red, either in fonts or as a background colour, because it is aggressive and difficult to see and read. Colours, generally, should be used sparingly and consistently. For example, you might choose one colour for all your titles and a somewhat darker or lighter shade of the same colour for the rest of your text.

Last but certainly not least, we come to the most important aspect of your presentation: the content. The mistake many people make is to try and place too much text on the screen. You should try and abbreviate your message, keep it easy to understand and not write everything out in complete sentences. A good idea is to try and follow the "7 x 7" rule, i.e. to create slides with a maximum of seven words across and seven lines down. After all, the idea of a presentation is that you, the presenter, can and should elaborate verbally on the information provided in the form of the concise text in the slides.

P **d** **Follow the suggested guidelines in the text above and create a software presentation with a partner about this topic. Present the results to the group. Whose presentation was the most effective? Why?**

4 Databases

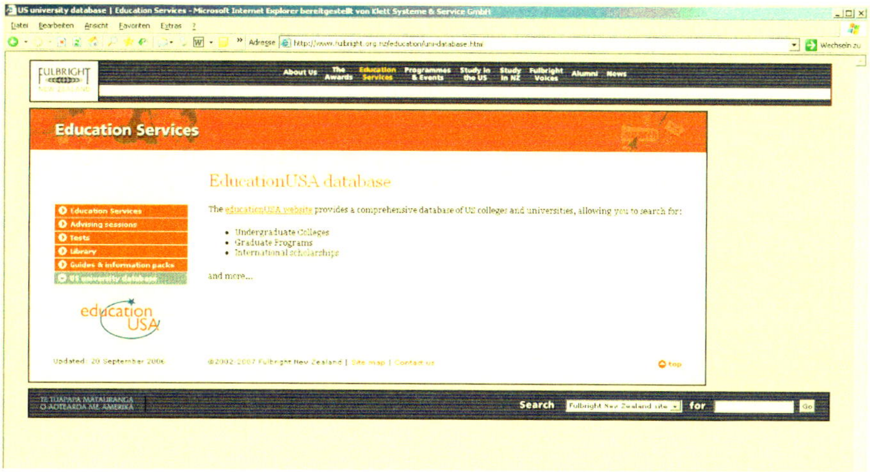

4.1 Introduction

When thinking about databases, the first thing that occurs to most people is their capability of storing huge amounts of data that a user can quickly access. How can a database process data so quickly? The reason is that a database "knows" where individual sets of data are stored; it does not have to first load all of the data and then start "looking" for what it wants, as one does when accessing conventional files or spreadsheets. Database technology allows you to radically reduce access time, as well as system resource needs, especially if large amounts of data are involved.

Another advantage to database systems is their logical versus physical structure. The user only deals with the logical structure of the data, a structure he designed himself in the process of creating the database. Storing the data physically is then done automatically by the system. This logical structure also enables the user to define links between data. This avoids redundancies and allows access to various new information, which otherwise would have to be collected manually – a rather tedious job without a database system.
A concrete example of how a retailer can store customer data and invoices in a database, and thereby optimize his data management, is illustrated below (DB-chart / image 1). Whenever he wants, he can create a list of his customers with their individual turnover by just typing in one command. If he used a spreadsheet he would need to find each customer's invoice and add up their totals. Of course, he could also make up a separate list with the customers' names, personal data and invoice totals, but such a list would have to be updated every time an item was sold or a customer's data changed, costing additional time and money. A database, in contrast, offers instant access to all data, and is capable of multi-linking them without incurring additional costs.
Database systems also offer real multi-user access. Hundreds of users can access a database simultaneously and everyone is treated as if he were the only user.
Furthermore, the right to access certain areas of a database can be defined individually for each user and each set of data. For example, one group of employees might be entitled to only access customer data such as name and address, while other employees would be allowed to see the customers' quarterly turnover or their account balance.

Another outstanding feature of databases are their superior backup facilities. While it is possible, of course, to save copies of your spreadsheets, this would involve transmitting the whole file every time you wanted to do a backup. Database systems, in contrast, support "replication". This means that every time data changes in the database, just the changes – and not the whole system – are transmitted to another server. This allows a second server to hold an exact copy of the original database at any given moment. If anything goes wrong on the primary database server, all requests can simply be redirected to the backup server.

To ease work with databases, SQL (standard query language) – a universal database language – was declared standard by the American National Standards Institute (ANSI) in 1986. It was also accepted by the International Organization for Standardization (ISO) in 1987. It is a powerful programming language whose syntax is based on everyday English and which is independent of different software products.

R **a** **Answer the following questions on the text (4.1 Introduction).**

1. What is the advantage of a database over a conventional filing system? Why?
2. Why is a logical structure advantageous for a database system?
3. Look up the meaning of "redundancy" in a dictionary. How does it relate to a database system?
4. Explain how using a database system can optimize customer data management.
5. What two advantages does multi-user access have?
6. How does the process of replication guarantee a backup at any given moment?
7. What is SQL?

R **b** **Find the English equivalents for the phrases below in the text.**

1. Das Erste, was einem einfällt …
2. Mit Datenbanktechnologie kann man die Zugriffszeiten entscheidend verringern.
3. Eine Datenbank bietet schnellen direkten Zugriff auf alle Daten und kann diese in jeder beliebigen Weise verknüpfen.
4. Jeder wird so behandelt, als ob …
5. Zugriffsrechte können eingeschränkt werden …
6. Ein herausragendes Merkmal …
7. Um die Arbeit zu erleichtern …
8. Zum Standard erhoben …

R **c** **Match the database features to their advantages.**

1. logical and physical data structure 2. redundancy 3. multi-user access 4. authorisation 5. network security 6. backup 7 replication	a. It is possible to regulate access to data on an individualized basis. b. Queries can be made by relating different sets of data with one command. c. Data loss can be prevented by mirroring the whole database on a second server. d. Lets the user define links between data to avoid redundancies. e. Loss of data can be prevented by making a copy of just one central file – the database. f. Many people can use the same database system at the same time without interference. g. Encrypted queries are possible in LANS as well as via internet.

4.2 Making use of databases

Scenario: In a database a retailer stores all the data relating to the products he sells, his customers and his invoices. The database also allows him to assess his business from different perspectives. For example, he could link data to find his top 10 customers or produce a list of his 10 best selling articles.

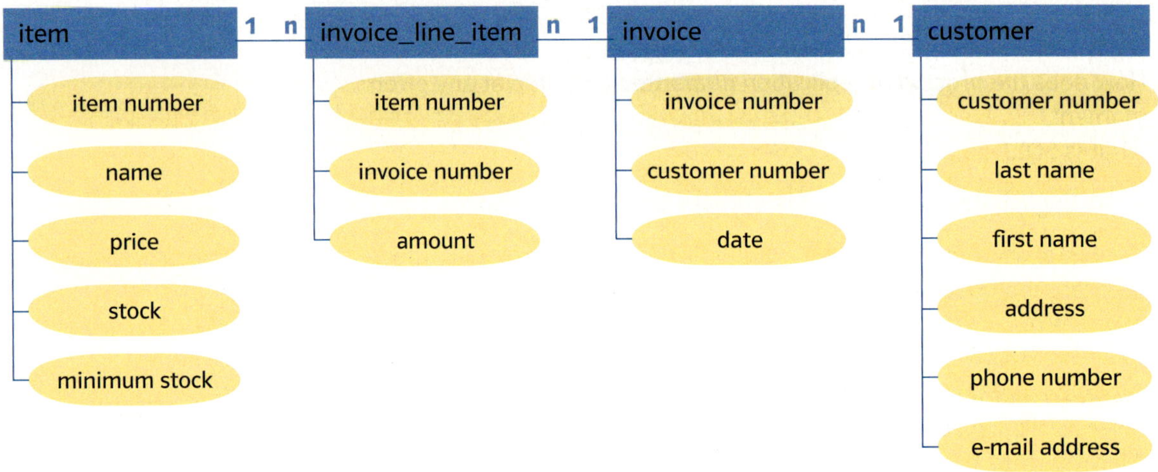

The following is an example in SQL for possible database queries using the above chart.
For resource planning there is supposed to be a definite number of each item in stock. With an SQL-Database one can find out this information with one command and within seconds:

```
SELECT "item number", "name", "minimum stock" - "stock" AS "amount"
FROM item
WHERE "minimum stock" > "stock"
ORDER BY "amount" desc;
```

R **How does this translate into "human" English?**
Match the correct pairs!

1. Browse through all your items in the warehouse.
2. Note item numbers, names, minimum stock for each item.
3. The actual stock you find is to be defined as "amount".
4. Whenever the actual stock is smaller than the defined minimal stock, give out the difference in numbers as an order.
5. Sort your order list with the highest number on top, the others descending.

a.	SELECT… - "stock" AS "amount" FROM item
b.	SELECT … FROM item WHERE "minimum stock" > "stock"
c.	SELECT… FROM item
d.	ORDER BY "amount" desc;
e.	SELECT "item number", "name", "minimum stock" - "stock" AS "amount" FROM item

5 Further reading: Data mining

Data mining uses data analysis tools to determine previously unknown, valid patterns and relationships in large data sets. Such tools can include statistical models, mathematical algorithms and machine learning methods. The latter are algorithms that improve their performance automatically through experience. Data mining is more than a matter of just collecting and managing data since it also encompasses analysis and prediction.

Data mining applications employ different parameters to examine the data such as association, sequence or path analaysis, classification, clustering, and forecasting. Association are patterns where one event is connected to another and sequence patterns where one event leads to another event. Classifications involves identifying new patterns and clustering finding and documenting groups or clusters of previously unknown facts. Forecasting means finding patterns on the basis of which reasonable predictions can be made.

In contrast to other data analysis applications, data mining uses a discovery rather than a deductive approach. This entails algorithms being used to examine a number of multi-dimensionsal data relationships simultaneously in order to find out those that are unique or which occur frequently. Due to this complexity, successful data mining calls for two important prerequisites: a clear formulation of the problem and access to relevant data.

A number of advances in technology and business processes have contributed to the growth of data mining. Among them are the expansion of computer networks which can be used to connect databases, better search techniques such as neural networks and advanced algorithms, and the increased ability to combine data from very different sources into a single searchable source. At the same time, there has been an enormous increase in the volume of accessible information collected and stored, while the costs for its storage have decreased dramatically. Data mining is used for many purposes in both the private and public sectors. Insurance companies and banks, for example, use data mining to detect fraud and assess risks, while retailers collect information through affinity programs (e.g. frequent flyer points, and preferred customer programs) to market their products and increase sales. ▶

In the wake of the threat of global terrorism the scope of data mining in the public sector has been greatly enhanced. It can be a potential means, for example, to identify terrorist activities, such as money transfers and communications, and to identify and track individual terrorists themselves through travel and immigration records.

While data mining application can be very powerful analytical tools, they do have their limitations. To be successful, data mining requires skilled technical and analytical specialists who can structure the analysis and interpret the output that is created. That is because, although data mining can help reveal patterns and relationships, it does not tell the user the value or significance of these patterns. Similarly, the validity of the patterns discovered is dependent on how they compare to "real world" circumstances. For example, while a data mining application might be able to create a profile of a "typical terrorist" – based on data about known terrorists – it won't be able to identify a suspect whose behaviour doesn't conform to the profile.
Furthermore, while data mining can identify connections between behaviors and/or variables, it cannot necessarily identify a causal relationship. For example, a data mining tool might discover that the propensity to purchase airline tickets just shortly before the flight is scheduled to depart, is related to factors such as income, level of education, and age. The question of why certain people buy last-minute flights, however, is not answered.

There are also a number of overriding issues in connection with data mining. One question concerns the accuracy and completeness of the collected data, another has to to do with the interoperability of data mining software and databases from different sources and agencies. The issues of mission creep, using the the data for other than the original stated purpose, and privacy are also matters of controversial debate.

(adapted from Data Mining and homeland security – an Overview, 2007)

M/R **Read the text above and answer the following questions in German.**

1. Was, sowohl ganz konkret als auch im weiteren Sinne, beinhaltet *Datamining*?
2. Welche Art analytischer Werkzeuge werden zum *Datamining* verwendet?
3. Beschreiben Sie die fünf Parameter, die zum *Datamining* verwendet werden.
4. Welche Herangehensweise wird in *Datamining* benutzt und was beinhaltet sie?
5. Welche Voraussetzungen erfordert *Datamining*?
6. Welche Faktoren trugen zum Zuwachs von *Datamining* bei?
7. Nennen Sie drei Beispiele für den Einsatz des *Datamining*.
8. Wie kann *Datamining* im Kampf gegen den Terrorismus helfen? Nennen Sie zwei Beispiele.
9. Welchen Einschränkungen unterliegt *Datamining* in Bezug auf Muster?
10. Welcher zusätzlichen Einschränkung unterliegt *Datamining*?
11. Welche Fragen lässt *Datamining* offen?

6 Language and grammar

6.1 Active and passive

INFO BOX Active/Passive

The passive puts the spotlight on the person or thing something is happening to rather than the agent of an activity.
Example: Active: People really like John. → Passive: John is well liked

Note: John, the object of the active sentence becomes the focus or subject of the passive sentence. The subject or agent of the active sentence, people, can be dropped, as if often the case in passive sentences. Another minor change is *well* instead of *really* liked because it sounds better in the passive.

a Convert the following active sentences into the passive.

1. In the future we won't need a keyboard to input data.
2. My voice mail program automatically downloads incoming messages.
3. They must take measures to protect the system against viruses.
4. The authorities don't seem to be doing anything about it.
5. People are buying more and more merchandise online.
6. Somebody might help us if we asked.
7. What can anyone do to help?
8. Some guy always takes care of all the travel arrangements.

b Match the following functions/features to the correct category of software: Note: Some features might be true of more than one category.

1. grammar exercises are featured	a. Database
2. visual representations of values, for example, in the form of pie charts, can be made	b. Spreadsheets
3. large amounts of data are stored digitally	c. Word-processing
4. information can be presented in an attractive and concise manner	d. Presentation software
5. maps can be displayed	e. Route Planners
6. different types and sizes of fonts can be used	f. Language-learning software

C Now use the clues below to form passive sentences to describe further application software features.

Example:
Database: changes, any number of records, at one time / information, retrieve, easily
→ Changes can be made in any number of records at one time and information easily retrieved.

1. Spreadsheets: change, width of columns/calculate values
2. Word processors: create more attractive print texts/mail merging, send
3. Presentation software: slide show prepare/animate, text and graphics
4. Route planners alternative routes, suggest/directions give
5. Language-learning software: vocabulary, practice/spelling and grammar mistakes, check

6.2 Infinitive or "ing"-form?

INFO BOX Infinitive and "ing"-form

Most adjectives are followed by the infinitive form of the verb.
Example: He's afraid to say anything.

However, if the adjective is coupled to a preposition the ing follows.
Example: He's always afraid of saying the wrong thing.

Choose the infinitive or ing form of the verbs in brackets of the following sentences.

1. After do my morning exercises, I always feel ready take on a new day.
2. We're sorry about have push back the deadline but our team just isn't capable of work any faster.
3. Sorry interrupt but I'm finding it difficult follow your train of thought.
4. Our firm is proud announce the upcoming merger with Nevertell.
5. It's rather surprising hear that the firm which has a reputation for be ruthless is now interested in compromise.

6.3 Prepositions

Complete the following sentences with the appropriate preposition.

from • after • till • at • in • per • of(2x) • within • during

1. A spreadsheet consists 1 a number of columns across the top of the sheet and rows down.
2. The amount of money spent 2 annum 3 $ millions is along the left hand side of the graph.
3. Please return the attached form 4 eight days to receive your free sample copy 5 PAC magazine.
4. You'll be able to contact me anytime 6 the fifth 7 the Hilltown Hotel. I'm staying there 8 the fair 9 Wednesday 10 Tuesday the 11th.

Unit 5
LANs, WANs and GANs

1 Networks

R **a** **Match the answers with the questions.**

1. It's two or more computers linked together.
2. The first connects computers within a limited area, while the latter links computers across a much larger space.
3. It covers an unlimited geographical area.
4. This is the main computer that stores the files of a network system.
5. Time and money can be saved by allowing workers to pool and exchange information more easily, as well as sharing resources such as printers.
6. They are points on a junction of communication lines in a network, in other words the various interconnected computer devices.
7. It is a network that is composed of different interconnected computer networks (WANs).

a. What is a global area network (GAN)?
b. What are nodes?
c. What is a file server?
d. What is the difference between a LAN and a WAN?
e. What is a network?
f. What are the advantages of LANs and WANs?
g. What is the range of a global area network?

R **b** **LAN versus Intranet**

Read the following text and answer the questions below.

A local area network is a short-distance network. It is used in many offices or administrative buildings to link a group of computers together within the same building. The costs for LANs are relatively low, but their range is usually limited to distances of less than 500 metres. A LAN is economical as it allows many users to share printers, scanners, etc. Using the LAN, employees in a company can communicate with each other very easily. Though the terms LAN and intranet are sometimes used interchangeably they are not the same. In brief, an intranet is a private computer network that employs internet protocols and network connectivity to allow employees access to an organization's pool of information or operations.

1. What does the acronym LAN stand for?
2. What is the advantage / disadvantage of a LAN?
3. What is the difference between a LAN and an intranet?

1.1 Network topologies

R **a** **The shape of a network is called its topology. The topology describes how different nodes in a network are connected to each other. The diagrams below show some of the most common network topologies. Match the texts below to the correct diagrams.**

1. All workstations and peripherals are linked to the central host computer which controls the activities of the network and through which all messages are routed.
2. All workstations are linked together in a circular manner. Each member of the loop or ring can process data directly as well as share applications and data along the network.
3. A single two-directional cable is used which is capable of sending information between two attached devices very quickly.
4. Every computer is connected to every other computer by a separate cable.

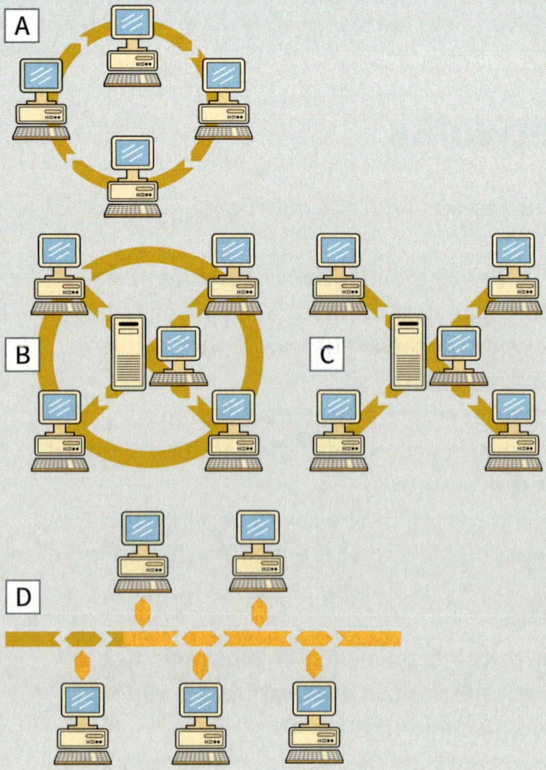

R **b** **Which of the diagrams on page 94 depicts which type of topology: Ring, Mesh, Star or Bus?**

R **c** **Find words in the text on page 92 (1.1) with the same or similar meanings as the following:**

1. reach	6. comparatively
2. principal	7. configuration
3. connect	8. independent
4. way, form	9. drawback
5. connected	10. cost-effective

R **d** **Put the jumbled sentences into the correct order to find out what is characteristic of the different topologies.**

1. which is an / has a / device. / at the centre / hub / electronic / A star topology
2. special unit of data. / has a token / A ring / which is a
   as a key / other devices. / It acts / to access
3. has the elements / A bus / connected / along a cable. / of its system
   can only / one at a time. / Messages / be sent
4. computer / more complicated / interconnected system / A mesh is a / in
   which each / is connected to the others.

1.2 Networking

R **a** **Match the network terms on the left to their synonyms on the right.**

1. gateway	a. authorization
2. token	b. rules
3. cable	c. connectors
4. nodes	d. information centre
5. protocol	e. portal
6. transceiver	f. on / off
7. file server	g. junctions
8. mail server	h. „walk-talky“
9. switch	i. post office

R **b** **Match the actions to the consequences.**

1. Inputting the wrong password	a. Can interconnect different types of networks
2. Installing a hub	b. The whole network crashes
3. Having a gateway	c. No access to the network
4. Possessing the token	d. No exchange between different systems
5. Using a faster modem	e. No effect on the other computers
6. A main cable breaks	f. Can establish a star topology
7. Removing a computer from a star topology	g. Save on telephone bills
8. Ignoring protocols	h. Can transmit on the network

R **C** **Read the short information in the Info Box below, then study the following statements dealing with various aspects of networking and decide if they characterize a peer-to-peer network or a client-server network.**

INFO BOX Peer-to-peer and client server networks

A network can be organized by setting up either a peer-to-peer or a client server structure. Computers in the former share each other's resources. There is no central computer which controls the network's activities. In the latter there is a powerful central computer, the server, which offers access to all workstations that have a client program. A server needs special server software, for example, a web-server. This software can be used by client software such as a browser.

1. Relationship of the PCs to each other	
a. A group of user oriented PCs work together on an equal basis whereby each can be a client and a server.	b. It consists of a group of user oriented PCs or clients who request and receive the services of special computers called servers.
2. Resource administration	
a. A host of servers can provide optimal network services for the Workstations.	b. The Workstations share common resources such as data and printers with access granted via special passwords or codes.
3. Data security	
a. Access to specific network resources can be limited via user accounts which are stored in a user database on the main server.	b. Security is limited due to the fact that individual access rights can't be granted.
4. Operating System	
a. No special network operating system is required.	b. A special network operating system is required such as Linux or Novell.

2 Wide Area Network (WAN)

A LAN links computers, printers and other devices located in a building or an office. A wide area network is used for greater distances and to connect local area networks.

R **a** **Study the following table listing the pros and cons of various wiring options for computer networks. Select the correct option from the choices below by matching the letter with the numbers.**

1. Phone	a Pros: no new wires, outlets widespread Cons: slow, liable to interference
2. Coax	b Pros: Uses same wire for data and voice Cons: outlets limited, expensive technology
3. Digital wireless	c Pros: no wires, supports portable devices Cons: insecure if not properly installed
4. Powerline	d Pros: High speed, business-tested Cons: expensive installation
5. Ethernet	e Pros: Backward-compatible, easy installation Cons: limited range and capacity

R **b** **Study the illustration below and read the following seven steps involved in making voice calls using IP (=Internet Protocol) telephony. Put the steps into the correct order. Listen and check.**

1. The sound waves are received from the IP gateway and forwarded to the final destination.
2. The sound waves are converted into binary digits, broken into packets, addressed and sent across private networks and the Internet.
3. Using a conventional phone, you dial into a central office. Your voice is sent as an analog sound wave over the regular phone lines.
4. Based on their address and sequence, the packets of data are reassembled and converted back into analog waves.
5. The person you wanted to call picks up the receiver of their phone and hears your voice.
6. Your call is received and forwarded, along with data from other sources such as fax machines or computers, to an Internet Protocol Gateway.
7. The packeted data is able to travel through cyberspace along various routes due to the IP.

R **C** **WAN Terms**

Find the 12 words and abbreviations related to networking in the puzzle below. Use them to complete the reading text .

N	**E**	**T**	**W**	**O**	**R**	**K**	I	S	S	N
V	I	A	B	P	O	W	E	R	A	Q
D	S	B	A	N	D	W	I	D	T	H
A	H	A	R	S	S	E	S	A	E	O
T	B	S	O	E	L	R	D	T	L	X
A	A	E	U	N	H	P	N	A	L	O
P	S	R	T	T	L	O	F	A	I	B
E	E	D	E	E	P	S	A	S	T	U
L	A	X	R	K	R	O	D	T	E	W
E	L	I	N	E	S	S	S	R	I	A
T	M	O	D	E	M	E	L	B	A	N

An integrated network of computers over long distances is a **1** or a Wide Area **2**. Networks are generally linked using either telephone **3** or fibre-optic cables. At present the international standard for transmitting **4** via the former is called **5** which stands for integrated service digital network. The latter uses FDDI, fibre distributed data interface, whose wide **6** permit high speed transmission. Via a **7** and either phone lines or cables, computers can also be linked to aerial dishes. These are equipped to relay signals to a **8** to be amplified and sent on to distant workstations. Along the way a device called a **9** determines exactly which path that a signal should take.
New options which would radically reduce download time of videos from minutes to seconds are being currently tested. The **10** 6000 digital subscriber line permits rapid transmission of data over ordinary telephone wires. With speeds of 46 MB per second is the cable modem option. Things would slow down, however, if some of the other subscribers you share the line with also took advantage of the service at the same time.
Satellite broadcasters which offer faster data transmission than ISDN lines could fuel the Internet drive. Another intriguing option would be to take advantage of the existing **11** lines for electricity. Such a system would require a **12** station in the network and a box in the home.

3 Telecommunications

P **a** **We combine tele which means "far" to form many words. How many can you think of? Use your dictionary if necessary.**

R **b** **Read the following definition. What is being described?**

It's a device for reproducing sound, especially that of the voice, at a distance using electricity; it consists of a transmitter and receiver connected by wires.

R/I **c** **Discuss in groups which of the statements below refer to which of the following telecommunication devices?**

Video conferencing • VoIP • screen phones • mobile phones • set-top boxes / Web-TV

1. Protocols are used to carry voice signals over the Internet or any other IP-based network.
2. It's a form of communication in which voice and data are emitted, transmitted and received via microwaves.
3. It's a device for reproducing sound like a telephone but also offers Internet access and e-mail.
4. It includes voice, data and image or video transmission.
5. They provide interactive services and Net access.
6. You can receive incoming phone calls wherever you connect to the Internet.
7. Broadcast capability is needed to transmit to multiple sites simultaneously.
8. No complicated software is needed.
9. Wireless Application Protocols allow users to access text information from the Internet.
10. It learns what you like and provides recommendations.
11. They come with a smart card reader for online shopping direct from your kitchen.
12. Phone service is generally virtually free or costs very little.
13. They feature a colour touchscreen for easy use.
14. Viewers can pause, rewind or instant replay live broadcasts.
15. It allows people to converse and / or transmit and receive data while moving from place to place.
16. It requires highly compressed image information and synchronisation.

P **d** **Using a selection of statements above write your own definition for one or more of the telecommunication devices.**

4 Further reading: Future technologies

Bluetooth & UWB – A Future of Unlimited Possibilities

Bluetooth and Ultra-Wideband-enabled devices offer enhanced capabilities that will make possible new applications and change the way people collect information.

By Tom Siep, Cambridge 2007

There are many ways to exchange information between 1 devices. Cell phones, laptops, PDAs, MP3 players and desktop computers all have increasingly large 2 of data to transfer. Normally, a single technology is used between any two devices at any one time. Previously it was wires, but increasingly there are a number of wireless options such as Wi- Fi, Bluetooth or proprietary 3 . In the future, very fast and efficient movement of data will be 4 by a combination of Bluetooth and the new Ultra-Wideband (UWB) technology. Bluetooth brings an established, accepted technology for low power connectivity, while UWB provides an extremely fast data transfer rate, 5 new applications requiring large but brief wireless transfers, such as downloading video.

UWB – One of the Future Wireless Technologies We all know there are many kinds of wireless communications in use today. As users find themselves in situations and/ or using different applications, they will choose the particular flavor of communications that 6 their needs.

▶

The IEEE1 (Institute of Electrical and Electronics Engineers) divides the wireless world into five classes based on the coverage:

- Wireless Personal Area Networks (WPANs)
- Wireless Local Area Networks (WLANs)
- Wireless Metropolitan Area Networks (WMANs)
- Wireless Regional Area Networks (WRANs)
- Wireless Global Area Networks (WGANs)

WPANs typically cover 10 meters or less, WLANs generally **7** at 10 times the power and cover about 100 meters in ideal situations. WMANs are also about an order of magnitude larger than its **8** . The WRANs and WGANs are each about two orders of magnitude larger than the next smaller footprint technology. All of these technologies are evolving and each has an expanded role for endusers in the future. The technology that will change most radically is in the WPAN arena. The **9** of that change will be the introduction of UWB capability. UWB has the potential to radically **10** how individuals gather and save information that is directly under their control.

UWB wireless communications technology sends data using high frequency, low-energy pulses. It differs from other wireless technologies by **11** communication at transmit levels below the noise floor— sophisticated receivers in UWB radios **12** signals at levels below normal background interference. For users, UWB offers incredibly low power and high speed, and **13** hundreds of simultaneous channels. It attains very high data rates of up to 400Mb/s in a scaleable architecture. In addition, it offers the potential of very good coexistence with other wireless technology because UWB signals do not **14** with each other or with conventional RF carriers, and the UWB signals are difficult to detect beyond the range of the WPAN technology.

R **a** **The following words and phrases appeared in the text. Choose the correct definition.**

1. **at any one time** means (at a given time/if there is enough time)
2. **low power connectivity** means (weaker links/less energy required for links)
3. **an order of magnitude** means (twice as much/to the power of ten)
4. **scaleable architecture means the size can be (measured/changed)**
5. **below the noise floor** means (coming from underneath/undetectable)
6. **smaller footprint technology** refers here to the (network range/the basic network steps)

R **b** **Read the article about Bluetooth & UWB on pages 98-99 and complete it. Choose the correct word from A,B,C, or D to fill in each gap.**

	A	B	C	D
1.	handy	private	personal	residential
2.	sorts	types	amounts	values
3.	ideas	schemes	patterns	theories
4.	launched	detailed	concentrated	facilitated
5.	using	enabling	providing	offering
6.	feeds	meets	melts	feels
7.	communicate	transmit	receive	transfer
8.	predecessor	successor	former	prearrangement
9.	thrust	locomotive	engine	motorway
10.	twist	manipulate	transfer	alter
11.	receiving	achieving	reaching	introducing
12.	determine	look after	decide	detect
13.	aids	supports	helps	oversees
14.	interrupt	interfere	coexist	interchange

R **c** **Answer the following questions.**

1. What used to be the standard technology for transmitting data?
2. What is expected to improve wireless transmission of data?
3. What are the respective advantages of Bluetooth and UWB technologies?
4. What is the range of distance covered by the various classes of wireless networks?
5. In which area of wireless technology can we expect the greatest innovation and why?
6. What is the difference between UWB and other wireless technologies?
7. What are the advantages of UWB for consumers?
8. Is UWB compatible with other technologies? Why or why not?

5 Language and grammar

5.1. Conditional sentences

INFO BOX If- sentences

There are three types of "if" or conditional sentences:

Type I (likely):
Example: If I have time I'll call.
(= At the moment I have no time but I will probably call later.

Type II (possible but unlikely):
Example: If I had time I would call.
(= I don't expect to have time to call but it is theoretically possible.)

Type III (merely speculative):
Example: If I had had time I would have called.
(= I didn't have time and now it's too late to do more than speculate).

A **mix of Type II and III** establishes a bridge between the present and the past.
Example: If they hadn't married so young, they would be happy now.

a Put the verbs in the following conditional sentences into their correct form.

1. Where be we without computers today?
2. If he work just a bit harder, he would now be graduating with the rest of the class.
3. If I had known then what I know now, I buy shares in one of the new start-up companies and be a rich man / woman.
4. I ask him, if I were you.
5. He wouldn't have shut down the system unless he have a good reason.
6. Who think such a thing possible 20 years ago?
7. He be a lot richer if he had discovered the goldmine first. Yes, but I don't think he be any happier.
8. If you use Google, you find the information more quickly.

b Complete the conditional sentences with the most suitable conjunction: if, in case, provided, when, unless, on condition that.

1. … of emergency call the following number: 891 552.
2. … we don't hear from them by Monday, I'm afraid the deal's off.
3. He'll supply the capital for the joint venture … we all agree to his conditions.
4. You should always be careful … you get an attachment from an unknown sender.
5. They're going to miss their plane … they get moving soon.
6. Write your credit card number on a separate piece of paper … it should get stolen.

c Complete the conditional sentences below with the most suitable conjunction: if, in case, provided, when, unless, on condition that.

INFO BOX Conditional sentences (provided - when - unless - in case)

Students of English sometimes don't recognize conditional sentences as such because the condition is not ushered in by "if" but one the following conjunctions or phrases:

1. provided/providing = if and only if
   Example: I will only sign the contract, provided you are willing to pay half the costs.
2. When = at the time at which
   Example: Let me know when the package arrives.
3. Unless = if ... not/except in the case that
   Example: Unless we're told otherwise I think we should just stick to the rules as stated.
4. In case = for fear that/ because ... perhaps
   Example: Here's my number in case you need to reach me in a hurry.

1. ... of emergency call the following number: 891 552.
2. ... we don't hear from them by Monday, I'm afraid the deal's off.
3. He'll supply the capital for the joint venture ... we all agree to his conditions.
4. You should always be careful ... you get an attachment from an unknown sender.
5. They're going to miss their plane ... they get moving soon.
6. Write your credit card number on a separate piece of paper ... it should get stolen.

d Put the verbs in brackets into their correct forms.

1. Here's my card, in case you ever (need) a good system administrator.
2. If people are willing to buy expensive DVDs, it (be) no wonder their prices are still high.
3. Unless you (work) with this program before, I'm afraid you are going to have some problems.
4. If she hadn't gotten cold feet and sold all her Internet stock she (be) a millionaire.
5. Give me a call when you (arrive) at the airport.
6. If you want to interrupt the transfer you (have to) click "stop".
7. I wonder what they would say if they (know) the truth?
8. I think most people (work) even if they didn't have to.

Unit 6
The Internet and globalization

1 The Internet

1.1 Internet terms

R **a** **Match the Internet terms to their definitions.**

1. A button that you can click that connects you directly to another website.	a. online banking
2. Lets private persons buy and sell generally used goods to the highest bidder.	b. browser
3. Unwanted, unsolicited e-mail, usually advertisements, i.e. online junk mail.	c. search engine
4. Allows you to pay bills and transact other financial business online.	d. online auctioning
5. Software which helps users find information and resources on the Internet.	e. blog
6. A place on the web where like-minded people can engage in real-time communication.	f. chatroom
7. A company which offers you a connection to the Internet for a fee.	g. spam
8. Software which helps you to find and display web pages.	h. service provider
9. A small file which tells a web server if you have visited their site before.	i. link
10. An online journal in which an individual can express their personal opinions.	j. cookie

P **b** **Write short definitions for other Internet terms.**

Example: hacker, blogroll, zero-day, newsgroup …

It's a person who … / It's a place on the web where …
It's a service/company/device which … / It's software/hardware which …

1.2 A short history of the Internet

R **a** **Complete the following TIMELINE by matching the information below to the correct text segments.**

1. **Late 50's and early 60's** the ARPA (=Advanced Research Projects Agency) is established within the Department of Defense as a reaction to the so-called Sputnik Scare. …
2. **In the early 70's** ARPAnet continues research into networking and the first computers are linked together…
3. **In the early 80's** networking develops from having just one big time-sharing computer at each site to connecting entire local networks. ARPAnet is broken down into three different sub-nets, …
4. **In the mid-80's** the DNS (=Domain Name Service) is introduced and the NSF(=National Science Foundation) net establishes five super computer centers …
5. **The late 80's** sees the first worm affect 6,000 of the now over 60,000 hosts and the IRC (=Internet Relay Chat) is developed. Germany joins the net and …
6. **In the early 90's** "The world comes on-line" with the first commercial provider of Internet dial-up access and the release of Tim Berners-Lee's WWW (=World Wide Web). …
7. **The mid-90's** sees the emergence of a whole series of new technologies such as …
8. **In the late 90's** emerging technologies include XML (Extended Mark-up Language), net cell phones and embedded computing and intrusion detection while consumer oriented services such as …
9. **In the first years of the 21st century** web size passes the 1 billion benchmark and …
10. **In 2004** media companies start selling music and video online as broadband becomes more widespread. The former file-sharing Napster is relaunched as a paid operation in competition to iTunes, …
11. **More recently,** in 2006, two major dictionaries added the word "google" ot their works…
12. **In the year 2007** internet TV is launched. With their Joost solution the founders of Skype, Janus Friis and Niklas Zennstrom make it possible …

a. … vBNS (=very high speed Backbone), search engines, the Internet phone and mobile code such as JAVA and JAVAscript.
b. … allowing for an explosion of connections, especially at universities.
c. … The term "surfing the net" is coined and the benchmark of over one million hosts is reached.
d. … The first theoretical papers and discussion about networking follow.
e. … of which one is reserved for the military and another is open to the general public.
f. … and new domain names (.aero/.biz/.coop/.eu/.info/.museum/.name/.pro) are introduced.
g. … The concept of networking is further developed and spread: the first international connections occur.
h. … is assigned the domain name .de just in time for reunification.
i. … online banking, E-commerce, E-auctions and mp3 really take off.
j. … Apple's music download store, as well as other media giants.
k. … to watch TV on your computer screen in a quality comparable to regular TV.
l. … in the meaning "to use the Google search engine to obtain information on the Internet" just two years after the company's IPO on August 19th, 2004.

P **b** To summarize create a timeline diagram with a brief (1–2 word) slogan for each time slot.

Example:

1950-1960 …

ARPA

early 70s

P/I **c** Create your own Internet timeline charting when you first went online, visited a chatroom etc. Either present to the class as a whole or exchange information with a partner.

2 Internet software and hardware

2.1 Internet software

R **a** Look at the section of a web browser page below and identify the following features.

a. scroll bar
b. minimize
c. toolbar
d. links
e. address box
f. enlarge

I **b In pairs take turns describing and having your partner guess the basic functions of the toolbars.**

Example:
A: You use it to update a page.
B: Refresh?
A: That's right.

2.2 Internet hardware

R **a Listen to the following sales dialogue and make a list of the Internet terms mentioned.**

R **b Listen to the dialogue again and answer the following questions.**

1. How long has the customer had his present computer?
2. Why does he want to go online?
3. What does he know about downloading? What is downloading?
4. Has the salesman ever used the Internet? If so, what has he used it for?
5. What does the salesman claim about freeware?
6. What expenses are involved in using the Internet?
7. What does the salesman recommend his customer?

3 Searching the web

3.1. From maps to navigation systems

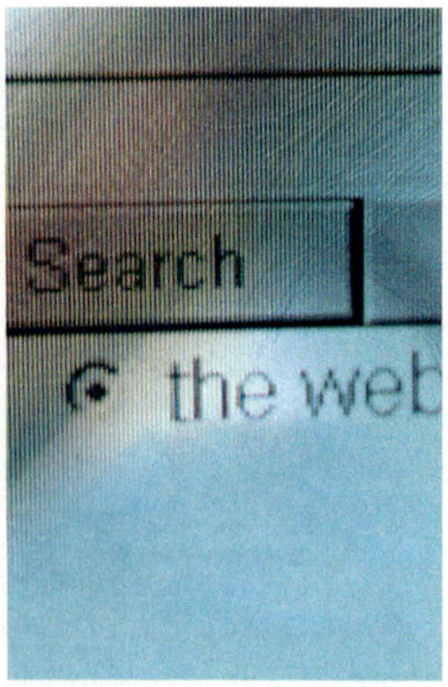

When you surf the WWW your starting point in most cases is a search engine. This software can be seen as a kind of map for travelling the web, guiding you to exactly where you want to go. Without a search engine one would have to click blindly from website to website, following links you came up across by chance.

The web held only approximately 130 websites when it was established in 1993. Despite it's fairly small size, though, it already had the first web crawler called 'The Wanderer'. This programme browsed through the whole web every six months indexing new websites which had not yet been catalogued.

Launched in the same year, a second search engine, 'Aliweb', operated on a different basis. Instead of indexing the web independently, it requested the operators of web servers to offer files containing a description of their services. Today's volume of new or modified sites make catalogues like Aliweb obsolete. A map is no longer adequate; a proper navigating system is required. Using programmes such as GoogleBot, search engines now continually browse through the web collecting the latest data. But all this data cannot be simply indexed and presented because the 33,500,000 hits, the result of a typical web search, would be far too overwhelmingly for the human user. Nowadays a search engine must have a rating system for its results which requires unimaginable calculation power. Google, for example, has to rate 8 billion websites and answer over 200 million queries in real time a day.

The following figures give you an idea of the dimensions of Google`s hardware:

- At the time of their first listing on the stock market in 2004 Google employed 126,544 CPUs.
- These CPUs had a combined clock frequency of 253 Terahertz, 127 Terabyte RAM, and 5 Petabyte storage capacity.
- This enormous calculation power is used to solve 1.6 million equations with 1.6 million variables each to determine the rank of every single website.

In comparison, your average home PC would need almost 24 hours to perform the same operation that the combined CPUs in Google take one second to caluculate.

R **a** **Answer the following questions on the above text.**

1. What are search engines compared to? Do you think they are apt comparisons?
2. How did the two earliest search engines differ?
3. Why can web data no longer simply be catalogued? What is needed?
4. How many CPUs does Google use today?
5. How much memory capacity did Google have when it was first launched?
6. How does the calculation power of a normal PC compare to that of Google?

P **b** **In the text above a number of comparisons are made. Make up sentences comparing the following pairs of items to each other. Make up your own pairs.**

1. doing research in a old-fashioned library/looking up a topic on the internet
2. using a paperback dictionary/using an online dictionary
3. consulting a map/using an online route planner
4. advertising your used furniture in the local paper/using eBay to sell the items
5. asking people about a certain book or movie/submitting the title to a search engine

I **c** **Discussion: As a webmaster how might you manipulate the results of a search engine? Discuss the possibilities with your teacher.**

3.2 Search engines

R **a** **Find the missing words of the text below in the following word square.**

P	V	J	W	R	P	D	C	D	A	B	F	M	A	M
H	R	D	E	G	R	E	E	L	Z	Y	A	D	M	T
P	A	O	B	S	Q	B	G	S	Y	W	J	L	O	A
A	N	D	S	K	C	O	N	T	E	N	T	B	R	H
R	K	X	I	N	R	Q	I	B	E	H	O	Y	D	Y
S	I	X	T	I	E	U	S	E	A	R	C	H	E	P
I	N	D	E	X	F	I	R	E	V	E	F	T	R	E
N	G	H	S	R	T	C	A	S	T	O	Y	H	A	R
G	M	L	X	E	U	K	N	R	R	K	Z	D	N	L
S	G	X	Y	P	E	L	K	R	E	A	V	D	K	I
P	G	X	W	Y	C	Y	I	O	D	X	E	E	I	N
M	U	X	V	H	Y	Y	N	B	X	X	Q	R	N	K
W	N	C	F	W	A	L	G	O	R	I	T	H	M	S
C	R	X	K	R	L	I	H	T	H	Q	C	Q	A	Q
S	T	O	R	A	G	E	L	E	R	N	U	W	L	A

Internet search engines were developed to **1** through the Internet's huge collection of data and to provide **2** to websites containing relevant information. Popular search engines are Google, Yahoo, MSN, Lycos, Alta Vista and Ask Jeeves.

Although each search engine employs different **3** and techniques, they all have the same basic functions of collecting, indexing, and storing web **4** and then delivering the results.

The term crawling or spidering refers to the process of following the links on different websites and gathering their contents for storage in gigantic search engine databases. The crawler, also called a web **5** or web spider, is the software program used to download the web pages, images, documents and other files and then follow the **6** to other sites. They are highly efficient and can crawl through multiple websites simultaneously, collecting billions of **7** contents.

Search engines also **8** the content of the gathered material. This means building a catalogue of the all the words that appear on each web page, the number of times they occur and so on. The first step in indexing is **9** which means extracting the key information of a page by excluding irrelevant words and characters. After indexing the results are stored in sorted **10** which makes it easier to retrieve information quickly.

Search engines also store individual pages and have huge **11** capacities. The problem, though, is being able to retrieve relevant data **12** and efficiently which requires special data storage functionality. When you enter search keywords this activates the engine's search algorithm which looks up the indexes for **13** to the given keywords. The search engine also tries to provide the most relevant contents first. The **14** of relevance is often given in percentages. Different search engines employ various search algorithms for relevance matching. Google is so popular because it can deliver more relevant answers to search queries. Advanced search engines also use a relevance **15** system based on such factors as content analysis, linking structure and page ranking.

R **b** **All search engines recognize the following "search engine maths". Match the equations on the left with the correct results on the right.**

1. history+Internet	a. documents containing this exact phrase
2. history+Internet+search engines	b. documents mentioning the first two but excluding the third
3. history+Internet-search engines	c. documents mentioning all three
4. history-Internet	d. documents mentioning both
5. "Internet history"	e. documents including the first but not the second

R **c** **Match the following search engine terms to their correct definition.**

1. spider trap	a. Software that searches documents for specific keywords and delivers the results
2. deep link	b. Gives information about a webpage but cannot be seen
3. meta tag	c. A program that runs without human intervention
4. robot	d. A connection either on a Web page or in the results of a search engine query to a non-home page
5. search engine	e. A condition in which a search gets entangled in an endless loop of code.

P/I **d** **Find out about the following in the Internet. Use various search engines. Discuss your findings in the group.**

1. The number of Internet users in the USA, Europe and worldwide
2. Details of the latest SEOs (=search engine optimization) tools available.
3. Translation programs
4. Cultural events in London this month.
5. Cultural events in your area this month. Is the information available in English as well as German?
6. Computer fairs around the world.

3.3 Google Earth

M **Mediation**

Your German colleague has some questions about Google Earth which your English colleague knows the answers to. Unfortunately, neither speaks the other's language. Mediate between the two friends.

German colleague	You	English colleague
Wann wurden die Bilder aufgenommen?	→ ? →	
		Sometime in the last three years.
	← ? ←	
Wie oft werden sie aktualisiert?	→ ? →	
		The images are updated on a rolling basis.
	← ? ←	
Zeigt Google Earth in Echtzeit an?	→ ? →	
		No. The images are photographs taken by satellites and aircraft sometime in the last three years.
	← ? ←	
Warum sehe ich nur verschwommene Bilder von meinem Haus?	→ ? →	
		Google Earth combines data of different resolutions to offer a seamless viewing experience, and some locations may look a bit blurry.
	← ? ←	
Läuft Google Earth auf meinem Computer?	→ ? →	
		If you are using an older machine, or a notebook computer that does not have 3D graphics capabilities, you may not be able to run the application.

4 E-mail

R **a** **Look at the e-mail address below and identify its different elements by matching the numbers with the letters below.**

1: patbalsamo 2: @ 3: jcpenny 4: .com 5: .uk patbalsamo @ jcpenny.com.uk	a. country code b. user name or identity c. means "at" d. domain e. type of organization

R **b** **Match the Internet codes on the right (a.–f.) with the numbers (1.–6.) below.**

1. aviation industry	a. biz-
2. network provider	b. aero-
3. business	c. ae-
4. United Arab Emirates	d. coop-
5. commercial organization	e. com/co
6. non-profit organization	f. net

P **c** **What are the Internet codes for the following countries?**

1. Australia
2. Austria
3. China
4. Canada
5. Ireland
6. Iran

P **d** **Look at the collection of e-mail addresses below. What can you reasonably assume or guess about the users?**

Example: kerstin.namuth@folkuniversitetet.edu.se → Kerstin works for some kind of university in Sweden.

1. irene.schmitt@vhs.or.at
2. hal.taylor@usafa.af.mil
3. luckbug@donau.net.de
4. 1pondelik@mciworld.com
5. maryjones@whitehouse.gov.us

I **e** **Interview your partner about his/her Internet habits. Ask questions such as the following and then report back to the class:**

- How long have you had e-mail?
- How often do you use the net?
- Have you ever e-mailed someone in another country?
- Have you ever emailed anyone in English? In another language another than your own?
- What is the most distant point you have ever sent an email to?
- Have you ever e-mailed someone you've never met?

5 Negative aspects of the Internet

5.1. Internet crime

Internet crime eclipses burglary in survey of perceived risks

Worries grow as more shop and bank online
Only card fraud causes greater concern

Fear of internet crime is now more prevalent than concerns about more conventional crimes such as burglary, mugging and car theft, according to a report published today. And criminals are increasingly targeting cyberspace as more and more people shop online and use internet banking services.

The study was conducted by Get Safe Online, a UK internet security awareness campaign launched last year by the government, the Serious Organised Crime Agency and big online companies.

More than a fifth of internet users (21 %) feel more vulnerable to electronic crime than any other type of criminal activity. It is second only to bank card fraud (27 %) as the type of crime to which survey respondents felt most exposed. Internet crime has overtaken burglary (16%) as one of the crimes people feel most at risk of.

Big online threats include phishing, where a hoax e-mail asks the recipient to update his or her account details. Losses from online phishing scams in the UK almost doubled to £23.2 m during 2005.

Pharming is another online scam, in which hackers download "crimeware" to the user's computer. The rogue software gathers personal information. Other internet threats include identity theft, viruses, hacking and cyber-bullying.

More than half of internet users do their banking online, with roughly the same volume using community and social networking sites, according to the report. Nearly a third (32%) pay their utility bills online and 23% buy their groceries online. But fear of internet crime is preventing some customers from carrying out any transactions on the internet.

Almost a quarter (24%) of respondents had been put off internet banking, while 18% would not shop online because of fear of crime. Another 17% had been deterred from using the internet altogether.

"Fear of online crime is an important issue that must not be ignored. Otherwise we will lose out on the enormous economic and social benefits that the internet provides," commented Patrick McFadden, a junior minister at the Cabinet Office. "Provided they take sensible precautions to protect themselves, there is no reason why the overwhelming majority of people should not be able to enjoy the internet safely."

Get Safe Online's managing director, Tony Neate, said it was vital to make people aware of resources such as to ensure they continue to use the internet safely and confidently.

"Get Safe Online is committed to this long-term awareness campaign," he said. "It is about education and making people aware that ... armed with the right knowledge, we can all continue to enjoy using the internet securely."

The report commissioned an ICM survey of 1,317 adults with internet access, which was carried out last month.

This week marks the start of Get Safe Online Week, which will involve a series of events, roadshows and training sessions nationwide. Experts will be giving advice and information on online protection programmes and systems.

October 9, 2006; The Guardian

R **a** **Based on the text below decide if the following statements are true (t), false (f), or the information is not contained in the text (nt):**

1. People are more afraid of internet crime than any other kind of crimminal activity.
2. *GetSafeOnline* is a British government agency for fighting online crime.
3. Web companies are concerned about the abuse of the internet.
4. People fear being mugged more than having their car stolen.
5. Misuse of bank cards is more prevelent than internet crime.
6. According to the survey, one in five Britains feels exposed to electronic crime.
7. Phishing scams doubled during the year 2005.
8. Phishing and pharming are the two main types of internet crime.
9. Some 50% of the internet users visit online social and community sites.
10. More than a fifth of the population pay their bills and buy food online.
11. Almost 20% of internet users refuse to buy anything online.
12. The government regards internet use postively.
13. *GetSafeOnline's* director claims it is safe to use the internet provided one uses caution.

R **b** **Look back over the text and find synonyms for the following words:**

1. sham
2. worry
3. focus on
4. consciousness
5. defenseless
6. poll
7. bypass
8. criminal
9. collect
10. terrorize
11. approximately
12. inhibit
13. topic
14. advantages
15. important
16. safely

5.2 Spyware

M **a** **Answer the following questions in German.**

1. Für welchen Zweck wird Spyware eingesetzt?
2. Auf welche Weise kommt Spyware auf Ihren Computer? Ist dies zwangsläufig so?
3. Wie gelangt Spyware an die Daten?
4. Welche Art von Informationen wird ermittelt?
5. Warum soll man Spyware meiden?

Spyware

One of the most controversial aspects of the Internet is spyware. Spyware secretly collects information about a user through their Internet connection, usually for advertising purposes but sometimes also with criminal intent. Typically spyware is embedded as a hidden element of freeware or shareware programs that one can download from the Internet, though not all or even the majority of such applications include spyware.

Once installed, the spyware can monitor your Internet activities. Since spyware is an independent executable program it can monitor keystrokes, scan files, spy out other applications such as chat programs or word processors, or read cookies. It can thus find out e-mail addresses, passwords or even credit card numbers and then relay that information back to the spy author who either uses it for marketing purposes or sells the information to a third party. Aside from the abuse of one's privacy, spyware also exploits the memory and system resources of your computer and can lead to system crashes.

R/I **b** **The following quotes touch on some positive and negative aspects of the internet. Which ones do you agree with most, least? Why?**

1. "The beautiful thing about the internet is that you can be in touch with the whole world just sitting at home with your laptop on the kitchen table."…

2. "The problem with the web is that it is addictive and prevents people, especially teens, from engaging in social activities."

3. "No doubt about it, the internet is a total information overload with content that is often tasteless, foolish, uninteresting or just plain wrong."

4. "With the internet you can network, swap files, chat, video conference, play games – you name it – where`s the disadvantage?"

5. "I refuse to use the internet because the minute you go online your every step and move can be tracked – I don't want people having access to my private affairs."

R/I **c** **Match the following characteristics of the internet to the correct explanations. Which are positive/negative? Discuss which outweighs the other.**

1. current	a. minority views are given a platform
2. disorganized	b. able to download and edit all kinds of file
3. no standards	c. information is very up-to-date
4. easy to use	d. can access from almost anywhere
5. unplanned	e. need only very basic computer skills
6. convenient	f. searches are often hit and miss and non-productive
7. diverse	g. no checking for the accuracy of the informaton
8. transient	h. fees are often charged for specialized information
9. costs	i. addresses and sites change, come and go
10. electronic access	j. lack of overriding principles for choosing content

6 Further reading: The internet and intercultural communication

R **a** **Read the following text and answer the questions on page 117.**

The internet and intercultural awareness

Whether right or wrong, globalization, as one writer puts it sounds unstoppable. Mass tourism, the interdependency of world markets and the Internet with its cheap and instant links to even the remotest corners of the globe have all contributed to an upgrowth in intercultural communication. In the course of their daily working lives more and more people over the world are confronted with the task of communicating with people from cultures very different from their own.

English, often not native to either speaker, is most frequently the language employed on the internet, i.e. the lingua franca. Yet the language itself is almost the least of it; intercultural awareness and tolerance play a central role in making global communication work.

How we express our needs, desires and feelings, however, is determined by the cultural context in which we operate. Caution is called for, though, in jumping to the conclusion that certain behavior is typically American, Malaysian or Swedish. We should also be aware that age, sex, regional differences, economic status and just plain personality differences also influence our communication patterns.

Certain core competences such as open-mindedness, respect, flexibility, and the ability to tolerate different habits can facilitate intercultural communication. More specifically, awareness and respect for the cultural differences in such areas as degree of formality, styles of addressing your counterpart, and time-management are helpful.

1. Does everyone agree on the import of globalization? If not, how do opinions differ? What do you, personally, think?
2. What factors have played a role in the spread of international contacts between people? What are the consequences? And for you personally?
3. What is meant by the term lingua franca?
4. Aside from being able to speak the other person's language, what do you need in order to deal with foreigners? Can you think of one example?
5. What factors determine how we speak to other people?
6. What makes it easier to talk to people from other parts of the world?
7. Can you think of any ways in which formality or style of address might differ from one country to the other?
8. In what way does the Internet influence intercultural communication.

I **b** **Interview your partner about experiences he/she might have had while living abroad, travelling or in contact with people from different cultures. Ask questions such as the following:**

Have you ever been surprised, shocked, confused or frightened by something you experienced while travelling abroad or in contact with people from other cultures? What happened? What did you do? How did the other people react? Report back to the class.

I **c** **Read the following blogs concerning English as the global language. Discuss which one you agree/disagree with most.**

With the boom in IT, English is no longer a matter of choice, it is de rigeur. Notwithstanding linguistic chauvinists, it is only a question of time before English becomes the first language of choice at least in India and perhaps the world.

The utility of a language is in the fact that the sender can encode his thought into a common medium/protocol for the recipient. If no one speaks Finnish or Estonian then what does it mean in real terms for the rest of us?

This really is an unfortunate inevitability. The only thing that can slow it is a fierce, near-religious commitment to preserving a language in its native-speaking population – but even then, it's a losing battle.

I'm not happy about the use of any national language as an international one because of all the cultural imperialism that goes with it and because it gives an unfair advantage to native speakers.

It is no longer just a foreign language. It has become a cultural technique, just like using the phone or sending e-mails.

P **d** **Now write your own blog expressing your own personal opinion about the role English plays in today's global world.**

7 Language and grammar

7.1. Tenses: Present perfect

LANGUAGE AND GRAMMAR BOX Present Perfect: Simple or continuous?

There is not a clear-cut line between simple and continuous form of the present perfect; both describe an ongoing activity which began in the past. The continuous form simply emphasizes the "active" nature of the proceedings. There is no essential difference between the statements *I have worked here for years* and *I have been working here for years*. Logically, since the emphasis in the continuous is on the "action", it is generally not used with intransitive verbs such as *be* or *exist*.

Complete the sentences with either the present perfect simple or present perfect continuous form of the verb in brackets. Give reasons for your choices.

1. We work on the Webpage project since July but still finish.
2. He be rather nervous lately due to his upcoming exams.
3. She live all her life here but think recently about moving.
4. Though Larry and Andrea marry for two years they still decide whether they want to buy a house or not.
5. In the meantime they live with her parents.

7.2. Present perfect or simple past

LANGUAGE AND GRAMMAR BOX Present perfect or simple past?

The present perfect, as the term in English implies, very much has to do with the present which is one reason why the German translation *zweite Vergangenheit* is misleading. In German it is a matter of regional differences whether a speaker says "*ich tat*" or "*ich habe getan*", both describe a past event or activity. In contrast, we use the simple past "did" to describe a past activity but the present perfect to describe the following activities, states, or events:

Look at the following examples of present perfect sentences in English. Decide 1. if the sentence describes experience, development, unfinished past or current information/news and 2. how you would translate the tense into German.

1. We've always lived near the center of town.
2. Stop complaining – I've closed the window like you wanted me to.
3. Mary's gained almost ten pounds since her first trimester.
4. I went to the seminar last week but I haven't had a chance yet to go over my notes.
5. A: Have you heard? They've fired Fred!
   B: Who's Fred? I've never met a Fred around here.

Unit 7

Programming

R **a** **Look at the following examples of different computer codes. Can you identify any of them?**

```
.MODEL tiny
.CODE
        ORG 100h
HELLO  PROC
        MOV   AH,09h
        LEA   DX,msg
        INT   21h        ;Display Hello World
        MOV   AX,4C00h;Exit to DOS
        INT   21h
HELLO  ENDP
        msg   DB         'Hello World$'
        END   HELLO
```

```
#include <iostream.h>

void main()
{
cout << "Hello World" << endl;
```

```
public class Hallo {

public static void main(String[] args) {
System.out.println("Hallo Welt!");
   }
}
```

R **b** **What is programming?**
Select the best option from the choices below to come up with a good definition for programming.

1. Programming is the idea / process of designing / producing a set / list of protocols / instructions written in code / symbols to make a computer / machine perform / entertain a specified / difficult problem / task.
2. Using a computer language / set of icons such as Basic / Windows the programmer can control / help what the computer thinks / does.

R **c** **Rewrite the following programming steps in the correct order:**

1. Compile the program
2. Write the code
3. Provide documentation
4. Analyse the problem
5. Get feedback from the users
6. Design the program
7. Test and correct the program
8. Train the users

R **d** **Match the definitions on the right to the corresponding basic programming terms on the left.**

1. algorithm 2. comments 3. variable 4. data 5. coding 6. debugging 7. structogram / flowchart	a. The process of writing instructions in a specific programming language b. A method to solve a problem systematically step by step c. The graphical representation of an algorithm d. Serve to explain other parts of the program e. Consists of a name, memory address and a value f. Finding, analysing and correcting errors in a program g. Information whose meaning has been agreed upon

1 Programming logic

a **Every program logic consists of three main structural elements: Sequence, Selection and Iteration (loop). Which is which?**

a. … is a series of commands whereby B automatically and necessarily follows A.
b. … repeats a given sequence of commands as long as given conditions exists or until a given condition is fulfilled.
c. … executes one of two or more possible functions in a program depending on whether a given condition has been fulfilled or not.

b **Structogram elements**

Match the following illustrations to the correct programming elements of a structogram.

1
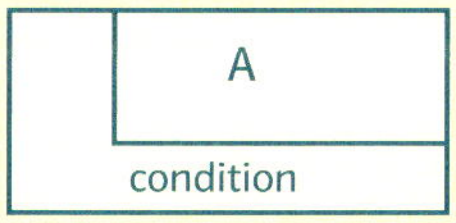

2
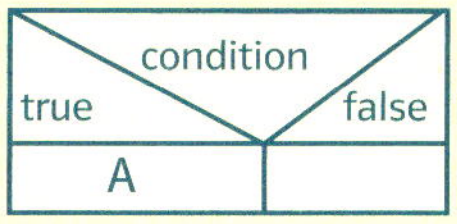

3
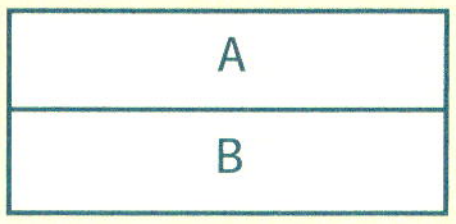

4
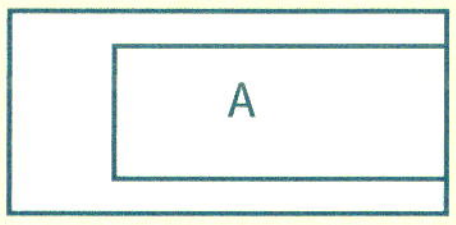

5
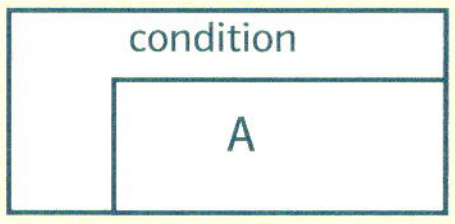

6
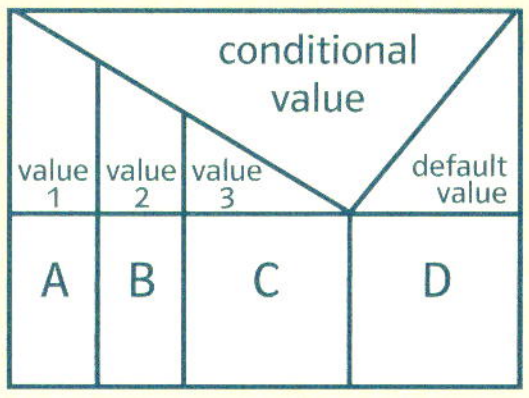

7
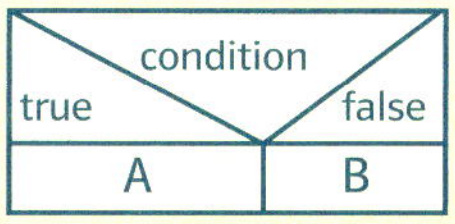

8

9

a. Dyadic selection checks a condition and, if it is true executes A in the true branch of the selection and if it's false executes B in the false branch.

b. A foot controlled **loop** around A checks the exit condition **just before leaving the structure**. The contained **structures** are executed once and a new cycle entered only if the exit condition is true.

c. Sequence is a series of commands whereby B automatically and necessarily follows A.

d. A multiple selection doesn't just have a *yes* or *no* condition but is required to interpret specific values. Each branch contains **structures** that are executed only if the associated value is entered as a condition. If none of the values equals the conditional value, the structure located in the default column on the right is executed.

e. Symbol for a call of a sub-routine, procedure or function. After this processing the program returns to the call point and proceeds with the following structure block of instructions.

f. The break or exit represents the end of part of a program. It should not interpreted as an unconditional jump.

g. A continuous looping has an entrance but no exit and keeps cycling the contained structures. All you have to do is use one or the other loop and make sure the loop condition is always true.

h. A monadic selection checks a condition and, if it proves true executes A located in the true branch, while the false branch of the selection remains empty.

i. A head controlled loop around A checks the exit condition right after entering the structure. The contained structures / conditions are only executed and a new cycle entered if the condition is true.

2 Basic programming

Before you actually start programming it is advisable to analyse the problem and to generate a flowchart of the process (see below).

a **You work for a building society and have developed a software tool for your customers to calculate how many months they will need to pay back their mortgages. The total sum of money that needs to be borrowed, the current interest rate and how much the customer can afford in monthly payments have to be taken into consideration. Complete the flowchart below with the correct terms from the box on the right.**

message • amount • instalment • debt • rate • display • increase • read • counter • increase

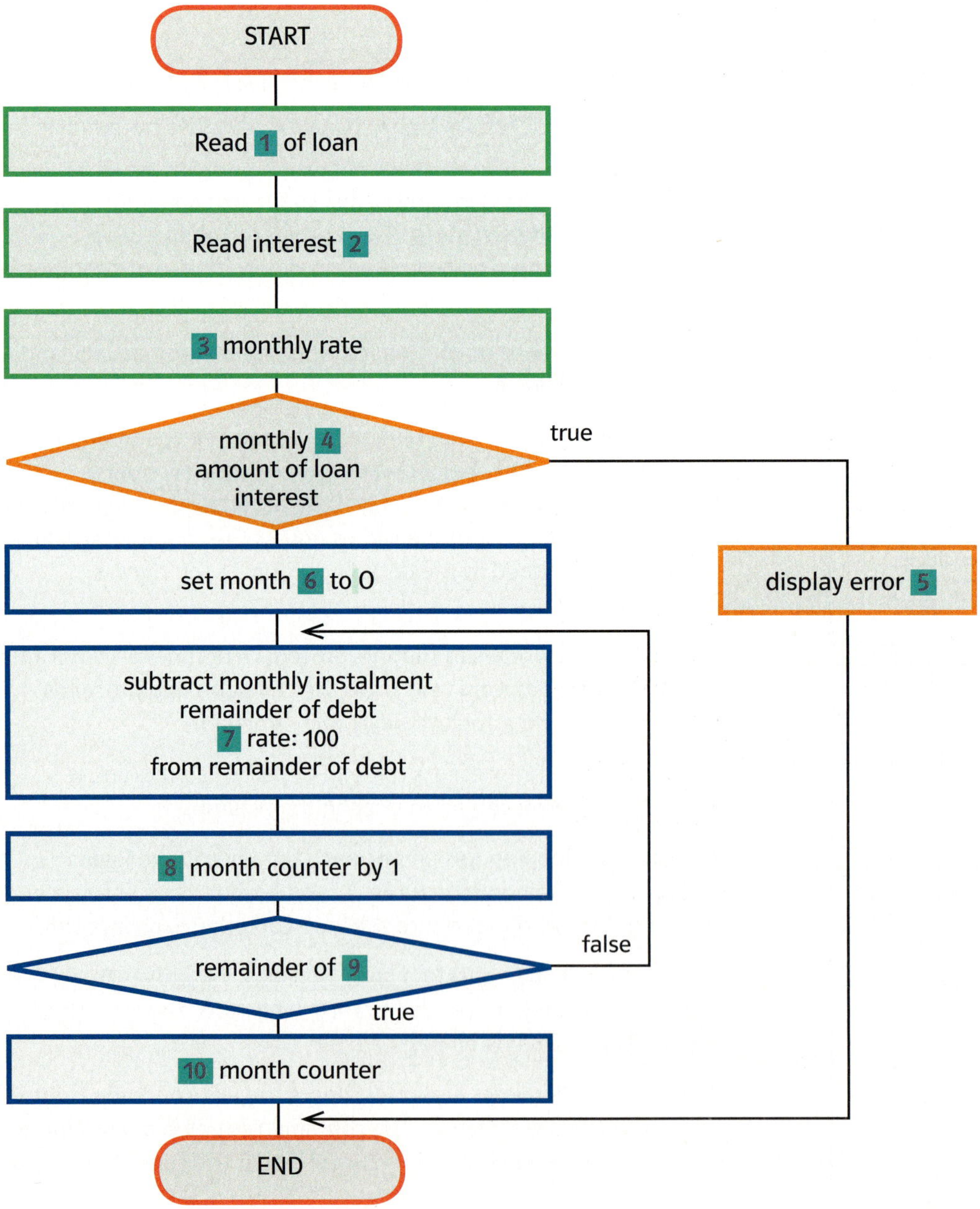

R **b** **Study the flowchart on page 122 again. Which colour represents the following procedures?**

1. Calculation and output of data
2. Data input
3. Check for validity of data

M **c** **Find the English equivalents for the following German terms in exercise a.**

1. Hypothek
2. Bausparkasse
3. Darlehen
4. geliehen
5. Zinsrate
6. Schulden
7. Zähler
8. zeigen

3 Programming languages

Over the years thousands of programming languages have been developed to fulfill many different purposes. Many languages are now obsolete and new ones are created every year. In the course of their careers programmers might use a dozen languages or more, so it's a good idea to keep on top of things.

R **a** **Match the following programming languages to their main purpose or feature.**

1. Java
2. PHP
3. Visual Basic
4. Fortran
5. C / C++
6. C#
7. Javascript
8. Perl

a. Developed for research purposes
b. Designed for processing text, popular for writing CGI scripts
c. Originally designed for programming small handheld devices
d. Efficiently control hardware and are platform independent
e. Provides a graphical programming environment, easy to learn
f. For creating dynamic Web pages, compatible with a variety of databases
g. A hybrid Microsoft product to improve development of Web applications
h. A scripting language developed to design interactive sites

R b **Read the following brief history of computer languages and use the information to complete the table of programming languages on page 125.**

A short history of programming languages

The only language computers really understand is machine code, i.e. a series of binary digits. Assembly languages which use abbreviations such as ADD and MOV to represent instructions were developed to make things easier. A special program called *assembler* then translates the abbreviations or mnemonic codes into machine code.

During the fifties and early sixties a number of new, so-called high-level languages, as opposed to the earlier low-level languages, were designed. Problem rather than machine oriented, programs in these languages are easier to write and are not restricted to just one type of computer. Known as source programs, they are converted into machine code using a compiler generating the object program. Examples are COBOL (= Common Business Orientated Language), FORTRAN (= FORmula TRANslation), developed for scientific programming and BASIC (= Beginner's All Purpose Symbolic Instruction Code) which was originally designed for teaching programming. Pascal, a third generation language designed for the development of structured applications, appeared relatively late in 1968.

Various languages had brief walk-ons during the sixties and seventies (Logo, Prolog, APL, PL1, ADA), but it was the programming language C in 1972 which took and was able to hold center stage with the development of C++, an OOPL (= Object Oriented Programming Language) in the early 80's. Designed for systems programming, it is an efficient hardware controller and is portable, i.e. programs written in C++ can easily be changed to run on many different types of systems.

Turbo Pascal introduced an Integrated Development Environment (IDE) in the mid-eighties that allowed you to edit the code while running the compiler which made the language very popular on the PC platform.

In the mid-nineties a row of new programming language entered the scene. Java is a stand-alone programming language originally designed for programming small electronic devices and to create applets for web pages. Simpler in design and use is Javascript which is embedded in HTML documents and allows authors to incorporate some functions inside web pages.

Visual Basic is a programming environment which uses the language BASIC and predefined objects chosen from a toolbox to write general purpose programs for Window applications. Derived from Turbo Pascal, Delphi first appeared in 1995. It is a powerful, object oriented Windows and Linux development tool with very fast compilation and execution.

The development of the Unified Modeling Language (UML) also began at this time. It is used to construct and document the artifacts of software systems, as well as for business modeling and other non-software systems. As the name implies, UML represents the best engineering practices for the modeling of large and complex systems.

high-level languages	dates developed	uses	characteristics	associated languages
1	59-61	business / administration	easy, English-like syntax	
FORTRAN	54-57	**2**	supports use of formulas	
Logo, APL Prolog,, PL1,	60-70	various	no longer widely used	
3	64	teaching, general purposes	relatively easy	Visual Basic
Pascal	68	structured applications	3rd generation language	**4**
C	**5**	system programming	compact code, simple structure	C++ / C#
C++	80's	system programming, efficient hardware controller	**6**	C / C#
Visual Basic	94	teaching, general applications	**7**	Basic
Java	95	**8**	stand-alone program	
Javascript	95	create interactive webpages	**9**	embedded in HTML documents
Delphi	95	**10**	visual programming language	Pascal
UML	95	modelling complex systems	unifies a number of object oriented languages, standardized collection of diagrams	

R **C** **Answer the following questions on the text on page 124.**

1. What is the difference between low-level and high-level programming languages?
2. What is a source program as opposed to an object program?
3. What different tasks do assemblers and compilers perform?
4. How does C differ from C++?
5. How does Visual Basic compare to BASIC? Delphi to Pascal?
6. Why is UML an apt name for this tool?

P **d Decide with a partner which language you would choose for the following tasks and / or users. Give reasons for you choices.**

Example: We would recommend C++ for … because it's portable and …

1. Integrating a database with a website.
2. To program games and extra software for mobile phone devices
3. To develop an operating system.
4. To teach young students programming.
5. To produce animation for a website.
6. To write database software.
7. To write anti-virus software.
8. To automate system administrative procedures, e.g. creating user accounts.
9. To create an interactive graphics program with sound, video and animation.
10. To write business applications such as accounting programs.

4 Error alert!

R **a Complete the following table by matching the definitions, examples, consequences and tactics to the different types of programming errors.**

	run-time errors	syntax errors	logic errors
A Definitions	2. errors that occur while the program is running		
B Examples			
C Consequences			2. program does not run …
D Tactics		1. avoid: dot your i's, deal: read error messages carefully	

A Definitions
1. grammar mistakes due to misspellings, false punctuation
2. errors that occur while the program is running
3. mistakes caused by using a false sequence of instructions

B Examples
1. contradictory or dead-end statements:
```
count = 0;
while (count > 15){ //does nothing because
condition is false
do something count++;}
```
2. missing closed bracket in line
3. "Segmentation Fault"

C Consequences
1. sometimes causes the program to crash
2. program does not run as expected
3. translator programs reject lines with such mistakes

D Tactics
1. avoid: dot your i's carefully, deal: read error messages carefully
2. avoid: plan program carefully (see structogram), deal: use debugger to trace program
3. avoid: provide code to check availability of resources, deal: use debugger to help locate error

R **b** **Complete the following text using the information from the previous page and the words in the box. Listen and check.**

translator • structogram • message • grammar • illogical • debugger • crash • program • sequence • bracket • run • spelling

Run-time errors are errors which occur while the 1 is running. An example would be "Segmentation Fault!" (Windows = bluescreen). They can sometimes cause a program to 2 . One way to avoid run-time errors is to provide code to check for the availability of resources. If a run-time error occurs you can use a 3 to help you locate the error.

Syntax errors are mistakes due to faulty 4 and false punctuation. An example would be to forget to set a closed 5 at the end of data you wanted to set in brackets. 6 programs reject lines with these kinds of mistakes which gives you a chance to repair the damage. Of course, it's better to avoid problems right from the start by being careful in points of grammar, 7 and punctuation when writing code. Once a mistake has occurred read the error 8 carefully to rectify the matter.

Logic errors are mistakes caused by using 9 instructions or a false 10 of instructions. They are especially tricky because the program can still 11 but it won't be doing its job properly. An example would be to write instructions that depend for their execution on conditions that, based on logic, simply cannot be fulfilled. To avoid such problems one should plan a program carefully in advance with a good 12 , for example. Once an error occurs you can use a debugger to help trace the source of the trouble.

P **c** **Complete the following sentences about programming errors in your own words. Consider the consequences, respectively what you should avoid or countermeasures when dealing with such errors.**

1. If your program crashes, it …
2. To avoid run-time errors you …
3. To help pinpoint run-time errors …
4. If you forget to set a necessary slash in a line of code …
5. You can reduce syntax errors by …
6. You will receive an error message …
7. If you use a false sequence of instructions …
8. If your program contains a logic error, it … but …
9. You should use a structogram …

5 COBOL Code

a **Study the following lines of COBOL-Code and answer the questions below.**

```
000010 PROCEDURE DIVISION.
000020 BEGIN.
000030       OPEN    INPUT  CITIES
000040               OUTPUT PRINTFILE
000050       MOVE    ZERO TO LINE-NR
000060       READ    CITIES AT END GO TO FINISH END-READ.
000070 LOOP.
000080       PERFORM UNTIL CITYNAME = HIGH-VALUES
000090               MOVE SPACES TO PRINTLINE
000100               ADD 1 TO LINE-NR
000110               MOVE LINE-NR TO PRINT-NR
000120               MOVE CITYNAME TO PRINT-NAME
000130               MOVE POPULATION TO PRINT-POP
000140               COMPUTE FINAL-VALUE ROUNDED = POPULATION
000150               PERFORM VARYING J FROM 1 BY 1 UNTIL J > FINAL-VALUE
000160                   MOVE "*" TO BAR (J)
000170               END-PERFORM
000180               WRITE PRINT-BUFFER FROM PRINTLINE AFTER 1
000190               READ CITIES
000200                   AT END MOVE HIGH-VALUES TO CITYNAME
000210               END-READ
000220       END-PERFORM.
000230 FINISH.
```

**Though COBOL is no longer widely used, we chose it as an example for code because its syntax is very much oriented on English and can be understood even if one hasn't learned to program in this language.*

Example of output:

1	New York	12	************
2	Mexico City	15	***************
3	Berlin	4	****
4	London	10	**********

1. Find the statements which start the outer and the inner loop respectively.
2. Which lines contain commands that lead to the computer performing calculations?
3. Which command brings the program to an end?
4. Which command transfers data within the RAM?
5. Which command transfers data from the file CITIES into RAM?
6. Find the statement which leads to the output of data.
7. What do you think is the purpose of the above sequence of statements?

P **b** **Computer task**

Design a plan (= structogram / flowchart) for a program to calculate the average grade of the class' last English test. If you already know a programming language well, write the script code and see if you can get the program to run.

R **c** **Software problems**

Listen to the following discussion between the senior developer and the applications engineer of a software firm about one their firm's newest products. Decide if the following statements are true or false.

1. Hothouse is a firm which produces design software.
2. Sleekware was written for a single, specific purpose.
3. Tom blames faulty hardware for Sleekware's printing problems.
4. Jerry reports that the people at Hothouse are completely dissatisfied with the Sleekware program.
5. Tom is annoyed that the Hothouse people didn't follow his hardware recommendations.
6. The hothouse people were eager to buy Sleekware.
7. There is nothing Tom can do or suggest to help Jerry with the problem.

6 Website design

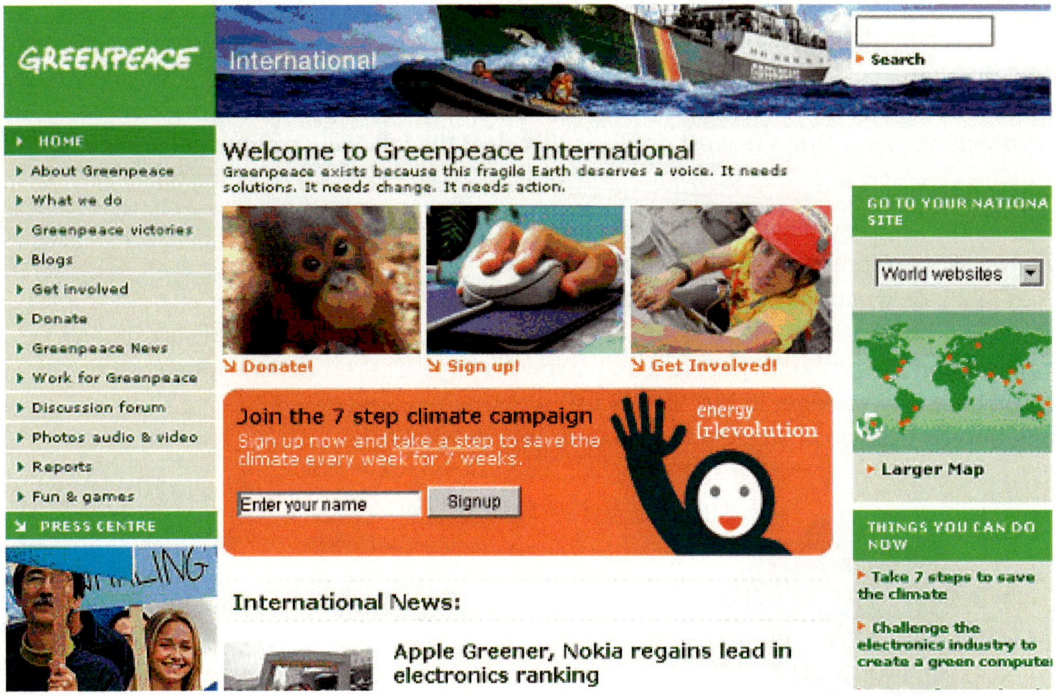

R **a** **Put the recommended steps for designing a web page in the correct order.**

1. sketch a rough plan or design
2. encode HTML
3. check and correct content
4. make final check
5. find cliparts and / or graphics
6. upload website
7. set objectives
8. create content, e.g. write texts, take photos

P **b** **Where can you click on the Greenpeace webpage above if you want**

1. to give the organisation money?
2. to join Greenpeace?
3. to help advertize Greenpeace?
4. to give active support?
5. to find out about activities in Germany?
6. to get tips on how to save electricity?

P **c** **Write a brief description and analysis of the Greenpeace webpage in terms of its design elements, i.e. visuals employed, basic layout, use of fonts and colours etc. Say what you like/dislike about the design and give it a rating (1-10). What would you do differently?**

M **d** **Translate the following description of a webdesign guide into German.**

Build a dynamic, high-impact Website with the remarkable power of Dreamweaver CS3 and the latest version of this top-selling guide from well-known Dreamweaver guru Joseph Lowery. Packed with hands-on instruction and step-by-step tutorials, this comprehensive manual starts you on the basics of Web design and moves to advanced techniques in no time. From quick design prototyping to ongoing Website management – plus a special focus on Dreamweaver CS3's new features for CSS, Flash video, code development, and more – this professional guide is a must for Web masters and developers.

Inside, you'll find complete coverage of Dreamweaver CS3

- Create dynamic Web pages using Cascading Style Sheets
- Punch up your page with progressive or streaming video
- Build interactive forms and client-side image maps
- Insert, delete, and update data in your Web pages
- Improve your HTML coding with the new Coding toolbar
- Integrate with Photoshop(r), Flash(r), Fireworks(r), ColdFusion(r), and other apps
- Use templates and the Library to unify and update your pages
- Extend Dreamweaver's power by creating your own custom tags and behaviors

P **e** **Make a rough outline or design of your own personalized website and present the results in the form of a short oral report, possibly with back-up visual aids, to the rest of the class. Alternatively, you could design a website for a cause or organization you are especially interested in.**

Consider the following points:

- What are my objectives? What impression would I like to convey to visitors to the site?
- Should the focus be on my professional or personal life?
- How should the content be organized? Would a longer text or smaller sections be better?
- What types of graphics – photos, cliparts, sketches – would be most appropriate? Decide whether they would provide additional impact or simply clutter.
- How many and what types of links could be included?
- For the presentation itself what visual back-up material might be useful? A sketch of the layout? Sample graphics?

7 Further reading: The problem with programming

R **a** **In the following interview Bjarne Stroustrup who designed and implemented the C++ programming language is talking about programming. The questions are in mixed order. Match them to the correct answers.**

Questions (Technology Review):

1 Why is most software so bad?

2 How can we fix the mess we are in?

3 The idea behind C++ was that programmers would work harder in return for more-efficient code. Today, there are a lot of software developers and computers are very fast. Does that vitiate the point of C++?

4 In retrospect, in designing C++, wasn't your decision to trade off programmer efficiency, security, and software reliability for run time performance a fundamental mistake?

5 What do you regret the most?

6 How do you account for the fact that C++ is both widely criticized and resented by many programmers but at the same time very broadly used? Why is it so successful?

Answers (Bjarne Stroustrup):

B C++ has indeed become too "expert friendly" at a time where the degree of effective formal education of the average software developer has declined. However, the solution is not to dumb down the programming languages but to use a variety of programming languages and educate more experts. There have to be languages for those experts to use – and C++ is one of those languages.

A No regrets! Well, of course I dream of what I might have done differently and better, but seriously, who am I to second-guess, say, 1984 vintage Bjarne? He may have been less experienced than I, but he was no less smart, probably smarter, and he had a better understanding of the world of 1984 than I have. C++ has been used to build many systems that enhance our lives, and it has been a significant positive influence on later languages and systems. That's something to be proud of.

C Some software is actually pretty good by any standards. Think of the Mars Rovers, Google, and the Human Genome Project. That's quality software! On the other hand, looking at "average" pieces of code can make me cry. The structure is appalling, and the programmers clearly didn't think deeply about correctness, algorithms, data structures, or maintainability. I think the real problem is that "we" (that is, we software developers) are in a permanent state of emergency, grasping at straws to get our work done. We perform many minor miracles through trial and error, excessive use of brute force, and lots and lots of testing, but – so often – it's not enough.

D In theory, the answer is simple: educate our software developers better, use more-appropriate design methods, and design for flexibility and for the long haul. Reward correct, solid, and safe systems. Punish sloppiness. In reality, that's impossible. People reward developers who deliver software that is cheap, buggy, and first. That's because people want fancy new gadgets now. They don't want inconvenience, don't want to learn new ways of interacting with their computers, don't want delays in delivery, and don't want to pay extra for quality.

E The glib answer is, there are just two kinds of languages: the ones everybody complains about and the ones nobody uses. The purpose of a programming language is to help build good systems, where "good" can be defined in many ways. My brief definition is, correct, maintainable, and adequately fast. Aesthetics matter, but first and foremost a language must be useful; it must allow real-world programmers to express real-world ideas succinctly and affordably. The main reason for C++'s success is simply that it meets its limited design aims: it can express a huge range of ideas directly and efficiently. C++ was not designed to do just one thing really well or to prevent people doing things considered "bad." Instead, I concentrated on generality and performance.

F Well, I don't think I made such a trade-off. I want elegant and efficient code. Sometimes I get it. These dichotomies (between efficiency versus correctness, efficiency versus programmer time, efficiency versus high-level, et cetera.) are bogus.What I did do was to design C++ as first of all a systems programming language: I wanted to be able to write device drivers, embedded systems, and other code that needed to use hardware directly. Next, I wanted C++ to be a good language for designing tools. That required flexibility and performance, but also the ability to express elegant interfaces. My view was that to do higher-level stuff, to build complete applications, you first needed to buy, build, or borrow libraries providing appropriate abstractions. Often, when people have trouble with C++, the real problem is that they don't have appropriate libraries – or that they can't find the libraries that are available.

(Technology Review Tuesday, November 28, 2006 by Jason Pontin – excerpts)

R **b** **Study the interview with Bjarne Stroustrup and answer the following questions:**

1. What does Bjarne Stroustrup think of modern software?
2. What does he criticize about some programmers? Why does he think this is the case?
3. What does he think should be done to improve the quality of programming work? Why, in his opinion, isn't it done?
4. Does he think C++ is still a relevant programming language? For whom?
5. Does he feel he compromised on the design of C++? Why or why not?
6. What aims did he have in mind when designing C++?
7. What does he think is the underlying problem many people have with C++?
8. What comprises a "good" programming language, in his opinion?
9. Why does he think C++ is so successful?
10. Is Bjarne Stroustrup 100 % satisfied with his achievements?

M **c** **In the interview Bjarne Stroustrup uses a number of colloquial expressions. How would you translate or explain the following terms in German?**

1. to fix the mess
2. to trade off … for
3. How do you account for
4. is this a joke?
5. glib answer
6. first and foremost
7. "the crowd"
8. grasping at straws
9. brute force
10. sloppiness
11. buggy
12. 1984 vintage
13. to dumb down
14. for the long haul

I/P **d** **Bjarne Stroustrup makes some pretty strong statements. Discuss with a partner whether you agree wholeheartedly, in part or not at all with the following. Report back to the group.**

- Software developers are not as well-trained as they used to be.
- There should be special programming languages just for experts.
- The average software is poorly programmed.
- Programmers are put under pressure to deliver the goods as quickly as possible.
- People just want quick, easy solutions to their computer needs.
- Programmers often don't make efficient use of libraries.
- There is no basic contradiction between efficiency versus correctness or efficiency versus time invested regarding programming work.

8 Language and grammar

8.1. Conjunctions

Join the following sentences with a suitable conjunction from the box.

while • but • before • although • because • so • that

1. Sam wanted to e-mail you. He claimed he didn't have your address.
2. I haven't had a steady job. I graduated from college two years ago. I have been travelling all around the world.
3. A client called. You were out for lunch.
4. It's such an easy programming language. Even a child could learn it.
5. This time get them to sign the contract. They change their minds.
6. People want the latest information. You should update your homepage on a regular basis.

8.2 Word families

With a partner try and come up with as many variations as you can for the following base words. Afterwards, join another pair and compare results.

Example: code – coding – coder; decode – decoder – decodeable

program • base • bug • compile • browse • hack

8.3 Acronyms

Often confusing but admittedly convenient at times, acronyms and abbreviations abound in the computer world. Do you know what all the letters in the ones below stand for? With a partner see how many you can identify correctly within a set time period – without looking back at the glossary.

WLAN • ALU • BASIC • BIOS • CAD • CAM • CAE • CD • CD-ROM • CPU • bps • DTP • DVD • FAQ • CGI • FTP • GB • GUI • HTML • Hz • HTTP • I/F • I/O • IP • IRC • DSL • ISP • IT • LAN • MB • MP • OCR • OS • PL/1 • PPP • RAM • TCP/IP • URL • WAN • WWW • PIN • VGA • VR • ppi

Unit 8
System administration and security

1 A system administrator

The job of a system administrator (sysadmin) is to maintain and troubleshoot a computer system. A sysadmin can have a wide range of duties that differ widely, depending on the type and size of an organization. Basic responsibilities often include training and supporting staff, installing, maintaining and upgrading both software and hardware, doing research and troubleshooting, documenting the network and supervising databases.
A qualified sysadmin should have a well-founded knowledge and experience of the type of network in place, standard office applications, network solutions and hardware installations. Technical know-how is a must, of course, but soft skills are also important since a sysadmin's duties usually involve teaching and training others.
On a day to day basis a sysadmin might be called on to make backups of computers and servers, add or delete new users, maintain effective and up-to-date virus protection and troubleshoot any problems the staff can't solve on their own.

Even the best sysadmins, though, aren't usually able to solve each and every computer problem. Consultants or specialists might sometimes be required for more complex problems or services. The sysadmin should also not be the only person who understands how the computer system functions. Skills and information should be shared with other members of the staff through training measures and thorough documentation of the system.

M/R **a** **Read or listen to the text above, draw a table like the following and complete the table in German:**

Zuständigkeiten des Systemverwalters	
Qualifikationen des Systemverwalters	
Tägliche Aufgaben	
Beschränkung – Gegenmaßnahme(n)	
Gefahr – Gegenmaßnahme(n)	

R **b** **A systems administrator is typically responsible for the following tasks. Finish the sentences with the correct endings.**

1. Setting up, deleting, modifying	a. passwords
2. Installing and configuring	b. the spread of viruses
3. Performing procedures to prevent	c. of data
4. Resetting	d. new hardware and software
5. Troubleshooting	e. user accounts
6. Answering	f. new workstations
7. Performing backups	g. any reported problems
8. Adding and configuring	h. up and running
9. Keeping the network	i. technical queries

R **c** **Defining users rights – determining who is allowed to do what on a system is an important element of a sysadmin's job.**
Match the users to their rights.

1. Administrators	a. can share directories and printers
2. Backup operators	b. have access with minimal privileges and lowest level of network rights
3. Guests	c. can support file replication in a domain
4. Power users	d. can bypass file security to make copies of files
5. Replicators	e. have ordinary rights
6. Users	f. can fully administrate computer/domain: can assign user rights, create and manage user accounts and local groups, maintain local profiles, share network resources, define network resource permissions, and lock the server.

M **d** **The administrator obviously has the most powerful account. Translate into German the rights of a system administrator as detailed in exercise c above.**

2 Working as a system administrator

M **a** **You have been asked to act as a "mediator" for an interview with a system administrator who only speaks English. Translate the questions into English and the answers into German.**

Interviewer	Mediator	System administrator
Wie lange arbeiten Sie schon als Systemadministrator?		
		Just over one year now. I was hired, in fact, to more or less set up the present system from scratch.
Klingt recht anspruchsvoll.		
		It was, though now a lot of my work is routine.
Wie groß ist das von Ihnen betreute Netzwerk?		
		We started with only 5 workstations and have now got about 60. The workstations are organized into 8 or 9 user groups with a data rate of approximately 300 megabyte per second.
Welche Topologie ist im Einsatz?		
		With this size network and the turnover a star topology on a client-server basis was the only logical choice.
Welche Art Server verwendet das System?		
		Well, there are the two main file servers, one for all the financial software – the payroll, spreadsheets and databases – and the other for everything else. And then there's the mail server and the Internet server.
Wie steht's mit dem Drucken?		
		There are some 20 local printers connected to individual workstations, of course, as well as about six what I would call real print servers including one super laser printer.
Wieviel Programmierarbeit müssen Sie leisten?		
		Very little real programming as such, but I often have to write smaller scripts in connection with system management.

P/I **b** **Interview your partner about a network(s) they are part of or familiar with. Report back to the class. Ask questions such as the following:**

1. How large is the network?

2. What's its topology?

3. What services does it offer?

4. Do you need a password to access the system? Is it user defined or assigned?

5. What would you change or add to the network and why?

3 Networking

3.1 Project role play – Case studies

P/I **Study the profiles of the three work groups on the next page and follow the steps of the project:**

Stage 1:
Choose one of the three work groups below and in groups of 3-4 hold a meeting to discuss proposals on how to best meet current as well as near future computer needs. At the "meeting" each group member should take over one of the following roles:

IT manager/secretary: Your job is to coordinate the discussion, take notes and present the final report.
Software specialist: You are responsible for proposing software solutions, i.e. specific software program packages.
Hardware specialist: You should make suggestions to meet the hardware needs of the work group.
System administrator/trainer: You should consider the networking needs and outline a training program for the work group.

Stage 2:
After a specified time each of the different specialists should meet with their opposite numbers, i.e. all the IT managers together, all the software people in another group and so on, to exchange ideas and tips.

Stage 3:
Each of the specialists then reports back to their original group which then works out the final draft of their computer plan of action to be presented to the whole group.

Work Group 1

A consulting firm specializing in joint ventures and foreign acquisitions wants to computerize their practice. The staff consists of four full-time partners/consultants, two freelance consultants paid on a project basis, a research assistant and a foreign trainee from Hong Kong. Till now two secretaries and a student working part-time after school have kept the office running, but they are sadly overworked. From time to time help from temp agencies has been recruited but it generally takes more time to train them than is worth the while The support staff in particular hope to see a reduction in their workload from the proposed computerization of the firm. On the other hand, there is some fear, especially on the part of the older secretary that she won't be able to cope with the new technology. This is also the secret fear of the oldest senior partner which expresses itself as scepticism regarding the cost efficiency ratio of the conversion. The agency has its office in a converted town house with old-fashioned panelling, wooden floors and winding staircases.

Work Group 2

A group of engineers who recently graduated from a college of applied sciences have decided to establish their own business. They would like to offer a broad range of technical services such as advice pertaining to compliance with environmental and workplace safety, health regulations and the application of technology. To have a cutting-edge in an already crowded and competitive field they plan to make the new information technologies an integral part of their business in terms of their marketing strategy, research, and for communicating with clients. Luckily they found a suite of reasonably priced office space to rent – three large rooms and a number of smaller cubicles. Unfortunately, they don't have a great deal of capital and don't want to run up too many debts.

Work Group 3

A medical team – two neurologists, one speech therapist, two physiotherapists, an ergotherapist, an occupational therapist, a registered nurse, a nurse's aid and a social worker – have been assigned the task of setting up a day clinic for stroke and brain-damaged victims. Initial plans call for a project on a smaller scale with just two large recreation rooms, a kitchen, a computer room and 6 smaller consulting/therapy rooms. Depending on funding, however, the project might later be extended to accommodate patients on a live-in basis.

3.2 Networking terms

R **Match the following networking terms with their definitions.**

Example:
1. kernel– f. is an essential part of an OS responsible for resource allocations, low-level hardware interfaces and security

1. kernel	a. is a computer connected to a network
2. trace route	b. is the effort to optimize the performance of a system
3. dump	c. is a tool to determine the path of a network connection
4. time-sharing	d. is an OS feature which allows several users to share a single CPU – multi-tasking for multiple users
5. hop	e. is the jump or connection from one server to another in a network (compare trace route)
6. host	f. is an essential part of an OS responsible for resource allocations, low-level hardware interfaces and security.
7. server	g. is a computer which runs programs that provide services for other computers (clients)
8. protocols	h. is a file that represents the memory content a program had when it crashed
9. client	i. is a computer which accesses programs run by a server
10. monitor	j. are the rules governing how data is transmitted, in particular in a network
11. accounting management	k. is to supervise or coordinate network activities
12. tuning	l. is the person who is responsible for establishing and running a web servers and/or the web pages of a website
13. webmaster	m. is the process of collecting information about and evaluating group and individual access to network resources
14. handshaking	n. consists of prearranged agreements regarding hardware or software activities in order to establish and maintain synchronization
15. audit	o. is a control program that manages the allocation of system resources

4 Error messages

a **Read the following explanations of error messages.**

1
Data error reading drive X
An area of the disk is unreadable. You can press R to retry, if that fails, press A to abort. Use a utility program to try and reconstruct the damaged area if there's no back-up and the data is important.

2
Duplicate file name not found
The referenced file doesn't exist or you are renaming a file to a file name that already exists.
It's also possible that the file you are renaming is in use by another user in the network. It would have to be closed by that person before you can rename it.

3
Exception error 12
DOS doesn't have enough space to deal with hardware interrupts. You should increase the number of stacks in the STACKS command in the CONFIG.SYS file.

4
Files not found
DOS cannot find the file named. Check the spelling using the Dir command or look in another directory.

5
Invalid parameter
DOS doesn't understand the command line which probably means that a switch is used incorrectly. With path names remember to use a backslash and a forward slash to enter parameters.

6
Not ready writing device PRN
Abort, Retry, Fail?
The printer is either switched off or unavailable. Either press A to cancel or turn the printer on and press R. Check the cable connection to the printer.

7
System halted
There is either a hardware or software problem due to one of the following causes: a memory parity error has been detected, a peripheral board is not in order, a bug or a virus.

8
Write protect error
Data cannot be recorded on a protected medium (e.g. floppy disk or tape). You have to either unprotect it or use another one.

R/M **b** **Now decide whether the German statements below are true or false.**

1. Data error reading drive X
a. Die Festplatte ist beschädigt.
b. Die eingegebenen Daten sind endgültig verloren.

2. Duplicate file name not found
a. Es gibt zwei mögliche Erklärungen.
b. Sie müssen die Datei schließen, um sie neu benennen zu können.

3. Exception error 12
a. Sie müssen mehr Platz schaffen.
b. Sie können die Anzahl von „Stacks" mit dem CONFIG.SYS Befehl vermehren.

4. File not found
a. Sie suchen möglicherweise in der falschen Datei.
b. Mit dem *Dir* Befehl können sie andere Dateien absuchen.

5. Invalid parameter
a. Deutet auf die falsche Verwendung einer Umschaltung.
b. Für Pfadnamen und die Eingabe von Parametern verwenden Sie einen „backslash".

6. Not ready writing device PRN
a. Der Drucker ist entweder nicht eingeschaltet oder nicht verfügbar.
b. Sie müssen A drucken, um den Auftrag zu stornieren und dann R, um es nochmals zu versuchen.

7. System halted
a. Ein Programmfehler verursacht einen Virus.
b. Speichermangel ist eine mögliche Ursache für die Meldung.

8. Write protect error
a. Diese Diskette ist geschützt.
b. Sie müssen eine neue Diskette benutzen.

M **c** **Translate the following terms/phrases often found in error messages into German.**

1. invalid
2. not found
3. doesn't exist
4. acess denied
5. login required
6. error occurred
7. not ready
8. system halted
9. exception
10. damaged

5 Computers and crime

5.1 Computer viruses

P **a** **Read the following text and make up headings for the eight paragraphs.**

1

Analogous to biological viruses, a computer virus is a program that searches out and "infects" other programs. It does this by embedding a copy of itself in the boot sector of a disk or to other widely used programs such as spreadsheets or database software. The virus itself is executed when an infected file is activated or when the computer is started from an infected disk.

2

Viruses are increasing at a mind-boggling rate. Though there was only one know virus in 1986, only four short years later they were being discovered at the rate of one per week. Today computer viruses are on the rise with up to 15 new viruses flaming up daily and annual growth rates of more than 100%. Naturally, an increase in the number of viruses at large in the computer world have led to a rapid spread in the rate of infections and the number of affected computers.

3

Originally viruses could not infect other computers without assistance. While disks were once the major source of infection, e-mail attachments soon replaced them as the bigger headache and were responsible for the sharp rise in infection rates. As opposed to diskettes, which are typical for boot-sector viruses, attachments are primarily responsible for the spread of macro viruses.

4

For some time now worms are on the rise. A worm uses a network to send a copy of itself to another computer. In other words, worms can spread on their own and don't need human help. Unlike viruses which infect or corrupt files, worms affect the network itself. Internet worms, for example, take advantage of "remote vulnerabilities" (security holes in programs) which is now the way most viruses and worms spread.

5
What exactly do computer viruses and worms do? Some are relatively benign and may result in nothing worse than "funny" messages or graphics popping up unexpectedly. Others are anything but harmless and can cause extensive damage, wasting time, money and countless hours of manpower.

6
Particularly malignant viruses can delete or block access to a user's files and cause damage to software, while worms can seriously harm networks, if nothing else by consuming bandwidth. Virus hoaxes claiming to warn other users of some lethal virus on the loose are almost as bad. They jam e-mail networks and lead to lost productivity and downtime.

7
Understandably, people tend to react emotionally when their files or network are threatened. It's therefore important, to remember a few points that run counter to the general myth building and media sensation surrounding viruses. Viruses don't infect write protected disks. With the exception of special types of hardware such as flash memory, they can't infect hardware.

8
Computer viruses can and do cause damage and call for effective countermeasures. Producing and peddling anti-virus software has become a lucrative business. Virus scanning and detecting can be done at intervals or each time a file is downloaded. As most people are aware, scanning e-mail attachments is also an important preventive measure.

R **b** **Match the following virus terms to their descriptions below.**

a. Trojan Horse
b. Worm
c. Benign virus
d. Malignant virus
e. Payload
f. Macro virus
g. File infectors
h. Boot infectors
i. Retro virus
j. Virus hoax

1. are annoying false alarms that waste time and jam up your mailbox.
2. is a category of virus which damages a computer system by corrupting files or destroying data.
3. are viruses which either latch onto or replace .COM and .EXE files as well as other extensions.
4. are designed to attack anti-virus programs and wipe out anti-virus data files.
5. are programs with a nasty surprise designed to cause harm, in contrast to viruses they can't make copies of themselves.
6. affect the boot program of the hard drive when the system is rebooted with a infected bootable storage medium in the drive.
7. are script based viruses and are spread generally via e-mail attachments and Internet downloads.
8. are programs designed to copy themselves from one computer to another, not from file to file, via a network system – this means they don't need humans to help spread and are, therefore, especially dangerous.
9. is a category of virus which cause no significant damage.
10. is the part of the virus that triggers the actual events.

5.2 Crimeware landmarks

R ■ **Match the name and date of the virus to its description.**

1. 1982 – Elk Cloner 2. 1986 – Brain 3. 1992 – Michelangelo 4. 1999 – Melissa 5. 2000 – Love letter 6. 2004 – MyDoom	a. One of the first viruses to get widespread media coverage, the reach of the "artist" – at one point predicted to hit 5m machines – turned out to be far smaller than anticipated. b. "She" took over e-mail programs, causing the internet to struggle under the weight of messages being sent. c. It spread on floppy disks that were used by the Apple II, a popular early home computer. d. A harmless but annoying virus which wasn't really as smart as its name implied. It spread worldwide in just a few months, making it the first widespread PC virus. e. A clever mass mailing worm, it currently holds the record for being the fastest-growing piece of malicious code. f. Disguised as a message saying "I love you", this virus is estimated to have caused more than \$10bn (£6bn) worth of damage, making it one of the most destructive pieces of crimeware ever written.

5.3 Protection

R a **Decode, i.e. put the words of the advice below into the correct order.**

Example: 1. Use your browser to dismantle "cookies" software

1. Use – browser – dismantle – your – "cookies" – software – to
2. Don't – unknown – from – open – attachments – sources – e-mail
3. Update – regularly – your – software – anti-virus
4. Keep – secret – a – password – your
5. Encrypt – sensitive – to – want – data – you – e-mail
6. Always – software – for – and – attachments – viruses – check – e-mail
7. Make – copies – files – important – of – back-up
8. Don't – virus – believe – hoaxes – and – pass – on

P b **Speculate about what could have been avoided if users had observed security measures.**

Example: Poor Dagmar. She lost all her current files when her computer crashed yesterday. → If Dagmar had made back-up copies she wouldn't have lost all her files.

1. The government cracked down on computer abuse in the 80's leading to the arrest of a number of infamous hackers.
2. She didn't bother to check the borrowed disk for viruses and caught a bug.
3. The teacher stupidly used his first name as a password which the students soon discovered.
4. Many users caught the "Iloveyou" virus because they blindly opened up the e-mail attachment it came in.
5. Greg was gullible and wasted half the morning passing on a warning about a new virus which turned out to be a hoax.

5.4 Cryptography

M **a** **Translate the following text into German.**

I **b** **Compare your translation to your partner's. What words or parts did you translate differently?**

Cryptography is the practice and study of encryption and decryption – encoding information so that it can only be decoded by certain individuals. A cryptosystem is one for encrypting and decrypting data. This generally involves an algorithm for combining the original data, called "plaintext", with one or more "keys". Keys are numbers or strings of characters which only the sender and/or recipient know. The output which results is called "ciphertext".

The security of a cryptosystem is usually dependent on the secrecy of some, more or all of the keys and not on the supposed secrecy of the algorithm. A good cryptosystem is in possession of a wide range of possible keys so that it is not feasible to simply try out all of them. This is known as the "brute force" approach. If a cryptosystem is strong, it will turn out ciphertext which appears random to standard statistical tests. A strong cryptosystem will be able to withstand cryptoanalaysis, i.e. all previously known methods of breaking code.

5.5 Passwords

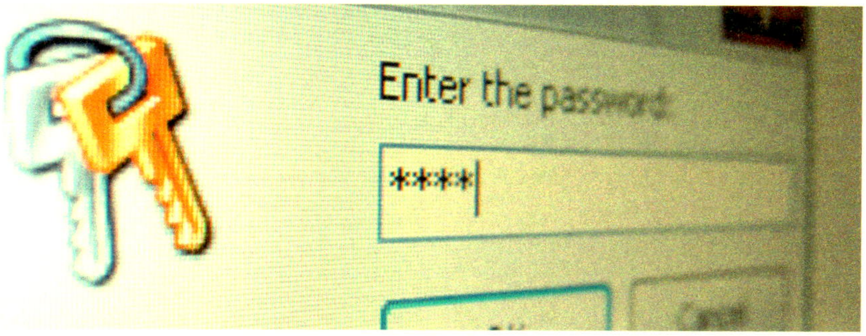

P **a** **Study the criteria below and reformulate them into rules for governing the use of passwords.**

Example: be easy to remember → A password should be easy to remember.

1. a word from the dictionary
2. contain both numbers and letters
3. include spaces, dots or symbols with special computing meanings
4. have both capital and small case letters
5. be a common word which is easy to guess
6. be told to your office colleagues
7. be jotted down somewhere near your computer
8. be reissued at regular intervals.
9. be at least six characters long.

A password shouldn't / should…

Don't …

You should avoid …

P **b** **Now consider the consequences if you don't follow the rules. Write one sentence per rule.**

Example: If the password isn't easy to remember, you'll soon forget it.

6 Further reading: Firewall

Firewall

A firewall is a system designed to prevent unauthorized access to or from a private network. Firewalls can be implemented in both hardware and software, or a combination of both. Firewalls are frequently used to prevent unauthorized Internet users from accessing private networks connected to the Internet, especially intranets. All messages entering or leaving the intranet pass through the firewall, which examines each message and blocks those that do not meet the specified security criteria.
There are several types of firewall techniques:

1. Packet filter: Looks at each packet entering or leaving the network and accepts or rejects it based on user-defined rules. Packet filtering is fairly effective and transparent to users, but it is difficult to configure. In addition, it is susceptible to IP spoofing.

2. Application gateway: Applies security mechanisms to specific applications, such as FTP and Telnet servers. This is very effective, but can impose a performance degradation.

3. Circuit-level gateway: Applies security mechanisms when a TCP or UDP connection is established. Once the connection has been made, packets can flow between the hosts without further checking.

4. Proxy server: Intercepts all messages entering and leaving the network. The proxy server effectively hides the true network addresses.

In practice, many firewalls use two or more of these techniques in concert. A firewall is considered a first line of defense in protecting private information. For greater security, data can be encrypted.
A technique used to gain unauthorized access to computers, whereby the intruder sends messages to a computer with an IP address indicating that the message is coming from a trusted host. To engage in IP spoofing, a hacker must first use a variety of techniques to find an IP address of a trusted host and then modify the packet headers so that it appears that the packets are coming from that host.

(Microsoft) Advertiser I

M **Read the text and explain the different types of firewall techniques in German.**

7 Language and grammar

7.1 Mixed tenses

Choose the correct form of the marked verbs in the following text.

1. English is essential in this help desk job. If you not know English you not be able to speak to half the callers.
2. In case I forget, remind me to send along copies to the rest of the staff.
3. Of course, it's important! If it not be a matter of top priority, we not put it on the agenda.
4. What like you to drink? – If you have red wine, I have a glass, otherwise just water, please.
5. If she take more computer courses when she be at college, she be in a better position now to find a good job.
6. If you ask me, the company be better off if they downsize earlier – now it be too late. – Nonsense! They be able still make a comeback if they act now.

7.2 Prepositions

Complete the sentences with the correct preposition.

(2x) for • up • of • between • by • (2x) on • in • over

1. They're offering discounts of ... to 10% off the regular price list.
2. It's a special offer – two ... the price ... one.
3. Charges ... express delivery vary ... 2% and 5%.
4. Payment is strictly ... a cash basis only.
5. Would you like to pay ... credit card or ... cash?
6. We're way ... budget and have to cut back ... spending to bring our debt balance down.

7.3 Idioms: to give

Complete the following sentences with the correct form of the phrasal verb.

give up • give away • give back • give in • give out (2x)

1. If I'd known you needed the scanner manual I would have ... it ... to you sooner.
2. ... to their every whim is not the answer to raising children properly.
3. He would have made a success of the venture if he hadn't gotten discouraged towards the end and ... the whole project.
4. In an effort to attract new subscribers, they're ... three free issues of ONLINE.
5. Cross your fingers and hope the car doesn't ... on us before we reach home.
6. Would you please ... these copies to the others?

Unit 9
Projects, meetings and presentations

1 Project management

P **a** **Based on the diagram below create a text describing project management.**

Example: Project management consists of applying …

R **b** **Put the following five major phases of project management in the correct order.**

1. planning/design
2. closure
3. control/monitoring
4. initiation/roll-out
5. execution

R **c** **Find the best match for project management related actions and aims.**

Example: 1. Planning and organizing – b. the work

1. Planning and organizing	a. risk
2. Analyzing and designing	b. the work
3. Assessing and mitigating	c. project execution
4. Estimating and allocating	d. objectives
5. Acquiring	e. tasks
6. Assigning	f. progress
7. Directing	g. based on the facts achieved
8. Controlling	h. resources
9. Tracking and reporting	i. human and material resources
10. Analyzing the results	j. activities

P **d** **Plan an English class project taking the points above into consideration, i.e. the aims of the project/required resources/range of activities/phases etc.**

Suggested projects:
- planning a classroom website
- setting up a dynamic database of English language learning materials
- a classroom outing
- arranging an exchange visit with English speaking vocational school pupils

R **e** **Complete the following advice for running an IT service unit with a suitable phrase from the box.**

1. Treat your end-users as …
2. Set … for IT service goals and capabilities.
3. Use … for customer relationship management.
4. Encourage and support …
5. Be proactive - take advantage of every opportunity for …
6. Pick an … designed to suit IT alignment goals.
7. Learn how to … to impractical service requests.
8. … to find "lessons" for performance improvement.
9. Engage and encourage …
10. Take a proactive approach to manage…

say no • Service Level Agreements • IT "added value" • end-user-training programs • strategic business partners • realistic expectations • „down-time" perceptions • Analyse IT service metrics • organizational model • end-user participation in IT projects

2 Meetings

2.1. The language of business meetings

R **a** **Complete the following business meeting quotations using the words or phrases in the box below.**

resolution • unanimous • chairman • out of order • agenda • motion • minutes • call • show of hands • business • to order • move • amend • adjourning • vote • amendment • committee • abstention

1. As … I would now like to … this meeting … Order, Ladies and Gentlemen!

2. The first item on today's … is Ms. Douglas' report on the new firewall installations.

3. If I could just have a quick … to see how many are in favour of taking a quick break.

4. George, I'm afraid you're … there and will have to yield the floor to Jane.

5. I think we can take the … of last week's meeting as read and proceed to today's first item of …

6. No objections? Good, then we're … in … the meeting till this time next week.

7. Ian: We're just going around in circles here – I … that we appoint a … of two or three to enquire into the facts of the case and report back to us.
Beate: I second the … and … that Ian himself head the committee.
Chris: I second the …

8. The … to form a committee of investigation is carried by a … of ten for, one against and one …

R **b** **At a business meeting, whether it's a session with a few colleagues or a formal gathering, you might hear a range of expressions.
Study the phrases below and list them under the following seven functions.
Note: There might be more than one way to express a certain function.**

1	2	3	4	5	6	7
Giving opinions	Agreeing	Disagreeing	Asking for clarification	Interrupting	Dealing with interruptions	Structuring

- There are several issues at hand here: One …
- Can you give an example?
- Can I just say something?
- As I see it …
- That's right!
- I couldn't agree more.
- Exactly!
- In my opinion/experience …
- Sorry, but could you repeat that, please?
- I didn't quite understand/get that …
- I'm not sure about that …
- Sorry, could I just finish?
- I'd like to make two points: First of all I'd say …
- It depends. On the one hand … on the other hand …
- I'm afraid I can't go along with that.
- I'd like to point out three main problems. Firstly, … , secondly … and finally …

2.2 Chairing a meeting

P/I **a** **A chairperson often plays a vital role in the success or failure of a meeting. Discuss with a partner and make a list of things a good chairperson should do during a meeting. Share with the group.**

R **b** **Now look at the following phrases (a.–h.) and decide what the chairperson would use them to do by matching the phrases with the speech functions (1. – 8.)**

Example: 1. refocusing the discussion: h. Perhaps we could get back to … / concentrate on the matter in hand.

1. refocusing the discussion 2. summarizing 3. opening the meeting 4. asking for opinions, information 5. asking for agreement 6. outlining the agenda 7. closing the meeting 8. moving on to the next point	a. Let's see where we are. Let me sum up … The consensus seems to be … b. Right, I think we're all here, so, ladies and gentlemen … I'd like to call the meeting to order. c. What do you think, Sandy? Mary, have you got anything to add? And what's your view? d. Are we all in favour? Can we agree? Can I have a show of hands? e. The problem we have to resolve is … There are three items on today's agenda. First … We're here to discuss the following points: … f. Well, that seems to wrap things up. Right, I think we've covered all the items on the agenda. I'd like to close the meeting at this point. Thank you. g. Let's move on, shall we? Okay. That seems clear. Now the third item on the agenda is … I think we should stop here and … h. Perhaps we could get back to … /concentrate on the matter in hand.

R **c** **Listen to the following meeting and identify the different phases or functions of the meeting as shown above. Who is speaking? (e.g. chairperson, participant, secretary, committee chairperson)**

R/I **d** **Discuss with your partner what you would do/say if the following things went wrong at a meeting.**

Example: If the schedule of the meeting was unclear, I would refer to the agenda.

1. If the chairperson didn't show up. 2. If, as chairperson, participants kept arriving late. 3. If the chairperson or one participant monopolized the meeting. 4. If the meeting dragged on and on. 5. If no one stuck to the agenda.	a. I would remind participants of the business at hand/request a second reading of the agenda. b. I would make a motion to adjourn the meeting. c. I would request members in future to arrive on time. d. I would suggest taking a short break or adjourning the meeting till a later date. e. I would suggest we listen to someone else's opinion for a change.

2.3 Role play: A business meeting

Hold a business meeting in groups of 5 – 7. Decide your own reason for the meeting or choose from one of the topics below. Before you start agree upon an agenda and who is to play any special role such as chairperson, secretary or committee chairperson. Keep in mind the various phases and functions of a meeting: opening, structuring, agreeing/disagreeing, summarizing, closing.

Meeting Idea 1

Your company specializes in developing and marketing software for printing purposes. A meeting has been called to develop a comprehensive in-company training program for staff members. Possible discussion points: Who needs training? What ? Trainers? When? Costs? Where?

Meeting Idea 2

You work for a middle-sized pharmaceutical company which wants to expand into E-commerce. A meeting has been called to discuss the necessary requirements: e.g. website with integrated database, retraining staff, hiring experts. Consider also your possible target market, e.g. wholesalers, retailers and individual customers as well as logistics.

Meeting Idea 3

Your consulting firm has been asked to work on a project aimed at the complete digitalisation of a small town with a population of 30,000. Possible points of discussion: hardware/software requirements, acclimatising the populace, financing.

3 Presentations

"It takes one hour of preparation for each minute of presentation time."
(Wayne Burgraff)

"There are always three speeches, for every one you actually gave. The one you practiced, the one you gave, and the one you wish you gave."
(Dale Carnegie)

3.1. Preparing a presentation

R/P **Read the following guideline and then summarize the main points as a list of dos and don'ts to keep in mind when preparing presentations.**

→ One of the first steps in preparing any kind of talk or presentation is to think about what you want to accomplish. Is the point to share information, convince your audience of your arguments or motivate them to undertake specific actions?

→ Once you have set your goals you have to think about your audience so you can customize your presentation to their needs. Will you be talking to experts or will your audience have little knowledge or experience about your topic? What are their expectations? What kind of questions might they ask?

→ After determining the focus of your presentation you will need to line up the facts to support your point of view or proposal. Your data, whether as text or in graphical form, should be accurate and complete to portray you as a reliable source of information.

→ You have to consider your priorities, your key points and just how much detail you want to include. Finding the right balance here isn't always easy; too much information and you'll overwhelm your audience, too little will leave them feeling they haven't been adequately informed.

→ One of the most essential aspects is not to ramble but to outline your talk and give your presentation a clear structure. The general rule of thumb is to tell them what you're going to tell them (forecast), tell them, and then tell them what you told them (summary).

→ A point that is sometimes overlooked but which is also important is the need to signpost your talk. This means indicating clearly to your audience what point in the presentation you are currently at, e.g. "My first point ....", "In conclusion ...".
→ As any successful speaker will tell you, rehearsing your presentation is an absolute must. Experts often recommend practising out loud in front of a mirror or even videotaping your practice sessions, keeping eye contact, body language, and pace in mind.
→ Last but not least, it's not a good idea to leave anything to chance. Make sure you know how to use the equipment without any problems and that it is set up and ready to run when you need it.

3.2. Making a presentation

R **a** **A number of factors generally contribute to the success of a good presentation. Match the topics to the suitable advice.**

1. appearance 2. posture 3. gestures 4. visuals 5. humor 6. eye contact 7. language 8. voice 9. time-management	a. Vary your volume and tone. Add life by emphasizing key words and phrases. b. Catch and hold your audience's attention by looking at them. c. Stand straight and relaxed. Don't fidget or lean forwards or backwards. d. Dress in a simple and professional manner. Avoid flashy colors and ornaments. e. Don't exceed the limit – aim for 80% of the allotted time. f. Create rapport by getting your audience to relax and laugh. g. Use your hands to add effect but don't overdo it. h. Use understandable, pronounceable words and phrases which are natural to you. i. Generate interest by making creative use of diagrams, graphics etc.

P/I **b** **List the above items in the order of importance for you personally. Compare and discuss with a partner. What points do you agree/disagree about? Report briefly to group.**

3.3 Presentation plan

R **a** **Choose the right category (1.–10.) for the examples (a.–j.) of presentation language below.**

1. Asking rhetorical questions 2. Describing results 3. Giving background information 4. Describing action taken 5. Opening strategies 6. Describing problems 7. Structuring 8. Forecasting 9. Summarizing 10. Closing	a. Did you realize … (quote unusual fact/figure)? As (famous person) once said … I'd like to start by telling … (joke, anecdote)
	b. Today I will be talking about … My talk will focus on the … I'm here today to tell you about …
	c. First, I'm going to … Then I'll give … Finally, I'd like … My presentation is divided into … First of all, … secondly, … after that …
	d. I'd like to begin by giving you some … Some time ago we were … Let's have a look at some background …
	e. So, what could we do? How did we deal with the problem? Where did we go from there?
	f. Well, the difficulty was … The problem we were facing … Our biggest challenge was …
	g. Therefore, we decided to … There were basically three choices of action: … Our first priority was to …
	h. Here are the preliminary results. If you look at this diagram, you can see … Have a look at the following outcome.
	i. To sum up … Let me briefly recapitulate: … In conclusion, …
	j. Thank you very much for time and attention. That brings me to the end of my talk. If you have any questions, I'll be happy to answer them now.

P **b** **Using the framework above prepare a short presentation. It can be about a computer problem you solved, a project you worked on or a personal challenge. Make brief notes and prepare simple visuals. Use the language above to structure your presentation but feel free to change it.**

4 Describing graphs and diagrams

Phrases **Describing graphs and diagrams**

↑ go up / rise / increase	Examples:
↓ decrease / fall / drop	There was a rise / an increase in server load to … MB/ s.
→ remain constant	There was a decline / fall / decrease in server load of 10 %.
↑ reach a high ↓ reach a low	Last year sales increased **slightly**. There was a **slight** increase of sales last year.
high enormously dramatically ↑ considerably slightly low hardly	

P **a** **Describe the following diagram dealing with the maximum load of four different servers.**

The server RS600A is the dark blue line. The server MC680 is the purple line. The server RS600B is the yellow line. The server GC100 is the light blue line.

Example:
The line graph shows the maximum load of … servers from … till … .
The first/second/third/fourth server starts off in the morning with a load of approximately … MB/s. After that ther's a slight decrease/increase/dip/rise/ drop in the server load till … when it reaches …

Time / Server	RS 600 A	MC 680	RS 600 B	GC 1000
08:00	12.0	8.6	18.9	0.0
09:00	13.4	15.9	13.2	4.5
10:00	9.5	11.9	21.6	5.6
11:00	8.3	13.8	14.3	11.1
12:00	6.4	16.8	6.7	17.3
13:00	9.7	17.3	9.2	19.4
14:00	14.5	20.0	19.4	19.5
15:00	12.1	17.4	24.1	21.2

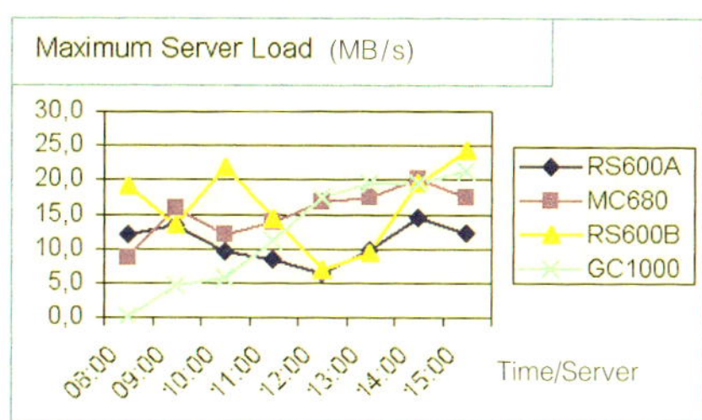

R/P **b** **Listen to the following report about the development of the stock market index from 2000 to April 2007. Draw a rough sketch of the development in the form of a line graph.**

5 Further reading: The ABCs of entrepreneurship

1. An 'entrepreneur' is a person who embodies certain 'enterprise skills and attitudes'. The skills include the willingness to take risks on new products or processes and the ability to deal with uncertainty and change in a competent manner. Determination, self-confidence and a strong work ethic characterize the attitude of the entrepreneur. The Program for Entrepreneurship Teaching (PET) wants to root enterprise in schools, so that students can learn about it and practise it in realistic situations. PET was established by a group of educators and business people in New York in 1986 and now teaches over 150,000 people worldwide about entrepreneurship.

2. The first step in establishing a successful business is to come up with a profitable idea. This might be a new product, something which you have seen when travelling and think you can introduce in your own country, or you can even build on the back of something else (such as products to go with cell phones). A new business idea could also be the opportunity to buy into someone else's good idea through a franchise.

3. Research can help the budding entrepreneur to work out if the idea has potential. It is a support in understanding and accessing customers' needs. Research helps to break the market down into smaller parts, or segments, so that they can be more easily targeted. Entrepreneurs often use a SWOT analysis to evaluate new business ideas. This has a closer look at the **S**trengths and **W**eaknesses of the idea, and the external **O**pportunities and **T**hreats. Students of PET workshops often come up with a wide range of business ideas. These are ideas for selling both goods and services – goods such as post-its and mousepads, and services such as setting up a swap shop so that other students in the school can sell and buy used text books at discounted prices.

4. When establishing a business one must differentiate between start-up costs, which only have to be paid initially, and running costs, which are needed to maintain the continued operation of the business. Running costs are usually further divided into direct costs, which are linked to output (such as material costs), and indirect costs – which are usually referred to as overheads (such as energy or interest rates). Entrepreneurs also need to estimate future cashflows using cashflow forecasts. They need to know if receipts will be greater than payments or if they will need to take out more in loans to make up for the deficit should payments be greater than receipts.

5. The students involved in PET projects are supported with a £50 loan to start the business. In normal businesses the most usual sources for start-up costs are owners' funds, i.e. the owners use their own savings or bank loans or overdrafts. Other possibilities are venture capital in which speculators risk their money by investing in businesses or so-called trade credit in which the new business pays for ordered goods at a later date.

6. The students report that they benefit enormously from their PET experiences. They feel they learn to work in teams, manage their time better and develop many other positive qualities. They feel that they would not have been able to develop many of these skills through the normal curriculum. In conclusion we can claim that PET helps young people to implement business ideas which use skills beyond those of the traditional curriculum. Students learn how to set up a business, manage market research, cash flow, work in teams and manage production, thus preparing them for the real world of business and work.

R **a** **Read the text above and choose the best title for each of the numbered paragraphs from the following list.**

A Students sell good and services
B New ideas offer chances
C Stages in establishing a business
D Business person profile
E PET realizes business ideas
F Entrepreneurship is a global concern
G Students profit from project
H Calculating costs
I Student loans
J Initial capital vs overhead
K Financing a business
L Market analysis

R **b** **Using the information from the text complete each of the sentences (1.-4.) with a suitable phrase (a.-g.) from the list below.**

1. A SWOT analysis involves ...
2. Through the project students felt they learned things that ...
3. An entrepreneur needs to estimate costs in advance in order to be able ...
4. To be successful a entrepreneur needs a good idea and, above all, ...

a. a willingness to take chances, adapt to new situations and work hard.
b. to distinguish between start-up costs and running costs.
c. assessing the positive and negative aspects of a business idea.
d. to know whether the business will make a profit.
e. are not usually taught in classes.
f. will help them find a job after completing the business curriculum.
g. deciding which business ideas are good and developing strategies to deal with competitors.
h. careful planning and new products ideas.

6 Language and grammar

Gerund or infinitive?

Complete the following sentences using either the "ing" or "to-infinitive" of the verb.

1. He has trouble admitting **make** mistakes.
2. Grace Hopper began **program** one of the very first computers in 1943.
3. Can we really afford **lose** any more money on such unproductive processes?
4. The alarm function on my wristband helps me not to forget **take** my pill every six hours.
5. They'll have to decide what **do** sooner or later.
6. As expected, he denies even **know** the names of any of the donaters.
7. Did you ever try **do** any meditation exercises?
8. Please excuse my **take** so long **get** back to you but I had a horribly busy morning.
9. That's the bottom line: You have to learn **pretend** **like** the way things are run here or find yourself a new job.
10. I can't imagine **risk** my career on an off chance like that.

INFO BOX "-ing" or "to"

Verbs can be followed by "ing":
Example: I don't mind picking you up first.

Or they can be followed by "to":
Example: They've decided to reorganize the whole department – again!

Some verbs are followed by either "ing" or "to" with virtually no difference in meaning:
Example:
He loved to drink beer. = He loved drinking beer.

A few verbs can be followed by either "ing" or "to" but with a difference in meaning:
Example:
She stopped to talk to him. (= She broke off whatever she was doing in order to talk to him.)
She stopped talking to him. (= She refused or discontinued speaking to him.)

Unit 10
Jobs in computing

According to the U.S. Bureau of Labor Statistics Information Technology (IT) is the fastest growing sector in the economy with a 68% increase in output growth rate projected between 2002 and 2012. Employment opportunities are expected to be good in the IT industry as demand for computer-related occupations increases due to rapid advances in computer technology, continuing development of new computer applications, and the growing significance of information security.

More than 90% of IT workers are employed outside the IT industry, which makes it necessary for them to have both IT and complementary training in their respective business sectors such as health care, manufacturing, or financial services. Employers are also looking for well-developed soft skills, transferable IT skills and adaptability in their workforce.

IT remains a critical aspect of work in all industries and sectors, as well as an industry in its own right. However, America continues to suffer from a shortage of qualified IT workers with flexible and portable skills who can readily adapt and respond to ever-changing IT demands and processes.

P/I **Read the text above and discuss the following questions.**

1. What are the job chances for IT specialists in the near and far future?
2. Where do the majority of them work?
3. What other job skills are required of IT-workers?

1 Job advertisements

R **Study the following job advertisements. List which of the following are required / offered in each of the advertised positions:**

	personal qualities	professional abilities	job duties	benefits
example	team oriented	fluent in German	manage sales force	bonus structure

1

Commensurate with skills

Junior C++ Developer, Brighton ,
C++, Competitive Salary

Based in Brighton our firm offers an excellent opportunity for a C++ developer to join its team of dynamic application developers. We specialise in the development of applications for the retail branch and are currently recruiting for a Junior C++ Developer. You need to have a good understanding of C++ and mainframe computers and be a good team player. This is a great chance to work on cutting-edge software and profit from some of the best developers in the industry. You will receive in-house training and benefit from external training courses paid for by the company. Please contact Portia Green at portia.green@apa.com.uk to find out more information.

2

Web Developer

The person in this position would work as a part of a larger web development team. Tasks include all aspects of web application development, from gathering and documenting user requirements to the database design.
Proficiency with Microsoft Visual Studio, ASP.NET, VB.NET, Microsoft IIS, SQL Server required. Microsoft Certified Application Developer certification helpful.
IT training or CS degree required, experience as web master a bonus.
As a dynamic and still expanding web firm, we offer self-starters with a strong sense of team spirit: responsibility, fascinating opportunties and a wide scope for the development of creative potential. Please visit the Careers section at websouth.com to submit your résumé for this position.

3

megamedia.com

IT sales professional Needed

Our sales team is looking for an experienced IT sales professional. You will be required to give detailed information and demonstrate technical specifications to meet customer needs. In addition, you will calculate prices and costs, make offers and advise customers about financing and services. Your tasks will also include follow-up technical support such as solving faults, maximising features and giving training advice.
Vocational computer / technical training or similar required, along with enthusiasm for the IT world and solid commercial background. The position calls for courtesy, good customer management skills, and team spirit. Flexibility and willingness to work evenings and at the weekends a must.
We offer a good base salary plus commission, opportunities for advancement, and a profit sharing program.
Please submit your application with the usual documents (cover letter, CV, references, certificates) online to shelly.winter@megamedia.com

4

Fairview Technology is a leading ASIC design service vendor.

ANALOG DESIGN ENGINEERS

Responsibilities: Design and evaluate high speed circuits, experience with flash, sigma-delta and other ADCCs, oscillators and voltage references. Candidate should have experience with CMOS technologies. Work effectively in multi-cultural team.
Requirements: BSEE / MSEE / PHD (or equivalent). Proficient in analog circuit design and analysis along with CAD / CAE design tools. Good oral and written communication skills.
We offer competitive salary, fabulous workplace employee benefits
· internal and external training
· English, Chinese and Japanese language classes
· bonuses
· maternity / parental leave

If you'd like to join the best please send your resume to Fairview Technology GmbH
Fäustlestr. 33
81659 Munich
http://www.fairview.com.tw

2 Finding a job

Job profiles are undergoing rapid revision as the working world becomes ever more complex and computerized.

P/I **Choose or have your teacher assign you a selection of 3-4 job titles from the selection below. With a partner consider the following questions:**

1. What job duties could the position possibly entail?
2. What sort of qualifications, training or expertise might be required?
3. Would you personally be qualified / want to work in one of the positions? Why or why not?

Online project manager • key account manager • team assistant • software developer • IT consultant • front desk manager • customer service • webmaster • call center coordinator • NT / Oracle administrator • pricing manager • marketing-communications coordinator • finance specialist • contact coordinator • relocation counselor • office head • content manager • DTP-allrounder • software target integration • senior and junior helpdesk analyst • IS senior system trainer • carrier liaison manager • network planning manager • junior art director • IT supporter • strategic cable planner • online admanager

3 Applying for jobs

INFO BOX How to translate German job titles

The following examples are translations recommended by the German Chamber of Commerce:

Automobilkaufmann / -frau	→ Automobile Sales Management Assistant
Bankkaufmann / -frau	→ Bank Business Management Assistant
Bürokaufmann / -frau	→ Office Management Assistant
Fachkraft für Lagerwirtschaft	→ Management Assistant in Warehousing and Logistics
Hotelkaufmann / -frau	→ Management Assistant in Hotel and Hospitality
Informatikkaufmann / -frau	→ Management Assistant in Informatics
Industriekaufmann / -frau	→ Industrial Business Management Assistant
IT-System-Kaufmann / -frau	→ Management Assistant in IT-Systems
Kaufmann / -frau für audiovisuelle Medien	→ Management Assistant in Audio / Visual Media
Kaufmann / -frau für Bürokommunikation	→ Management Assistant in Office Communication

3.1. Schools and qualifications

R/M **The following table lists some German schools and qualifications and their American and British equivalents . Complete the table by matching the missing terms in the box below to the numbers (1–6) in the table.**

O (= ordinary)-level • full-time vocational school • comprehensive school • higher secondary school • technical school • A (= advanced)-level

 German	 American	 British
	Institutions	
1. Hauptschule	junior high school	secondary modern school
2. Realschule	high school	1
3. Gymnasium	high school	grammar school
4. Gesamtschule	high school	2
5. Berufsschule	vocational school	vocational school
6. Berufsfachschule	full-time vocational school	3
7. Fachoberschule	technical school	higher secondary vocational school
8. Fachschule	technical school	4
9. Fachhochschule	technical institute	university (polytechnic)
10. Universität	university	university
	Certificates and diplomas	
11. Hauptschulabschluss	junior high school diploma	school leaving certificate
12. Mittlere Reife	high school diploma-non-academic orientation	5
13. Abitur	high school diploma with college entrance qualification	6
14. Fachhochschulreife	advanced technical college entrance qualification	advanced technical college entrance qualification

3.2 Curriculum Vitae: The Europass CV

The Europass is designed to encourage mobility and lifelong learning in an enlarged Europe. It aims to help three million citizens make their qualifications and skills easily understood throughout Europe by the year 2010.
The Europass brings together into a single framework several existing tools for the transparency of diplomas, certificates and competences. Helping citizens to better communicate and present their qualifications and skills throughout Europe, the Europass will promote both occupational mobility between countries as well as across sectors, and mobility for learning purposes.

Anyone who wants to use the Europass can start by completing the Europass CV. The Europass CV enables you to make your skills and qualifications visible, and other Europass documents can be attached to the CV.
The Europass CV replaces the European CV, launched in 2002.

The Europass CV provides a standardised overview of an individual's education and occupational qualifications: language competences, work experience, education and training qualifications and other skills and competences gained outside formal training schemes.
The Europass CV is available in 13 languages and is frequently used across Europe.

M **a** **Answer the following questions on the Europass in German.**

1. Was wird durch den Europass CV ermöglicht?
2. Wann wurde der Europass CV gestartet? Was ersetzt er?
3. Worüber bietet der Europass einen Überblick?
4. Umfasst der Europass lediglich formale Qualifikationen?
5. In welchen Sprachen und Regionen wird der Europass verwendet?

R **b** **Match the jumbled data items below to the marked fields in the Europass CV on page 169.**

Example: a British – 7 Nationality

a British
b Setting up, maintaining network / second level support
c Remote connectivity, network architecture, security and maintenance, knowledge of LANs and WANs, ability to troubleshoot network problems, ability to understand technical information and terminology.
d International energy providing firm
e November 9th 1981
f Play the keyboard
g LTC Language School / London University / Leeds Grammar School
h Network technician
i English
j Male

europass 2003

Europass Curriculum Vitae	Insert photograph. Remove heading if not relevant
1 Personal information	
2 Surname(s) / First name(s)	Mellor, Timothy
3 Address(es)	Herzog-Heinrichstr. 10a, 93059, Regensburg, Germany
4 Telephone(s)	Mobile:0176-2273-9996
5 Fax(es)	
6 E-mail	timothy.mellor@econ-is.com
7 Nationality	British
8 Date of birth	
9 Gender	
10 Desired employment / Occupational field	17
11 Work experience	
12 Dates	. 2003 / 2002 / 1999
13 Occupation or position held	
14 Main activities and responsibilities	
15 Name and address of employer	a ECON- Information Services, Dr. Gesslerstr. 35, 93051 Regensburg
16 Type of business or sector	
Education and training	
17 Dates	
18 Title of qualification awarded	
19 Principal subjects / occupational skills covered	German as a foreign language / computer science / English, Maths, Physics, History
20 Name and type of organisation providing education and training	
Personal skills and competences	
21 Mother tongue(s)	
22 Other language(s)	
23 Self-assessment	

European level (*)	**Understanding**		**Speaking**		**Writing**
	Listening	Reading	Spoken interaction	Spoken production	
German	C1	C1	B1	B1	B2
French	B1	B1	A2	A2	A2

* Common European Framework of Reference for Languages

24 Social skills and competences	Good written and spoken communication skills in both mother tongue and German, high degree of intercultural competence
25 Organisational skills and competences	
26 Technical skills and competences	
27 Computer skills and competences	Web page designing, operating systems, C++
28 Artistic skills and competences	
29 Other skills and competences	

P **C** **Using the Europass form your teacher hands out to you create your own CV. Details can be based either on your own personal data or feel free to make up any details, as you like.**

3.3. Letter of application

I **a** **Discuss which of the following points should be included in a letter of application:**

name • age • salary • nationality • contact addresses • marital status • ages and sexes of any children • relevant experience • detailed description of your present job duties • reason you are applying for the job • a list of all the computer language courses you've ever taken • special skills • opinion of the company

P **b** **Now write your own letter of application for one of the posted jobs on pages 164 and 165.**

3.4 Researching jobs

P/I **a** **Research computer job offers on the Internet and report back to the class. Consider some of the following questions:**

1. Which site(s) did you find most / least useful?
2. If you had a position to offer someone would you place it online? On which site?
3. Did you (or would you) apply for any of the advertised jobs? What was your experience?

P **b** **Consider your own personal assets and strengths. Write (anonymously) your own advertisement seeking employment – 50 / 60 words – using the following guidelines:**

- Use direct, dynamic language
- Give your advertisement a structured outline
- Include details about key qualifications and experience
- Be brief

R/I **c** **Collect the advertisements and post them up on the walls of the classroom. Study them and discuss which one(s) you found most appealing and why.**

4 The interview

P/I **a** **Interview your partner about their first (computer) job and then report back to the class. Ask questions about the following:**

- qualifications needed / colleagues / boss / firm
- job duties – difficult, interesting, challenging, unpleasant
- benefits – pay, holidays, flexitime, amenities

P/I **b** **What advice would you give a friend going for an important job interview? Brainstorm with a partner and then share with the group.**

Example: Don't be late for the interview.

Don't …

Make sure …

Show …

Prepare a few …

Wear …

Be …

…

R/P/I **c Read the following typical "tricky" job interview questions. How would you, personally, answer each of them? Practise asking and answering the questions with a partner, making notes of your best ideas and answers.**

1. What would you consider to be your strongest asset / worst fault or weakness?
2. Where do you see yourself in ten years' time?
3. Why do you want to leave your present job?
4. How would you characterize your relationship with your colleagues / boss at your present job?
5. Tell me about yourself and your hobbies.
6. A number of people have applied for this position. Why should we choose you?
7. What is the most important thing for you in life: family, free time, status or money?
8. What recent achievements are you most proud of?

R **d Listen to the extracts from five interviews for the four jobs advertised on pages 164–165. Match the interview excerpts to the correct job. Note: One interview does not fit.**

I **e Take turns playing the role of the interviewer or, alternatively, the candidate for a computer related job.**

Role play: Job interview Follow these steps:
1. Working in groups of three write an advertisement for a job that might reasonably match the expectations and abilities of some or most members of the class group. Make copies or display your finished job ad so that the other members of the class have a chance to read it.
2. Choose one of the jobs advertised by another group. Apply for the job by writing a letter of application and submitting your CV. You will probably want to do this double task as homework and channel it through the teacher to ensure correctness and a smooth coordination of operations.
3. a. Interviewers: Back in your work groups read through the submitted letters of application and Cvs. Prepare a checklist of questions or topics you would like to cover in the interview: job experience, further training, health, language skills etc. b. Candidates: Prepare yourself for your upcoming interview. Once again go over the points of advice prepared and the tricky questions on the previous pages.
4. Conduct the interviews in rounds as outlined in the scheme on page 173. As interviewers make sure you take adequate notes.

The interview

First round
Each group consists of three people: A,B, C. In the first round all the A's are job candidates. They leave their groups to be interviewed by members of another group. The B's and C's stay behind to interview a person from another group.

Second round
In the second round the B's now leave the group to play the role of job candidates. The A's return to their original group and together with their C partners interview a B candidate from another group.

Third round
In the third round it's now the turn of the C's to be the candidates. They leave the group to be interviewed while the A's and B's stay behind to interview one of the C candidates from another group.

Fourth round
In the fourth round the original A,B,C work group meets to compare notes. They fill each other in on how the different interviews went (one member was always away being interviewed themselves) and choose the best candidate for the job.

Conclusion and discussion
After announcing the successful applicants discuss the following points:
1. Which role did you feel to be more challenging, that of the interviewer or that of the job applicant?
2. As a candidate what struck you as positive / negative / helpful / intimidating … about the different interviewers?
3. Did you feel the simulation was realistic? What would you do differently in a real life interview?

P **f** **Write an essay covering the following points:**

1. Where would you like to be / do you think you'll be in 5 / 10 / 15 years from now? (In terms of your career / family life / personal growth?)
2. In what ways might the one affect the other? Positively / negatively?
3. In what area would you like / do you think you'll need to invest more training? (Your language / communication skills / computer know-how?)

5 Future plans

1

2

3

4

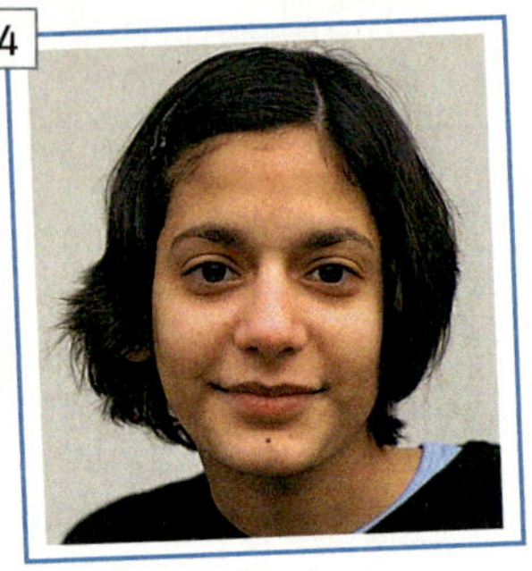

5

R **a Listen to five IT students talking about their plans after finishing their training. Which of the students talk about the following subjects:**

1. visiting English speaking countries
2. making money
3. reading in English
4. finding a job
5. working at home
6. working in an English speaking environment
7. moving to a new location
8. finishing their training
9. working for a company
10. family members

I **b Now interview your partner about his / her future plans. Ask questions such as the following:**

When are you going to finish your training?

What are you going to do first?

Do you think you'll need English on the job? What for?

Are you planning on relocating?

6 Further reading: Internship programs

Text 1

Wanting to go abroad?
Willing to work in a multicultural environment?
Would you like to make a big step forward?

Then our Internship Program is the right choice for you! At **Studios92.com Ltd.** we offer you the chance to gain practical international work experience that will definitely differentiate you from future competitors on the job market. Join our wide and dynamic international team! Our interns all come from vastly different cultures and countries, from all over Europe, thus giving you the distinct opportunity to improve your language skills in a familiar and relaxed atmosphere.

Our unique internship programme runs all through the year, lasting from 2 weeks up to 1 year, therefore giving you the freedom to choose your start and end dates yourself. You will be surrounded by young, dynamic and motivated people, establishing critical contacts and references for your future life and career. The practical work and communication skills that our internship will provide you with, along with an experience of learning how to live and work within diverse settings will prepare you for a successful future in all aspects of life.

http://www. …

Text 2

International Participation

We are seeking international organizations able to provide us with a source of qualified, enthusiastic, and well-educated trainees. Over 75 % of our trainees are international students and young professionals. **Internship4America** provides domestic and international Internships for students and young professionals from around the world. Our USA internships, summer internships, hospitality internships and international internships, provide housing, transportation and stipend for qualified trainees. We develop corporate internship programs. Our programs are designed to meet the US State Department Exchange Visitors Program criteria. Submit your résumé and application to be considered for our program.

http://www. … /

R **a** **Study the two texts on page 175 concerning internships and decide if the statements below are:**
a) true of both texts
b) true of neither text
c) true of text 1 only
d) true of text 2 only

1. The program is targeted towards college students / graduates.
2. The program gives young people the chance to work abroad.
3. It would be possible to do an internship during vacation break.
4. Internships are offered in countries all over the world.
5. Applicants are invited to send in their curriculum vitae.
6. The program arranges for a place to live and a small salary.
7. The program is in keeping with government regulations.
8. The program is headquarted in Europe.
9. People from all over the world participate in the program.
10. The program promises to improve your career opportunities

R **b** **Read the text again and find synonyms for the following words:**

1. opportunity
2. get
3. foreign country
4. crucial
5. rival
6. distinguish
7. allowance
8. various
9. zealous
10. standards

M **c** **Mediation**
Translate the following collocations (= established word combinations) from the text into German. Do the German translations also form collocations?

1. willing to work
2. big step forward
3. join our team
4. distinct opportunity
5. language skills
6. relaxed atmosphere
7. future life and career
8. from around the world
9. young professionals
10. submit your résumé

7 Language and grammar

7.1 Language of job advertisements

Match the words and phrases (1.-10. and a.-j.) often found in job advertisements.

Example:
1. design – a. new products / e. new software concepts

1. design	a. new products
2. experience with	b. customer contacts
3. responsible for	c. travel
4. develop	d. new growth
5. maintain	e. new software concepts
6. generate	f. system applications
7. operate	g. high standards
8. arrange	h. in international teams
9. willingness to	i. meetings and conferences
10. work	j. CNC meetings

7.2 Qualifiers

Find the best match for the job related nouns and their qualifiers below.

Example: 2. competitive – e. salary

1. broad	a. background
2. competitive	c. the computer industry
3. fluent	d. vendor
4. experience in	e. salary
5. thorough	f. area
6. ambitious	g. team
7. technical	h. English
8. effective	i. training
9. interesting	j. position
10. excellent	k. prospects

7.3 Prepositions

Complete the sentences with the correct preposition.

for • in • of (5x) • to (2x) • at • over • with

1. I have considerable expertise … the field … CAD design tools.
2. You would be responsible … the design and layout … mixed signal circuits.
3. All the candidates who have applied … date are … forty years old.
4. Applicants will be considered on the basis … their suitability, regardless … sex, race, nationality or age.
5. If you are good … people, like working in a team and are capable … working to tight deadlines, write … us … megamoney@alp.com.

Unit vocabulary

Introduction Computer basics and office skills

Page 8

variety [vəˈraɪətɪ]	Vielfalt
subject [ˈsʌbdʒekt]	Fach
database [ˈdeɪtəbeɪs]	Datenbank
customer [ˈkʌstəmə]	Kunde/Kundin
monitor (v) [ˈmɒnɪtə]	steuern
cash machine [ˈkæʃmə,ʃiːn]	Geldautomat
execute (v) [ˈeksɪkjuːt]	durchführen
receive (v) [rɪˈsiːv]	empfangen
order (v) [ˈɔːdə]	bestellen
goods [gʊdz]	Waren
administrate (v) [ədˈmɪnɪstreɪt]	verwalten
personnel [ˌpɜːsənˈel]	Personal, Personalwesen
data [ˈdeɪtə]	Daten
provide (v) [prəˈvaɪd]	zur Verfügung stellen
air pressure [ˈeə,preʃə]	Luftdruck
offer (v) [ˈɒfə]	anbieten
route [ruːt]	Route, Weg
handle (v) [ˈhændl]	handhaben, umgehen mit
spreadsheet [ˈspredʃiːt]	Tabellenkalkulation
drawing [ˈdrɔːɪŋ]	Zeichnung
forecast (v) [ˈfɔːkɑːst]	vorhersagen
flight [flaɪt]	Flug
traffic [ˈtræfɪk]	Verkehr
habit [ˈhæbɪt]	Gewohnheit
gist [dʒɪst]	das Wesentliche
decide (v) [dɪˈsaɪd]	entscheiden
statement [ˈsteɪtmənt]	Aussage
head [hed]	(hier) Leiter
purpose [ˈpɜːpəs]	Zweck
reason [ˈriːzn]	Grund
be in charge of (v) [bɪ‿ɪn ˈtʃɑːdʒ‿əv]	verantwortlich sein, leiten
related [rɪˈleɪtɪd]	verwandt
amount [əˈmaʊnt]	Menge
daily [ˈdeɪlɪ]	täglich

Page 9

peripheral device [pə,rɪfərəldɪˈvaɪs]	Peripheriegerät, Anschlussgerät
access [ˈækses]	Zugang
mainly [ˈmeɪnlɪ]	hauptsächlich
spend (v) [spend]	verbringen

Page 10

indispensable [ˌɪndɪˈspensəbl]	unverzichtbar
home appliance [ˌhəʊməˈplaɪəns]	Haushaltsgerät
process (v) [ˈprəʊses]	verarbeiten
file [faɪl]	Datei
GPS [ˌdʒiːpiːˈes]	weltumspannendes Ortungssystem, Navigationssystem
calculator [ˈkælkjəleɪtə]	Rechner
mean (v) [miːn]	meinen, bedeuten
tool [tuːl]	Werkzeug
basically [ˈbeɪsɪklɪ]	hauptsächlich, im Großen und Ganzen
feed (v) [fiːd]	füttern, zuführen
via [vaɪə] [ˈviːə]	mittels
keyboard [ˈkiːbɔːd]	Tastatur
device [dɪˈvaɪs]	Gerät
input (n) (v) [ˈɪnpʊt]	Eingabe; eingeben
manipulate (v) [məˈnɪpjəleɪt]	(Daten) bearbeiten
final (step) [ˌfaɪnl (ˈstep)]	letzter (Schritt)
output (v) (n) [ˈaʊtpʊt]	ausgeben; Ausgabe
store (v) [stɔː]	speichern
term [tɜːm]	Begriff
intangible [ɪnˈtændʒəbl]	nicht greifbar
refer to (v) [rɪˈfɜː tuː]	sich beziehen auf
image [ˈɪmɪdʒ]	Bild
instruction [ɪnˈstrʌkʃn]	Anweisung
opinion [əˈpɪnjən]	Meinung
involve (v) in [ɪnˈvɒlv ɪn/wɪð]	mit etw. zu tun haben
as opposed to [əzəˈpəʊzd‿tə]	im Gegensatz/ Vergleich zu
brief [briːf]	kurz
make up (v) [ˌmeɪk ˈʌp]	bilden, erfinden
random access [ˌrændəmˈækses]	wahlfreier Zugriff
oversee (v) [ˌəʊvəˈsiː]	überblicken
temporarily [ˌtempəˈrerɪlɪ]	vorübergehend
current [ˈkʌrənt]	aktuell
memory [ˈmemrɪ]	Speicher
operating system [ˈɒpəreɪtɪŋ,sɪstəm]	Betriebssystem
hard disk [ˈhɑːd‿dɪsk]	Festplatte
frequently [ˈfriːkwəntlɪ]	oft, häufig
link (n) (v) [lɪŋk]	Verbindung; verbinden
circuit [ˈsɜːkɪt]	Schaltkreis
interface (n) (v) [ˈɪntəfeɪs]	Schnittstelle; verbinden

Page 11

relationship [rɪˈleɪʃnʃɪp]	Verhältnis
broad [brɔːd]	breit
impact [ˈɪmpækt]	Wirkung
custom [ˈkʌstəm]	Gewohnheit
movement [ˈmuːvmənt]	Bewegung
trade [treɪd]	Handel
value [ˈvæljuː]	Wert
aim (n) (v) [eɪm]	Ziel; zielen
reinforce (v) [ˌriːɪnˈfɔːs]	verstärken
pool (n) (v) [puːl]	Zusammenlegung; zusammenlegen
transform (v) [trænsˈfɔːm]	verändern, wandeln
barrier [ˈbærɪə]	Hindernis
transfer (n) (v) [ˈtrænsfɜː](n) [trænsˈfɜː](v)	Übertragung; übertragen
include (v) [ɪnˈkluːd]	beinhalten
explain (v) [ɪkˈspleɪn]	erklären
overlap (v) [ˌəʊvəˈlæp]	überschneiden
ultimately [ˈʌltɪmətlɪ]	letzlich, letzten Endes

occur (v) [ə'kɜ:]	stattfinden
channel ['tʃænl]	Kanal
phenomenon [fɪ'nɒmɪnən] [fɪ'nɒmɪnə]	Erscheinung
introduction [ˌɪntrə'dʌkʃn]	Einführung, Vorstellung
speed up (v) [ˌspi:d 'ʌp]	beschleunigen
pace [peɪs]	Tempo
range [reɪndʒ]	Spektrum
allow (v) [ə'laʊ]	erlauben
spread [spred]	Verbreitung
incentive [ɪn'sentɪv]	Anreiz
adopt (v) [ə'dɒpt]	übernehmen
advantage [əd'vɑ:ntɪdʒ]	Vorteil
society [sə'saɪətɪ]	Gesellschaft
empower (v) [ɪm'paʊə]	ermächtigen

Page 12

participate (v) [pɑ:'tɪsɪpeɪt]	teilnehmen
compete (v) [kəm'pi:t]	wetteifern
flow [fləʊ]	Fluss
be cut off (v) [bɪ ˌkʌt 'ɒf]	abgeschnitten sein
rise [raɪz]	Zuwachs
consumer [kən'sju:mə]	Verbraucher(in)
previously ['pri:vɪəslɪ]	vormals
limit (v) ['lɪmɪt]	begrenzen
develop (v) [dɪ'veləp]	entwickeln
unprecedented [ʌn'presɪdentɪd]	noch nie da gewesen, beispiellos
nonprofit [ˌnɒn'prɒfɪt]	gemeinnützig
recruit (v) [rɪ'kru:t]	anwerben, einstellen
volunteer [ˌvɒlən'tɪə]	Freiwillige(r)
environmental [ɪnˌvaɪərən'mentl]	ökologisch, umweltpolitisch
raise money (v) [ˌreɪz 'mʌnɪ]	Geld sammeln
impart [ɪm'pɑ:t]	verleihen, geben
opportunity [ˌɒpə'tju:nətɪ]	Chance
edge [edʒ]	Rand, Überlegenheit
be readily available (v) [ˌredɪlɪ‿ə'veɪləbl]	leicht verfügbar sein
force (n) (v) [fɔ:s]	Kraft, Macht; zwingen
lose out (v) [ˌlu:z 'aʊt]	schlecht wegkommen
threaten (v) ['θretn]	bedrohen
undermine (v) [ˌʌndə'maɪn]	untergraben
overwhelming [ˌəʊvə'welmɪŋ]	überwältigend
working knowledge of [ˌwɜ:kɪŋ‿'nɒlɪdʒ‿əv]	Grundkenntnisse in
establish (v) [ɪ'stæblɪʃ]	einführen, etablieren
effect [ɪ'fekt]	Wirkung
refuse (v) [rɪ'fju:z]	ablehnen
impossible [ɪm'pɒsəbl]	unmöglich
prosper (v) ['prɒspə]	gedeihen, Erfolg haben
encompass (v) [ɪn'kʌmpəs]	umfassen
aside from [ə'saɪdfrəm]	abgesehen von
twin [twɪn]	doppelt
view (v) [vju:]	betrachten

Page 13

skill [skɪl]	Fertigkeit
tense [tens]	Zeitform, Tempus
check (v) [tʃek]	nachprüfen, kontrollieren
enquire (v) [ɪn'kwaɪə]	anfragen
whether ['weðə]	ob
permanent ['pɜ:mənənt]	fest, dauerhaft
freelance ['fri:lɑ:ns]	freiberuflich
depend (v) [dɪ'pend]	darauf ankommen
look forward (to) (v) [ˌlʊk 'fɔ:wəd]	sich freuen auf

Page 14

phrase [freɪz]	Formulierung
hold the line (v) [ˌhəʊld‿ðə'laɪn]	am Apparat bleiben
through [θru:]	durch
message ['mesɪdʒ]	Nachricht
appointment [ə'pɔɪntmənt]	Termin
set up (v) [ˌset 'ʌp]	vereinbaren
tricky business [ˌtrɪkɪ 'bɪznɪs]	schwierige Sache
diary ['daɪərɪ]	Terminkalender
practice (v) ['præktɪs]	üben
get together (v) [ˌget‿tə'geðə]	treffen, zusammenkommen
convenient [kən'vi:nɪənt]	passend
manage (v) ['mænɪdʒ]	einrichten
fit in (v) [ˌfɪt 'ɪn]	einen Termin geben
response [rɪ'spɒns]	Antwort, Reaktion
descending order [dɪˌsendɪŋ'ɔ:də]	absteigende Reihenfolge
politeness [pə'laɪtnəs]	Höflichkeit

Page 15

inconvenience (v) [ˌɪnkən'vi:nɪəns]	Umstände machen
instead [ɪn'sted]	stattdessen
catch (v) [kætʃ]	verstehen, mitbekommen
repeat (v) [rɪ'pi:t]	wiederholen
spell (v) [spel]	buchstabieren
speak up (v) [ˌspi:k 'ʌp]	lauter sprechen
busy ['bɪzɪ]	besetzt
prepare (v) [prɪ'peə]	vorbereiten

Page 17

suitable ['sju:təbl]	passend
complete (v) [kəm'pli:t]	vervollständigen
incorporated (company) [ɪn'kɔ:pəreɪtɪd]	eingetragene Aktiengesellschaft
rushed [rʌʃt]	unter Zeitdruck

Page 18

run into (v) [ˌrʌn 'ɪntu:]	zufällig treffen
request (n) (v) [rɪ'kwest]	Bitte, Anfrage; bitten
supplier [sə'plaɪə]	Lieferant(in)
championship ['tʃæmpɪənʃɪp]	Meisterschaft
sales representative ['seɪlzreprɪˌzentətɪv]	Vertreter(in)
purchasing ['pɜ:tʃəsɪŋ]	Einkauf
administrative [əd'mɪnɪstrətɪv]	Verwaltungs-
chief executive officer (CEO) [ˌtʃi:fɪgˌzekjətɪv'ɒfɪsə] [ˌsi:i:'əʊ]	Geschäftsführer(in)

Page 19

bracelet ['breɪslət]	Armband
put off (v) [ˌpʊt 'ɒf]	vertrösten, verschieben
get back to (v) [ˌget‿'bæk tu:]	zurückmelden

put on hold (v) [ˌpʊt‿ɒn 'həʊld]	zurückstellen
translate (v) [trænz'leɪt]	übersetzen
equivalent [ɪ'kwɪvələnt]	Entsprechung

Page 20

mouth (v) [maʊθ]	nachplappern, deutlich artikulieren
consideration [kənˌsɪdə'reɪʃn]	Rücksichtnahme
softening ['sɒfənɪŋ]	besänftigend
reject (v) [rɪ'dʒekt]	ablehnen
complain (v) [kəm'pleɪn]	sich beschweren
talking/speaking of ['tɔ:kɪŋ‿əv] ['spi:kɪŋ‿əv]	da gerade die Rede von … ist
remind (v) of [rɪ'maɪnd ɒv]	erinnern an
by any chance [baɪˌenɪ'tʃɑ:ns]	möglicherweise
lend (v) [lend]	leihen
actually ['æktʃʊəlɪ]	tatsächlich
fill (position) (v) [fɪl (pə'zɪʃn)]	(Position) besetzen
suggestion [sə'dʒestʃn]	Vorschlag
be of service (v) [bɪ‿əv'sɜ:vɪs]	helfen
no way [ˌnəʊ'weɪ]	keineswegs

Page 21

duty ['dju:tɪ]	Aufgabe
responsibility [rɪˌspɒnsə'bɪlətɪ]	Verantwortung
report to (v) [rɪ'pɔ:t‿tu:]	unterstehen, unterstellt sein
vocational training school [vəʊˌkeɪʃənəl'treɪnɪŋˌsku:l]	Berufsschule
overtime ['əʊvətaɪm]	Überstunden
troubleshoot (v) ['trʌblʃu:t]	Fehler suchen und beheben
headquarters [ˌhed'kwɔ:təz]	Hauptsitz
department [dɪ'pɑ:tmənt]	Abteilung
branch [brɑ:ntʃ]	Zweig
subsidiary [səb'sɪdɪərɪ]	Tochtergesellschaft
employ (v) [ɪm'plɔɪ]	beschäftigen
consist of (v) [kən'sɪst‿əv]	bestehen aus
accounts [ə'kaʊnts]	Buchhaltung
human resources [ˌhju:mən'ri:sɔ:sɪz]	Personalwesen
research and development [ˌri:sɜ:tʃəndɪ'veləpmənt]	Forschung und Entwicklung

Page 22

appropriate [ə'pəʊprɪət]	passend, angebracht
enclose (v) [ɪn'kləʊz]	beifügen, beilegen
invitation [ˌɪnvɪ'teɪʃn]	Einladung
payment ['peɪmənt]	Bezahlung
delivery [dɪ'lɪvərɪ]	Lieferung
advertisement [əd'vɜ:tɪsmənt] [ˌædvə'taɪzmənt]	Inserat, Werbung
dissatisfactory [dɪsˌsætɪs'fæktərɪ]	unzufriedenstellend
of late [əv'leɪt]	in der letzten Zeit
quote (v) [kwəʊt]	anbieten
discount ['dɪskaʊnt]	Nachlass
latest ['leɪtɪst]	neueste(r, s)
essential [ɪ'senʃl]	notwendig, erforderlich
cordially ['kɔ:dɪəlɪ]	herzlich
attend (v) [ə'tend]	teilnehmen
immediate [ɪ'mi:dɪət]	sofortig
reimbursement [ˌri:ɪm'bɜ:smənt]	Rückerstattung
as agreed [əzə'gri:d]	wie vereinbart
bankers draft ['bæŋkəzˌdrɑ:ft]	Überweisung
receipt [rɪ'si:t]	Empfang
invoice ['ɪnvɔɪs]	Rechnung
booth [bu:ð] [bu:θ]	Stand
terms of ['tɜ:mz‿əv]	Bedingungen
above all [əˌbʌv'ɔ:l]	vor allem
replace (v) [rɪ'pleɪs]	ersetzen
considered [kən'sɪdəd]	angesehen
acceptable [ək'septəbl]	annehmbar
agree (v) [ə'gri:]	einverstanden sein
at large [ət'lɑdʒ]	insgesamt, im Allgemeinen
proper ['prɒpə]	richtig
bother to (v) ['bɒðə‿tə]	sich die Mühe machen
count (v) [kaʊnt]	zählen, von Bedeutung sein
care (v) [keə]	sich kümmern
pass on (v) [ˌpɑ:s 'ɒn]	weitergeben, -leiten
permission [pə'mɪʃn]	Erlaubnis

Page 23

header ['hedə]	Kopf
recipient [rɪ'sɪpɪənt]	Empfänger(in)
drop a line (v) [ˌdrɒp‿ə 'laɪn]	kurz schreiben
figure on (v) ['fɪgər‿ɒn]	damit rechnen
asap = as soon as possible [ˌeɪeseɪ'pi:] [əz‿su:nəz'pɒsəbl]	so bald wie möglich
knock off (v) [ˌnɒk 'ɒf]	abziehen
assume (v) [ə'sju:m]	annehmen, vermuten
reach (v) [ri:tʃ]	erreichen
schedule ['ʃedju:l] ['skedju:l]	Terminplan
outline ['aʊtlaɪn]	Abriss
punctuate (v) ['pʌŋktʃʊeɪt]	Satzzeichen setzen

Page 24

complimentary close [ˌkɒmplɪmentrɪ'kləʊz]	Schlussformel
opening salutation [ˌəʊpnɪŋsæljə'teɪʃn]	Grußformel
subject line ['sʌbdʒektˌlaɪn]	Betreff
in reference to [ɪn'refrəns‿tə]	Bezug nehmend auf
confirm (v) [kən'fɜ:m]	bestätigen
be satisfied (v) [bɪ 'sætɪsfaɪd wɪð]	zufrieden sein
retail price [ˌri:teɪl'praɪs]	Verkaufs-, Ladenpreis
description [dɪ'skrɪpʃn]	Beschreibung
shipping ['ʃɪpɪŋ]	Versand
packaging ['pækɪdʒɪŋ]	Verpackung
selection [sə'lekʃn]	Auswahl
adventure [əd'ventʃə]	Abenteuer
note (v) [nəʊt]	beachten
require (v) [rɪ'kwaɪə]	benötigen

Page 25

extension [ɪk'stenʃn]	Durchwahl
disconnect (v) [ˌdɪskə'nekt]	unterbrechen
futile ['fju:taɪl]	nutzlos
ignore (v) [ɪg'nɔ:]	nicht beachten

claim (v) [kleɪm] behaupten
considerable [kənˈsɪdrəbl] beachtlich
several [ˈsevrəl] einige
occasion [əˈkeɪʒn] Gelegenheit
severely [səˈvɪəlɪ] schwerwiegend
shake (v) [ʃeɪk] erschüttern
due to [ˈdjuː tuː] aufgrund, wegen
downright [ˈdaʊnraɪt] ausgesprochen
rudeness [ˈruːdnəs] Unhöflichkeit
dealings [ˈdiːlɪŋz] Geschäfte
although [ɔːlˈðəʊ] obwohl
in stock [ɪnˈstɒk] auf Lager
available [əˈveɪləbl] verfügbar
case [keɪs] Fall
bill (v) [bɪl] berechnen
point out (v) [ˌpɔɪnt ˈaʊt] hinweisen (auf)
error [ˈerə] Fehler
completely [kəmˈpliːtlɪ] völlig
dial (v) [daɪəl] wählen
equally [ˈiːkwəlɪ] genauso
queue [kjuː] Warteschlange
treat (v) [triːt] behandeln
staff [stɑːf] Belegschaft, Mitarbeiterstab
forward (v) [ˈfɔːwəd] weiterleiten
deplorable [dɪˈplɔːrəbl] bedauernswert
state of affairs [ˌsteɪtəvəˈfeəz] Zustand
persist (v) [pəˈsɪst] anhalten
custom [ˈkʌstəm] Geschäft
overcharge (v) [ˌəʊvəˈtʃɑːdʒ] zu viel berechnen

Page 26

guideline [ˈgaɪdlaɪn] Richtlinie
topic [ˈtɒpɪk] Thema
bug-laden [ˌbʌgˈleɪdn] verseucht
high ranking [ˌhaɪˈræŋkɪŋ] hochgestellt
appalled [əˈpɔːld] entsetzt
stance [stɑːns] Haltung
faulty [ˈfɔːltɪ] [ˈfɒltɪ] fehlerhaft
deafening [ˈdefənɪŋ] betäubend
undertake (v) [ˌʌndəˈteɪk] unternehmen
to no avail [təˌnəʊəˈveɪl] erfolglos
hint (n) (v) [hɪnt] Hinweis; hinweisen, andeuten
worth [wɜːθ] wert
place the ball in their court [ˌpleɪsðəˌbɔːlɪnˈðeəˌkɔːt] den anderen die Schuld geben/den Schwarzen Peter zuspielen
deadline [ˈdedlaɪn] Frist, Fertigstellungstermin
threat [θret] Bedrohung
heading [ˈhedɪŋ] Kopfzeile, Überschrift
in advance [ɪnədˈvɑːns] im Voraus
paragraph [ˈpærəgrɑːf] Absatz
avoid (v) [əˈvɔɪd] (ver)meiden
flowery [ˈflaʊərɪ] blumig
circumlocution [ˌsɜːkəmləˈkjuːʃn] Umschreibung
clutter [ˈklʌtə] Unordnung
unnecessary [ʌnˈnesəserɪ] unnötig
aside [əˈsaɪd] Nebenbemerkung
mistake [mɪˈsteɪk] Fehler
courtesy [ˈkɜːtəsɪ] Höflichkeit

Unit 1 Hardware, bits and codes

Page 27

bit [bɪt] Bit
synchronize (v) [ˈsɪŋkrənaɪz] synchronisieren
jumper [ˈdʒʌmpə] Jumper, Steckbrücke
print (v) [prɪnt] drucken
contain (v) [kənˈteɪn] beinhalten
slot [slɒt] Schlitz
real-time [ˈrɪəltaɪm] Echtzeit
socket [ˈsɒkɪt] Anschlussdose
attach (v) [əˈtætʃ] anbringen, anbinden
interrupt (n) (v) [ˌɪntəˈrʌpt] Unterbrechung; unterbrechen
connector [kəˈnektə] Anschlussstecker
performance [pəˈfɔːməns] Leistung
bare bones [ˌbeəˈbəʊnz] Grundgerüst, Grundausstattung
ribbon cable [ˈrɪbnˌkeɪbl] Bandkabel
power supply [ˈpaʊəsəˌplaɪ] Energieversorgung
clock rate [ˈklɒkˌreɪt] Taktfrequenz

Page 28

bridge [brɪdʒ] Brücke
hold (v) [həʊld] halten
executable [ˌeksɪˈkjuːtəbl] ausführbar
mediator [ˈmiːdɪeɪtə] Vermittler(in)
designed [dɪˈzaɪnd] konzipiert
especially [ɪˈspeʃəlɪ] insbesondere
throughput [ˈθruːpʊt] Datendurchlauf, Durchsatz (rate)
demand [dɪˈmɑːnd] Anforderung
3-D graphics [ˌθriːdiːˈgræfɪks] 3-D-Bild
source [sɔːs] Quelle
plug in (v) [plʌg] einstecken
computing [kəmˈpjuːtɪŋ] Rechen-; EDV-
mass storage device [ˌmæs‿ˈstɔːrɪdʒdɪˌvaɪs] Massenspeicher
port [pɔːt] Port, Anschluss
switch off (v) [ˌswɪtʃ ˈɒf] ausschalten
settings [ˈsetɪŋz] Einstellungen
additional [əˈdɪʃənl] zusätzlich
portable [ˈpɔːtəbl] tragbar

Page 29

button [ˈbʌtn] Taste, Knopf
printout [ˈprɪntaʊt] Ausdruck
happen (v) [ˈhæpn] passieren
step [step] Schritt
order [ˈɔːdə] Reihenfolge
register (v) [ˈredʒɪstə] anmelden, erfassen
initiate (v) [ɪˈnɪʃɪeɪt] einleiten
finally [ˈfaɪnəlɪ] schließlich
path [pɑːθ] Pfad
thereby [ˌðeəˈbaɪ] dabei
pass through (v) [ˌpɑːs ˈθruː] passieren, durchlaufen
wait (v) [weɪt] warten
execution [ˌeksɪˈkjuːʃn] Ausführung
cause (v) [kɔːz] verursachen
character [ˈkærɪktə] Zeichen
buffer [ˈbʌfə] Puffer

monitor ['mɒnɪtə]	Bildschirm
imply (v) [ɪm'plaɪ]	andeuten, implizieren
examine (v) [ɪg'zæmɪn]	untersuchen
interpret (v) [ɪn'tɜ:prɪt]	auslegen, interpretieren
various ['veərɪəs]	verschiedene
perform (v) [pə'fɔ:m]	aus-, durchführen
operation [ˌɒpə'reɪʃn]	Arbeit
unit ['ju:nɪt]	Einheit
program counter ['prəʊgræmˌkaʊntə]	Programmzähler, Befehlszähler
main memory [ˌmeɪn'memrɪ]	Hauptspeicher
ever increasing [ˌevərɪn'kri:sɪŋ]	ständig steigend
gradually ['grædʒʊəlɪ]	allmählich
supplant (v) [sə'plɑ:nt]	ersetzen
apply to (v) [ə'plaɪ tu:]	anwenden auf
versus ['vɜ:səs]	verglichen mit, gegen

Page 30

accumulator [ə'kju:mjəleɪtə]	Akkumulator, Speicher
stack pointer ['stækˌpɔɪntə]	Stapelzeiger
instruction decoder [ɪn'strʌkʃndɪˌkəʊdə]	Befehlsdecoder
gate [geɪt]	Gate, Gatter
switch [swɪtʃ]	Switch, Schalter
ready (v) ['redɪ]	bereitstellen
comparison [kəm'pærɪsən]	Vergleich
result [rɪ'zʌlt]	Ergebnis
sequence ['si:kwəns]	Ablauf
sub-program ['sʌbˌprəʊgræm]	Unterprogramm
ensure (v) [ɪn'ʃɔ:]	sicherstellen
return (v) [rɪ'tɜ:n]	zurückkehren
leave off (v) [ˌli:v 'ɒf]	aufhören
interim ['ɪntərɪm]	vorläufig

Page 31

increase (n) (v) [ɪn'kri:s]	Anstieg; anheben
interpret [ɪn'tɜ:prɪt]	auswerten
according to [ə'kɔ:dɪŋ‿tə]	laut, nach, gemäß
contribution [ˌkɒntrɪ'bju:ʃn]	Beitrag
set theory ['setˌθɪərɪ]	Mengenlehre
computer science [kəmˌpju:tə'saɪəns]	Informatik
leader ['li:də]	Führer(in)
day trading [ˌdeɪ'treɪdɪŋ]	Day Trading, Tagesspekulationsgeschäft
key (information) [ki:]	entscheidende (Informationen)
keep in touch (v) [ˌki:p ɪn ˌtʌtʃ]	in Kontakt bleiben
pocket ['pɒkɪt]	Tasche
driving force ['draɪvɪŋˌfɔ:s]	Antriebskraft
progress ['prəʊgres]	Fortschritt
at face value [ət‿ˌfeɪs'vælju:]	für bare Münze
assurance [ə'ʃɔ:rəns]	Zusicherung
appear (v) [ə'pɪə]	erscheinen
screen [skri:n]	Bildschirm

Page 32

member ['membə]	Mitglied
report back (v) [rɪˌpɔ:t‿'bæk]	berichten
similar ['sɪmɪlə]	ähnlich
opposite ['ɒpəzɪt]	Gegenteil
time-saving ['taɪmˌseɪvɪŋ]	zeitsparend
expensive [ɪk'spensɪv]	teuer
reliable [rɪ'laɪəbl]	zuverlässig
exciting [ɪk'saɪtɪŋ]	aufregend
dependable [dɪ'pendəbl]	zuverlässig
old-fashioned [ˌəʊld'fæʃnd]	altmodisch
advantageous [ˌædvæn'teɪdʒəs]	vorteilhaft
handy ['hændɪ]	praktisch, handlich
boring ['bɔ:rɪŋ]	langweilig
maddening ['mædnɪŋ]	ärgerlich, unerträglich
progressive [prə'gresɪv]	fortschrittlich
successful [sək'sesfəl]	erfolgreich
timeless ['taɪmləs]	zeitlos
up-to-date [ˌʌptə'deɪt]	modern, zeitgemäß
valuable ['væljʊəbl]	wertvoll
user-friendly [ˌju:zə'frendlɪ]	benutzerfreundlich
concerning [kən'sɜ:nɪŋ]	betreffend
unauthorized [ʌn'ɔ:θəraɪzd]	unbefugt, unerlaubt
thought [θɔ:t]	Gedanke

Page 33

feature ['fi:tʃə]	Funktion, Eigenschaft
compromise (v) ['kɒmprəmaɪz]	Kompromisse machen
state-of-the-art [ˌsteɪtəvðɪ'ɑ:t]	auf dem neuesten Stand der Technik, hochmodern
security [sɪ'kjʊərətɪ]	Sicherheit
deny (v) [dɪ'naɪ]	verweigern, versagen
experience [ɪk'spɪərɪəns]	Erfahrung
cutting edge [ˌkʌtɪŋ'edʒ]	innovativ
advanced (technology) [əd'vɑ:nst]	hochmoderne, fortgeschrittene (Technologie)
superior [su:'pɪərɪə]	überdurchschnittlich
high-end [ˌhaɪ'end]	hochwertig, Spitzen-
support [sə'pɔ:t]	Unterstützung
slip in (v) [ˌslɪp 'ɪn]	gleiten lassen in
high-performance [ˌhaɪpə'fɔ:məns]	Hochleistungs-
boast [bəʊst]	sich rühmen
funky ['fʌŋkɪ]	flippig
edit (v) ['edɪt]	editieren, bearbeiten
application [ˌæplɪ'keɪʃn]	Anwendung
leading edge [ˌli:dɪŋ'edʒ]	Spitzen-
tailor-made [ˌteɪlə'meɪd]	maßgeschneidert
requirement [rɪ'kwaɪəmənt]	Anforderung
front side ['frʌntˌsaɪd]	Vorderseite
need [ni:d]	Bedürfnis
tuner ['tju:nə]	Empfänger
guide [gaɪd]	Führer
wealth [welθ]	Reichtum
combine (v) [kəm'baɪn]	kombinieren, verbinden
powerful ['paʊəfəl]	leistungsstark, -fähig
enhanced [ɪn'hɑ:nst]	verbessert
burn [bɜ:n]	brennen
labelling ['leɪblɪŋ]	Etikettierung
select (v) [sə'lekt]	auswählen
bright [braɪt]	hell
contemporary [kən'tempərərɪ]	zeitgemäß

addition [əˈdɪʃn]	Zusatz, Bereicherung
impressive [ɪmˈpresɪv]	eindrucksvoll
two tone [ˌtuːˈtəʊn]	zweifarbig
extend to (v) [ɪkˈstend‿tuː]	sich erstrecken bis
echo (v) [ˈekəʊ]	sich wiederholen
effortless [ˈefətləs]	mühelos

Page 34

tiny [ˈtaɪnɪ]	winzig
mean [miːn]	durchschnittlich, Mittelwert
full-scale [ˌfʊlˈskeɪl]	umfassend, in Originalgröße
infinitesimal [ˌɪnfɪnɪˈtesɪml]	unendlich klein
average [ˈævrɪdʒ]	durchschnittlich
middle-sized [ˌmɪdlˈsaɪzd]	mittelgroß
sizeable [ˈsaɪzəbl]	beträchtlich, ziemlich groß
minute [maɪˈnjuːt]	winzig
huge [hjuːdʒ]	sehr groß
intermediate [ˌɪntəˈmiːdɪət]	Zwischen-
prefix [ˈpriːfɪks]	Vorsilbe

Page 35

abbreviation [əˌbriːvɪˈeɪʃn]	Abkürzung
collection [kəˈlekʃn]	Sammlung
wire [waɪə]	Draht
represent (v) [ˌreprɪˈzent]	darstellen
simply [ˈsɪmplɪ]	einfach
string [strɪŋ]	Kette
arrange (v) [əˈreɪndʒ]	zusammensetzen, arrangieren
measure (v) [ˈmeʒə]	messen
originally [əˈrɪdʒɪnəlɪ]	ursprünglich
simplify (v) [ˈsɪmplɪfaɪ]	vereinfachen
gap [gæp]	Kluft
real [rɪəl]	tatsächlich
widen (v) [ˈwaɪdn]	ausweiten
measurement [ˈmeʒəmənt]	Messung
specify (v) [ˈspesɪfaɪ]	spezifizieren
multiple [ˈmʌltɪpl]	Mehrfach-
widely [ˈwaɪdlɪ]	weitgehend
continue (v) [kənˈtɪnjuː]	weitermachen
despite [dɪˈspaɪt]	trotz
lack [læk]	Mangel
body [ˈbɒdɪ]	Gremium, Organ
unambiguous [ˌʌnæmˈbɪgjʊəs]	eindeutig
notation [nəʊˈteɪʃn]	Bezeichnung

Page 36

equal (v) [ˈiːkwəl]	ergeben (Mathematik)
pixel [ˈpɪksəl]	Pixel, Bildelement
summary [ˈsʌmərɪ]	Zusammenfassung
pronounce (v) [prəˈnaʊns]	aussprechen
widespread [ˈwaɪdspred]	weitverbreitet
publish (v) [ˈpʌblɪʃ]	veröffentlichen
update (v) [ʌpˈdeɪt]	erneuern, aktualisieren
strictly speaking [ˌstrɪktlɪˈspiːkɪŋ]	streng genommen
specific [spəˈsɪfɪk]	bestimmt, spezifisch
digit [ˈdɪdʒɪt]	Zahl, Ziffer
pronunciation mark [prəˌnʌnsɪˈeɪʃnˌmɑːk]	Betonungszeichen
letter [ˈletə]	Buchstabe
depict (v) [dɪˈpɪkt]	darstellen
disadvantage [ˌdɪsədˈvɑːntɪdʒ]	Nachteil
incompatible [ˌɪnkəmˈpætəbl]	inkompatibel, unvereinbar
respectively [rɪˈspektɪvlɪ]	beziehungsweise
array [əˈreɪ]	Palette, Array
encoding [ɪnˈkəʊdɪŋ]	Kodierung
representation [ˌreprɪzenˈteɪʃn]	Darstellung
unique [juːˈniːk]	einmalig, einzigartig
glyph [glɪf]	Bildzeichen
multi-tiered [ˌmʌltɪˈtɪəd]	mehrstufig
saving [ˈseɪvɪŋ]	Einsparung
legacy [ˈlegəsɪ]	Vorläufer, Alt-
enable (v) [ɪˈneɪbl]	ermöglichen
target (v) [ˈtɑːgɪt]	abzielen, erreichen
platform [ˈplætfɔːm]	Plattform, Programm
language [ˈlæŋgwɪdʒ]	Sprache
re-engineer (v) [ˌriːendʒɪˈnɪə]	umarbeiten
corruption [kəˈrʌpʃn]	Verfälschung

Page 37

monochrome [ˈmɒnəkrəʊm]	einfarbig
dot [dɒt]	Punkt
correspond to (v) [ˌkɒrɪˈspɒnd‿tuː]	entsprechen
example [ɪgˈzɑːmpl]	Beispiel
primary [ˈpraɪmərɪ]	Grund-
display (v) [dɪˈspleɪ]	zeigen
convert (v) [kənˈvɜːt]	umwandeln
determine (v) [dɪˈtɜːmɪn]	festlegen

Page 38

boom [buːm]	Aufschwung
e-waste [ˈiːˌweɪst]	Elektroschrott
refuse [ˈrefjuːz]	Abfall
barely [ˈbeəlɪ]	kaum
equipped with [ɪˈkwɪpt‿wɪð]	ausgestattet mit
invent (v) [ɪnˈvent]	erfinden
lifespan [ˈlaɪfspæn]	Lebensdauer
shipbreaking [ˈʃɪpˌbreɪkɪŋ]	Schiffsverschrottung
recycling [ˌriːˈsaɪklɪŋ]	Wiederverwertung
involve (v) [ɪnˈvɒlv]	mit sich bringen
obsolete [ˈɒbsəliːt]	überholt, obsolet
ecology-minded [ɪˌkɒlədʒɪˈmaɪndɪd]	umweltbewusst
choose (v) [tʃuːz]	wählen
poverty [ˈpɒvətɪ]	Armut
poison [ˈpɔɪzn]	Gift
ferrous [ˈferəs]	eisenhaltig
lead [led]	Blei
cadmium [ˈkædmɪəm]	Kadmium
antimony [ænˈtɪmənɪ] [ˈæntɪmənɪ]	Antimon
beryllium [bəˈrɪlɪəm]	Beryllium
chromium [ˈkrəʊmɪəm]	Chrom
mercury [ˈmɜːkjərɪ]	Quecksilber
palladium [pəˈleɪdɪəm]	Palladium
platinum [ˈplætɪnəm]	Platin
pie chart [ˈpaɪˌtʃɑːt]	Tortendiagramm
dump (v) [dʌmp]	wegwerfen
toxicity [tɒkˈsɪsətɪ]	Giftigkeit

nonrecyclable [ˌnɒnrɪ'saɪkləbl]	nicht wiederverwertbar
plastic ['plæstɪk]	Kunststoff
flame-retardant ['fleɪmrɪˌtɑ:dənt]	Flammschutzmittel

Page 39

entire [ɪn'taɪə]	ganz
community [kə'mju:nətɪ]	Gemeinde
earn (v) [ɜ:n]	verdienen
livelihood ['laɪvlɪhʊd]	Lebensunterhalt
scavenge (v) ['skævɪndʒ]	ergattern
extract (v) [ɪk'strækt]	gewinnen, entnehmen
capacitor [kə'pæsɪtə]	Kondensator
melt down (v) [ˌmelt‿'daʊn]	schmelzen
charcoal ['tʃɑ:kəʊl]	Holzkohle
cord [kɔ:d]	Kabel
barrel ['bærəl]	Fass
expose (v) [ɪk'spəʊz]	bloßlegen, freilegen
copper ['kɒpə]	Kupfer
yield (v) [jɪ:ld]	ergeben
consider (v) [kən'sɪdə]	bedenken
emit (v) [ɪ'mɪt]	ausstoßen
toxic ['tɒksɪk]	giftig
volume ['vɒlju:m]	Menge, Umfang
remaining [rɪ'meɪnɪŋ]	übrig, restlich
heavy metal [ˌhevɪ'metl]	Schwermetall
donor ['dəʊnə]	Spender(in)
intended [ɪn'tendɪd]	beabsichtigt
scrap heap ['skræpˌhi:p]	Müllhalde
estimate (v) ['estɪmeɪt]	(ein)schätzen
at present [ət‿'prezənt]	zurzeit
amendment [ə'mendmənt]	Gesetzesänderung
pending ['pendɪŋ]	anstehend
ban (v) [bæn]	verbieten
hazardous ['hæzədəs]	gefährlich
disposal [dɪ'spəʊzl]	Entsorgung
implement (v) ['ɪmplɪment]	einführen
propose (v) [prə'pəʊz]	vorschlagen
skim (v) [skɪm]	überfliegen (Text)
landfill ['lændfɪl]	Deponie, Geländeauffüllung
prison labour ['prɪznˌleɪbə]	Arbeit von Strafgefangenen
findings ['faɪndɪŋz]	Ergebnisse

Page 40

conduct (v) [kən'dʌkt]	durchführen
survey ['sɜ:veɪ]	Umfrage
indicate (v) ['ɪndɪkeɪt]	andeuten
ownership ['əʊnəʃɪp]	Besitz
everyday speech [ˌevrɪdeɪ'spi:tʃ]	Alltagssprache
drop (v) [drɒp]	fallen lassen
task [tɑ:sk]	Aufgabe
occasionally [ə'keɪʒənlɪ]	gelegentlich

Page 41

common ['kɒmən]	weitverbreitet
switch (v) [swɪtʃ]	umschalten
issue (v) ['ɪʃu:]	erteilen
command [kə'mɑ:nd]	Befehl
fulfill (v) [fʊl'fɪl]	erfüllen
preposition [ˌprepə'zɪʃn]	Verhältniswort, Präposition

press (v) [pres]	drücken
recording [rɪ'kɔ:dɪŋ]	Aufnahme
flip down [ˌflɪp 'daʊn]	runterklappen
launch (v) [lɔ:ntʃ]	starten
campaign [kæm'peɪn]	Aktion

Unit 2 Input, output and storage devices

Page 42

host computer [ˌhəʊst‿kəm'pju:tə]	Hauptrechner, Hostcomputer
in order to [ɪn'ɔ:dətu:]	um (zu)
expand (v) [ɪk'spænd]	erweitern
ability [ə'bɪlətɪ]	Fähigkeit
mount (v) [maʊnt]	anbringen, installieren
case [keɪs]	Gehäuse
sheet [ʃi:t]	Blatt
come up with (v) [ˌkʌm 'ʌp wɪð]	sich ausdenken

Page 43

ergonomically [ˌɜ:gə'nɒmɪklɪ]	ergonomisch
wrist [rɪst]	Handgelenk
backwards ['bækwədz]	rückwärts
simultaneously [ˌsɪməl'teɪnɪəslɪ]	simultan, gleichzeitig
preview ['pri:vju:]	Vorschau
resolution [ˌrezə'lu:ʃn]	Auflösung
outfitted with ['aʊtfɪtɪd wɪð]	ausgestattet mit
pen-like ['penˌlaɪk]	stiftähnlich
move (v) [mu:v]	bewegen
index finger ['ɪndeksˌfɪŋgə]	Zeigefinger
space [speɪs]	Platz
multi-purpose [ˌmʌltɪ'pɜ:pəs]	Mehrzweck-
gaming device ['geɪmɪŋdɪˌvaɪs]	Spielegerät
examination [ɪgˌzæmɪ'neɪʃn]	Untersuchung
mammal ['mæməl]	Säugetier
rodent ['rəʊdənt]	Nagetier
control stick [kən'trəʊlˌstɪk]	Steuerknüppel
handheld [ˌhænd'held]	tragbar
cursor ['kɜ:sə]	Cursor, Positionsanzeiger
sound wave ['saʊndˌweɪv]	Schallwelle
relay (v) ['ri:leɪ]	leiten, weiterleiten

Page 44

touch pad ['tʌtʃˌpæd]	Cursor-Steuerungsfeld
recognition [ˌrekəg'nɪʃn]	Erkennung
virtual touch screen [ˌvɜ:tʃʊəl'tʌtʃˌskri:n]	Sensorbildschirm
voice [vɔɪs]	Stimme
upside down [ˌʌpsaɪd‿'daʊn]	verkehrt herum
positioning reference [pə'zɪʃənɪŋˌrefrəns]	Positionsbezug
generate (v) ['dʒenəreɪt]	erzeugen
digitized ['dɪdʒɪtaɪzd]	digitalisiert
pattern ['pætən]	Muster
light wave ['laɪtˌweɪv]	Lichtwelle
surface ['sɜ:fɪs]	Oberfläche
capacitive [kə'pæsɪtɪv]	kapazitiv
motion ['məʊʃn]	Bewegung

magazine article [ˌmægəˈziːnˌɑːtɪkl]	Zeitschriftenartikel
illustration [ˌɪləˈstreɪʃn]	Abbildung
unfamiliar [ʌnfəˈmɪliə]	nicht vertraut
independent [ˌɪndɪˈpendənt]	selbstständig
motor-impaired [ˌməʊtərɪmˈpeəd]	motorisch beeinträchtigt
handicapped [ˈhændɪkæpt]	behindert
limb [lɪm]	Glied
sketch [sketʃ]	Skizze
ease [iːz]	Leichtigkeit

Page 45

prefer (v) [prɪˈfɜː]	bevorzugen
insert (v) [ɪnˈsɜːt]	einfugen
delete (v) [dɪˈliːt]	löschen, entfernen
set [set]	Satz
upper [ˈʌpə]	obere(r, s)
instruct (v) [ɪnˈstrʌkt]	anweisen
in operation [ɪn ˌɒpəˈreɪʃn]	in Betrieb
certain [ˈsɜːtən]	gewisse(r, s)

Page 46

high volume [ˌhaɪˈvɒljuːm]	große Anzahl
snail mail [ˈsneɪlˌmeɪl]	"Schneckenpost" (normaler Postweg)
flyer [ˈflaɪə]	Flyer
placard [ˈplækɑːd]	Plakat
be on a low budget (v) [bɪ‿ɒnəˌləʊˈbʌdʒɪt]	sparen müssen
run out of the home [ˌrʌnaʊtəvðəˈhəʊm]	innerhalb der eigenen vier Wände geführt
precision equipment [prɪˌsɪʒnɪˈkwɪpmənt]	Feinmesszeug
sales force [ˈseɪlzˌfɔːs]	Verkaufsteam
acronym [ˈækrəʊnɪm]	Akronym, Abkürzungswort
stand for (v) [ˈstænd fɔː]	stehen für

Page 47

résumé [ˈrezjuːmeɪ]	Lebenslauf
dazzling [ˈdæzlɪŋ]	strahlend, umwerfend
hassle-free [ˌhæslˈfriː]	problemlos
layering technology [ˈleɪərɪŋtekˌnɒlədʒɪ]	Schichttechnologie
VAT = value added tax [ˌviːeɪˈtiː] [ˌvæljuːˌædɪd‿ˈtæks]	Mehrwertsteuer
breakthrough [ˈbreɪkθruː]	Durchbruch
ink [ɪŋk]	Tinte
oversized [ˌəʊvəˈsaɪzd]	überdimensional
emulation [ˌemjəˈleɪʃn]	Emulation, Nachahmung
tray [treɪ]	Ablage
duplexing [ˈdjuːpleksɪŋ]	beidseitig
expandable [ɪkˈspændəbl]	erweiterbar
envelope [ˈenvələʊp]	Briefumschlag
sleep mode [ˈsliːpˌməʊd]	Schlafmodus
feeder [ˈfiːdə]	Dokumentenzuführung

Page 48

maintenance [ˈmeɪntənəns]	Wartung
driver [ˈdraɪvə]	Treiber
dot-matrix (printer) [ˌdɒtˈmeɪtrɪks (ˌprɪntə)]	Nadeldrucker
ink-jet [ˈɪŋkdʒet]	Tintenstrahl-
keep in mind (v) [ˌkiːp ɪn‿ˈmaɪnd]	beachten
indicator [ˈɪndɪkeɪtə]	Hinweis
capture (v) [ˈkæptʃə]	erfassen
razor sharp [ˌreɪzəˈʃɑːp]	messerscharf
decent [ˈdiːsənt]	anständig, ordentlich
dynamic [daɪˈnæmɪk]	dynamisch, beweglich
top-of-the-line [ˌtɒpəvðəˈlaɪn]	anspruchsvoll, auf dem neuesten Stand
churn out (v) [ˌtʃɜːn ˈaʊt]	(in großen Mengen) ausstoßen, schnell herstellen
formatting [ˈfɔːmætɪŋ]	Formatierung
slow down (v) [ˌsləʊ ˈdaʊn]	verlangsamen
fortune [ˈfɔːtʃuːn]	Vermögen
obvious [ˈɒbvɪəs]	offensichtlich
overlook (v) [ˌəʊvəˈlʊk]	übersehen, vergessen

Page 49

ergonomics [ˌɜːgəˈnɒmɪks]	Ergonomie, körpergerechte Gestaltung
noise [nɔɪz]	Lärm
toner cartridge [ˈtəʊnəˌkɑːtrɪdʒ]	Toner-Kartusche, Patrone
repair [rɪˈpeə]	Reparatur
upkeep [ˈʌpkiːp]	Wartung
bypass (v) [ˈbaɪpɑːs]	überspringen
be in a hurry (v) [bɪ‿ɪnəˈhʌrɪ]	es eilig haben
expansion [ɪkˈspænʃn]	Erweiterung
issue [ˈɪʃuː]	Punkt
check out (v) [ˌtʃek ˈaʊt]	überprüfen
glossary [ˈglɒsərɪ]	Glossar, Worterklärungsliste
index [ˈɪndeks]	Inhalts-/ Stichwort-verzeichnis
guarantee (n) (v) [ˌgærənˈtiː]	Garantie; garantieren
distinguish (v) [dɪˈstɪŋgwɪʃ]	unterscheiden
pin [pɪn]	Nadel
carbon copy [ˌkɑːbnˈkɒpɪ]	Durchschlag, Kopie
carriage [ˈkærɪdʒ]	Wagen
construction [kənˈstrʌkʃn]	Bau
predominant [prɪˈdɒmɪnənt]	vorherrschend
project (v) [prəˈdʒekt]	spritzen, schleudern
droplet [ˈdrɒplət]	Tröpfchen
achieve (v) [əˈtʃiːv]	erreichen
drawback [ˈdrɔːbæk]	Nachteil
ink powder [ˈɪŋkˌpaʊdə]	Tintenpulver
operate as (v) [ˈɒpəreɪt‿əz]	fungieren als
priority [praɪˈɒrətɪ]	Priorität, wichtigste Sache
dispense with (v) [dɪˈspens wɪð]	verzichten auf
approximately [əˈprɒksɪmətlɪ]	ungefähr

Page 50

sensitive [ˈsensɪtɪv]	empfindlich
re-writable [ˌriːˈraɪtəbl]	wieder beschreibbar
back-up [ˈbækʌp]	Sicherungs-
vast [vɑːst]	umfangreich
subject to [ˈsʌbdʒəkt‿tuː]	abhängig von
distribute (v) [dɪˈstrɪbjuːt]	verteilen
density [ˈdensɪtɪ]	Dichte
removable [rɪˈmuːvəbl]	entfernbar, herausnehmbar
inexpensive [ˌɪnɪkˈspensɪv]	preisgünstig

Page 51

looks [lʊks]	Aussehen
triplet ['trɪplət]	Drilling
rely on (v) [rɪ'laɪ‿ɒn]	sich verlassen auf
pit [pɪt]	Vertiefung, Rille, Pit
spiral track [ˌspaɪrl'træk]	spiralförmige Spur
thick [θɪk]	dick
seamless ['si:mləs]	nahtlos
transition [træn'zɪʃn]	Übergang
tuning ['tju:nɪŋ]	Einstellung
track pitch ['træk‚pɪtʃ]	Spurabstand
tighter ['taɪtə]	enger
apart [ə'pɑ:t]	auseinander, voneinander entfernt
reduce (v) [rɪ'dju:s]	reduzieren
wavelength ['weɪvleŋkθ]	Wellenlänge
infrared [ˌɪnfrə'red]	infrarot
improve (v) [ɪm'pru:v]	verbessern
hub [hʌb]	Wickelkern, Mittelpunkt
instant ['ɪnstənt]	Moment
lens [lenz]	Linse
reflective layer [rɪˌflektɪv'leɪə]	reflektierende Schicht
relocate (v) [ˌri:ləʊ'keɪt]	neu zuordnen
optical pickup [ˌɒptɪkl'pɪkʌp]	optischer Lesekopf
distortion [dɪ'stɔ:ʃn]	Verkrümmung, Verformung
precision [prɪ'sɪʒn]	Genauigkeit

Page 52

depth [depθ]	Tiefe
travel through (v) [ˌtrævl 'θru:]	durchbohren
remain (v) [rɪ'meɪn]	bleiben
flat [flæt]	flach
withstand (v) [wɪð'stænd]	standhalten
bond (v) [bɒnd]	verbinden, verkleben
comparable [kəm'pærəbl]	vergleichbar
heavy-duty [ˌhevɪ'dju:tɪ]	Hochleistungs-
crude [kru:d]	grob
detection [dɪ'tekʃn]	Erkennung
embed (v) [ɪm'bed]	einbetten
possess (v) [pə'zes]	besitzen

Page 53

burst data transfer rate [ˌbɜ:st‿deɪtə'trænsfɜ:ˌreɪt]	Datenübertragungsrate, Burst-Data-Rate
average seek time [ˌævrɪdʒ'si:kˌtaɪm]	durchschnittliche Suchzeit
multi-segmented buffer [ˌmʌltɪsegˌmentɪd'bʌfə]	mehrfach segmentierter Puffer
rotation [rəʊ'teɪʃn]	Rotation, Umdrehung
areal density [ˌærɪəl'densɪtɪ] [ˌeərɪəl'densɪtɪ]	Flächendichte
moving parts [ˌmu:vɪŋ'pɑ:ts]	bewegliche Teile
consistent [kən'sɪstənt]	beständig
renowned [rɪ'naʊnd]	berühmt
loading mechanism ['ləʊdɪŋˌmekənɪzm]	Lademechanismus
prevent (v) [prɪ'vent]	verhindern
data loss ['deɪtəˌlɒs]	Datenverlust
power cut-off ['paʊəˌkʌtɒf]	Stromausfall
accidental [ˌæksɪ'dentl]	unbeabsichtigt
removal [rɪ'mu:vl]	Entfernung, Entnahme

Page 54

race [reɪs]	Rennen
broadcast ['brɔ:dkɑ:st]	Rundfunk, Sendung
mention (v) ['menʃn]	erwähnen
default document properties [ˌdi:fɒlt‿'dɒkjəmənt‿ˌprɒpətɪz]	Standardeinstellungen für das Dokument
mixed [mɪkst]	vermischt
toolbar ['tu:lbɑ:]	Werkzeugleiste
review [rɪ'vju:]	Besprechung, Rezension
tend to (v) ['tend‿tu:]	neigen zu
weigh [weɪ]	wiegen
competitive [kəm'petɪtɪv]	konkurrenzfähig
charge [tʃɑ:dʒ]	Kosten
just as ['dʒʌst‿əz]	genauso
just about any kind [ˌdʒʌstəˌbaʊt'enɪˌkaɪnd]	fast jede Art
reviewer [rɪ'vju:ə]	Rezensent(in)
number of ['nʌmbər‿əv]	Anzahl von, mehrere

Page 55

executive [ɪg'zekjətɪv]	Topmanager(in), Führungskraft
eventually [ɪ'ventʃʊəlɪ]	schließlich, endlich
mainstream ['meɪnstri:m]	etabliert
line [laɪn]	Produktpalette
competition [ˌkɒmpə'tɪʃn]	Konkurrenz
rock bottom [ˌrɒk'bɒtəm]	allerunterste(r,s)
take a pass (v) [ˌteɪk‿ə 'pɑ:s]	darauf verzichten
fall for (v) ['fel fɔ:]	es jmdm. angetan haben
vendor ['vendə]	Verkäufer(in), Lieferant(in)
lap [læp]	Schoß
lounge (v) [laʊndʒ]	entspannen, es sich bequem machen
adequate ['ædɪkwət]	ausreichend
unfortunately [ʌn'fɔ:tʃənətlɪ]	leider
puny ['pju:nɪ]	kümmerlich, winzig
replacement [rɪ'pleɪsmənt]	Ersatz
repeatedly [rɪ'pi:tɪdlɪ]	wiederholt
fade (v) [feɪd]	schwächer werden
sole [səʊl]	einzig
award [ə'wɔ:d]	Auszeichnung

Page 56

advise (v) [əd'vaɪz]	beraten
spend (v) [spend]	ausgeben

Page 57

magnetize (v) ['mægnətaɪz]	magnetisieren
detect (v) [dɪ'tekt]	aufspüren
spindle ['spɪndl]	Drehspindel
platter ['plætə]	Platte
coat (v) [kəʊt]	auftragen
spin (v) [spɪn]	drehen
modify (v) ['mɒdɪfaɪ]	ändern
common ['kɒmən]	gemeinsam
roughly ['rʌflɪ]	grob
numerous ['nju:mərəs]	zahlreich
region ['ri:dʒən]	Bereich
be composed of (v) [kəm'pəʊzd‿əv]	zusammengesetzt sein aus
grain [greɪn]	Korn

circulation [ˌsɜːkjəˈleɪʃn]	Kreislauf
cushion [ˈkʊʃn]	Kissen
keep free of (v) [ˌkiːp ˈfriː‿əv]	freihalten von
dust [dʌst]	Staub
damage [ˈdæmɪdʒ]	Schaden
seal (v) [siːl]	versiegeln
partition (v) [pɑːˈtɪʃn]	aufteilen

Page 58

vacation [veɪˈkeɪʃn]	Urlaub
cottage [ˈkɒtɪdʒ]	Ferienhaus
flexi-time [ˈfleksɪtaɪm]	Gleitzeit
express (v) [ɪkˈspres]	ausdrücken
exception [ɪkˈsepʃn]	Ausnahme
belong to (v) [bɪˈlɒŋ‿tuː]	gehören zu

Page 59

be used to (v) [ˈjuːst‿tə]	gewohnt sein
succeed (v) [səkˈsiːd]	Erfolg haben
insist on (v) [ɪnˈsɪst‿ɒn]	bestehen auf
difficulty [ˈdɪfɪkəltɪ]	Schwierigkeit
confuse with (v) [kənˈfjuːz wɪð]	verwechseln mit
emphasize (v) [ˈemfəsaɪz]	betonen
superlative [suːˈpɜːlətɪv]	Superlativ, 2. Steigerungsform
explanation [ˌekspləˈneɪʃn]	Erklärung
clearly [ˈklɪəlɪ]	eindeutig, offensichtlich
advancement [ədˈvɑːnsmənt]	Fortschritt, Verbesserung

Unit 3 Operating systems and software

Page 61

vary (v) [ˈveərɪ]	variieren, sich unterscheiden
keep (sth) running (v) [ˌkiːp (ˌsʌmθɪŋ) ˈrʌnɪŋ]	etwas am Laufen halten
system utility [ˌsɪstəmjuːˈtɪlətɪ]	Hilfsprogramm
file search [ˈfaɪlˌsɜːtʃ]	Dateisuche
backup program [ˈbækʌp‿ˌprəʊɡræm]	Sicherungsprogramm
govern (v) [ˈɡʌvən]	steuern
probably [ˈprɒbəblɪ]	wahrscheinlich
make or break (v) [ˌmeɪkɔːˈbreɪk]	entscheidend sein (für)
by heart [baɪˈhɑːt]	auswendig

Page 62

followup [ˈfɒləʊʌp]	Nachfolger
own right [ˌəʊnˈraɪt]	eigenständig
authentically [ɔːˈθentɪklɪ]	authentisch, echt
predecessor [ˈpriːdɪˌsesə]	Vorgänger
be prone to (v) [ˈprəʊn‿tuː]	anfällig sein für
conceive (v) [kənˈsiːv]	anlegen, konzipieren
capable [ˈkeɪpəbl]	fähig
offshoot [ˈɒfʃuːt]	Ableger

Page 63

initial [ɪˈnɪʃl]	anfänglich
level [ˈlevl]	Ebene
boot (v) [buːt]	starten (Computer), laden
load (v) [ləʊd]	laden
unalterable [ʌnˈɒltərəbl]	unveränderbar
erasable [ɪˈreɪzəbl]	löschbar
downside [ˈdaʊnsaɪd]	Nachteil
improperly [ɪmˈprɒpəlɪ]	unsachgemäß
counteract (v) [ˌkaʊntərˈækt]	entgegenwirken
in order [ɪnˈɔːdə]	in Ordnung
proceed (v) [prəˈsiːd]	fortfahren
further [ˈfɜːðə]	weiter
take over (v) [ˌteɪk ˈəʊvə]	übernehmen
bootstrap [ˈbuːtstræp]	Bootstrap, Ladeprogramm
hot plug [ˈhɒt‿plʌɡ]	Einbau bei laufendem Betrieb
matter [ˈmætə]	Angelegenheit, Frage
unusable [ʌnˈjuːsəbl]	nicht verwendbar, unbrauchbar
interplay [ˈɪntəpleɪ]	Zusammenspiel
inspect (v) [ɪnˈspekt]	untersuchen
terminate (v) [ˈtɜːmɪneɪt]	beenden
skip (v) [skɪp]	überspringen
log (v) [lɒɡ]	anmelden
pass over (v) [ˌpɑːs ˈəʊvə]	übergehen

Page 64

major [ˈmeɪdʒə]	größere(r, s)
upgrade (v) [ʌpˈɡreɪd]	verbessern, aufrüsten
disjointed [dɪsˈdʒɔɪntɪd]	unzusammenhängend
piece back together (v) [ˌpiːs bæk‿təˈɡeðə]	wieder zusammensetzen
hunt down (v) [ˌhʌnt‿ˈdaʊn]	Jagd machen auf
eliminate (v) [ɪˈlɪmɪneɪt]	beseitigen, entfernen
spot (v) [spɒt]	ausfindig machen, entdecken
superfluous [suːˈpɜːflʊəs]	überflüssig
space hogging [ˌspeɪsˈhɒɡɪŋ]	viel Platz einnehmend
compress (v) [kəmˈpres]	komprimieren
profiler [ˈprəʊfaɪlə]	Profilkorrektureinrichtung
interval [ˈɪntəvl]	Abstand, Interval
failure [ˈfeɪljə]	Ausfall
stream [striːm]	Datenkette
encryption [ɪnˈkrɪpʃn]	Ent-/Verschlüsselung
algorithm [ˈælɡərɪðm]	Algorithmus, Befehlsfolge zur Lösung eines Problems

Page 65

reminder [rɪˈmaɪndə]	Erinnerung
health [helθ]	Gesundheit
hidden [ˈhɪdn]	versteckt
duplicate [ˈdjuːplɪkeɪt]	Doppel-, doppelte(r, s)
recover (v) [rɪˈkʌvə]	wiederherstellen
protect (v) [prəˈtekt]	schützen
clean up (v) [ˌkliːn ˈʌp]	aufräumen
weed out (v) [ˌwiːd ˈaʊt]	aussondern
cookie [ˈkʊkɪ]	Cookie, Profildatei (kleine Datei, die den Besuch einer Website anzeigt)
pop up (v) [ˌpɒp ˈʌp]	plötzlich erscheinen
synch (v) [sɪŋk]	synchronisieren, abstimmen
snoop (v) [snuːp]	ausspähen
streamline (v) [ˈstriːmlaɪn]	optimieren
favo(u)rite [ˈfeɪvərɪt]	Lieblings-, bevorzugt
notify (v) [ˈnəʊtɪfaɪ]	benachrichtigen
colo(u)rful [ˈkʌləfəl]	farbenfroh, bunt

note [nəʊt]	Merkzettel
upcoming ['ʌp,kʌmɪŋ]	bevorstehend

Page 66

enjoy (v) [ɪn'dʒɔɪ]	genießen
reputation [,repjə'teɪʃn]	Ruf
restrict (v) [rɪ'strɪkt]	einschränken
property ['prɒpətɪ]	Besitz
stipulation [,stɪpjə'leɪʃn]	Bedingung
modification [,modɪfɪ'keɪʃn]	Änderung
license (v) ['laɪsəns]	lizenzieren, berechtigen
share [ʃeə]	gemeinsam benutzen, teilen
download (v) ['daʊnləʊd] [,daʊn'ləʊd]	herunterladen
manual ['mænjʊəl]	Handbuch
catch [kætʃ]	Haken
deny (v) [dɪ'naɪ]	verleugnen
challenge (v) ['tʃælɪndʒ]	herausfordern
steep learning curve [,sti:p'lɜ:nɪŋ,kɜ:v]	großer Lernaufwand
roll up one's sleeves [,rəʊlʌpwʌnz‿'sli:vz]	die Ärmel hochkrempeln
exasperating [ɪg'zæspəreɪtɪŋ]	ärgerlich
accommodating [ə'kɒmədeɪtɪŋ]	entgegenkommend, kulant

Page 67

resize (v) [,ri:'saɪz]	in der Größe anpassen
dedicate (v) ['dedɪkeɪt]	widmen, vormerken
recommend (v) [,rekə'mend]	empfehlen
walk you through (v) [,wɔ:kjə'θru:]	Schritt für Schritt durchführen
right away [,raɪtə'weɪ]	sofort
quiz (v) [kwɪz]	ausfragen
once [wʌns]	sobald
stage [steɪdʒ]	Stadium
settle for (v) ['setl fɔ:]	sich für etw. entscheiden
prompt [prɒmpt]	Eingabeaufforderung
directory [dɪ'rektərɪ] [daɪ'rektərɪ]	Verzeichnis
search for (v) ['sɜ:tʃ fɔ:]	suchen nach
manually ['mænjʊəlɪ]	mit der Hand
attribute ['ætrɪbju:t]	Attribut, Eigenschaft

Page 68

mail client ['meɪl,klaɪənt]	Mail-Client (Programm zur Inanspruchnahme von E-Mail-Diensten)
sound control ['saʊnd‿kən,trəʊl]	Ton- und Musikeinstellung
text editor ['tekst,edɪtə]	Texteditor (Programm zur Bearbeitung von Textdateien)

Page 69

minimize (v) ['mɪnɪmaɪz]	minimieren, verkleinern
enlarge (v) [ɪn'lɑ:dʒ]	vergrößern, erweitern
pull down (v) [,pʊl 'daʊn]	herunterziehen
arrow ['ærəʊ]	Pfeil
bottom ['bɒtəm]	unteres Ende
folder ['fəʊldə]	Ordner
lock (v) [lɒk]	sperren
log out (v) [,lɒg 'aʊt]	abmelden
make a jump (v) [,meɪk‿ə 'dʒʌmp]	überspringen
clue [klu:]	Hinweis

Page 70

long-awaited [,lɒŋə'weɪtɪd]	lang erwartet
promise (v) ['prɒmɪs]	versprechen
unveil (v) [ʌn'veɪl]	enthüllen
predict (v) [prɪ'dɪkt]	vorhersagen
in the making [ɪnðə'meɪkɪŋ]	in Bearbeitung
release (v) [rɪ'li:s]	freigeben, veröffentlichen
alongside [ə,lɒŋ'saɪd]	neben
flagship ['flægʃɪp]	Flaggschiff, Hauptprodukt
blog (v) [blɒg]	Blog (hiermit können Internet-Tagebucheinträge gemacht werden)
foundation [faʊn'deɪʃn]	Basis
subject ['sʌbdʒekt]	Thema
concerns [kən'sɜ:nz]	Bedenken
voice (v) [vɔɪs]	äußern
theft [θeft]	Diebstahl
insufficient [,ɪnsə'fɪʃənt]	unzureichend

Page 71

extensive [ɪk'stensɪv]	weitreichend, beträchtlich
join (v) [dʒɔɪn]	sich jmdm./etw. anschließen
stage [steɪdʒ]	Bühne
announce (v) [ə'naʊns]	bekannt geben
reunification [,ri:ju:nɪfɪ'keɪʃn]	Wiedervereinigung
smooth [smu:ð]	problemlos
century ['sentʃərɪ]	Jahrhundert
host (v) [həʊst]	veranstalten
generic [dʒə'nerɪk]	allgemein
venue ['venju:]	Veranstaltungsort
with regard to [wɪðrɪ'gɑ:d‿tu:]	bezüglich
manner ['mænə]	Art und Weise

Page 72

intend (v) [ɪn'tend]	vorhaben
careless ['keələs]	sorglos
regret (v) [rɪ'gret]	bedauern
trouble ['trʌbl]	Schwierigkeit

Unit 4 Application software

Page 73

sub-category ['sʌb,kætəgərɪ]	Unterklasse, Untergruppe
employ (v) [ɪm'plɔɪ]	verwenden
application suite [,æplɪ'keɪʃn,swi:t]	Anwendungspaket
bundle (v) ['bʌndl]	bündeln
educational [,edjʊ'keɪʃənl]	Lern-, Bildungs-

Page 74

row [rəʊ]	Reihe
make a typo (v) [,meɪk‿ə 'taɪpəʊ]	sich verschreiben
section ['sekʃn]	Abschnitt
paste (v) [peɪst]	einfügen
highlight (v) ['haɪlaɪt]	hervorheben

neat [niːt]	ordentlich
appearance [əˈpɪərəns]	Aussehen
hyphenation [ˌhaɪfəˈneɪʃn]	Silbentrennung
justification [ˌdʒʌstɪfɪˈkeɪʃn]	Blocksatz
comprehensive [ˌkɒmprɪˈhensɪv]	umfangreich
dictionary [ˈdɪkʃənrɪ]	Wörterbuch
constantly [ˈkɒnstəntlɪ]	dauernd
kick in (v) [ˌkɪk ˈɪn]	aktiviert werden
split (v) [splɪt]	trennen
space (v) [speɪs]	platzieren
evenly [ˈiːvənlɪ]	gleichmäßig
flush [flʌʃ]	bündig
margin [ˈmɑːdʒɪn]	Rand
full-featured [ˌfʊlˈfiːtʃəd]	voll ausgestattet
search and replace (v) [ˌsɜːtʃənrɪˈpleɪs]	suchen und ersetzen
word wrap [ˈwɜːdˌræp]	Zeilenumbruch
cut and paste (v) [ˌkʌtənˈpeɪst]	ausschneiden und einfügen

Page 75

font [fɒnt]	Schriftart
macros [ˈmækrəʊz]	Makros
merge (v) [mɜːdʒ]	zusammenfügen, mischen
spell checker [ˈspelˌtʃekə]	Rechtschreibprüfprogramm
footnote [ˈfʊtnəʊt]	Fußnote
references [ˈrefrənsɪz]	Quellenangaben, Referenzen, Empfehlungen
cross reference [ˌkrɒsˈrefrəns]	Querverweis
header [ˈhedə]	Kopfzeile
footer [ˈfʊtə]	Fußzeile
numbering [ˈnʌmbərɪŋ]	Nummerierung
thesaurus [θɪˈsɔːrəs]	Synonymwörterbuch
table of contents [ˌteɪbləvˈkɒntents]	Inhaltsverzeichnis
word completion [ˈwɜːdkəmˌpliːʃn]	Wortvervollständigung
layout [ˈleɪaʊt]	Layout, Design, Anordnung
synonym [ˈsɪnənɪm]	Synonym, alternative Bezeichnung
keystroke [ˈkiːstrəʊk]	Anschlag einer Taste, Tastendruck
indentation [ˌɪndenˈteɪʃn]	Einrückung, Einzug
misspell (v) [ˌmɪsˈspel]	falsch buchstabieren
bold [bəʊld]	fett
italics [ɪˈtælɪks]	kursiv
tailor (v) [ˈteɪlə]	maßschneidern, auf etw./jmdn. zuschneiden

Page 76

tab [tæb]	Tabulator
blank space [ˌblæŋkˈspeɪs]	Leerstelle
line-spacing [ˈlaɪnˌspeɪsɪŋ]	Zeilenabstand
scrolling [ˈskrəʊlɪŋ]	Scrollen
insertion point [ɪnˈsɜːʃnˌpɔɪnt]	Einfügestrich
adjust (v) [əˈdʒʌst]	anpassen
alignment [əˈlaɪnmənt]	Ausrichtung, Anordnung
redo (v) [ˌriːˈduː]	neu anfangen

Page 77

manage (v) [ˈmænɪdʒ]	etw. schaffen
feed in (v) [ˌfiːd ˈɪn]	eingeben
get the hang of sth. [ˌget‿ðəˈhæŋəvˌsʌmθɪŋ]	den Dreh bei etw. heraushaben
my pleasure [ˌmaɪˈpleʒə]	gern geschehen

Page 78

plain [pleɪn]	einfach, schlicht
underline (v) [ˌʌndəˈlaɪn]	unterstreichen
capital letter [ˌkæpɪtl‿ˈletə]	Großbuchstabe
quotation mark [kwəʊˈteɪʃn‿ˌmɑːk]	Anführungszeichen
(in) parenthesis [pəˈrenθəsɪs]	in Klammern, Parenthese
bracket [ˈbrækɪts]	Klammer
mortgage [ˈmɔːgɪdʒ]	Hypothek
utilities [juːˈtɪlətɪz]	Nebenkosten
fee [fiː]	Gebühren, Honorar
misc./miscellaneous [ˌmɪsəlˈeɪnɪəs]	Diverses, Verschiedenes
expenses [ɪkˈspensɪz]	Ausgaben, Auslagen
interest [ˈɪntrəst]	Zins
stocks [stɒks]	Aktien
rent [rent]	Miete
salary [ˈsælərɪ]	Gehalt
revenue [ˈrevənjuː]	Einnahmen

Page 79

column [ˈkɒləm]	Spalte
intersection [ˌɪntəˈsekʃn]	Schnittpunkt
exceed (v) [ɪkˈsiːd]	übersteigen
earnings [ˈɜːnɪŋz]	Einnahmen
seasonal [ˈsiːzənl]	saisonabhängig
fluctuation [ˌflʌktʃʊˈeɪʃn]	Schwankung
expenditures [ɪkˈspendɪtʃəz]	Ausgaben
delayed [dɪˈleɪd]	verzögert
affect (v) [əˈfekt]	beeinflussen
formula [ˈfɔːmjələ]	Formel
quarterly [ˈkwɔːtəlɪ]	quartalsweise, vierteljährlich
bar chart [ˈbɑːˌtʃɑːt]	Balkendiagramm
line graph [ˈlaɪnˌgrɑːf]	Kurvendiagramm
grid [grɪd]	Gitternetz

Page 80

over time [ˌəʊvəˈtaɪm]	im Zeitablauf
percentage [pəˈsentɪdʒ]	Prozentsatz
scalable [ˈskeɪləbl]	in der Größe veränderbar
variable [ˈveərɪəbl]	Variable
quadrant [ˈkwɒdrənt]	Quadrant
present (v) [prɪˈzent]	zeigen
divide (v) [dɪˈvaɪd]	aufteilen
segment [ˈsegmənt]	Segment, Abschnitt
figures [ˈfɪgəz]	Zahlen
exhibit (v) [ɪgˈzɪbɪt]	zeigen, darstellen
respective [rɪˈspektɪv]	jeweilige(r, s)
series [ˈsɪəriːz]	Reihe, Serie
market share [ˌmɑːkɪtˈʃeə]	Marktanteil
sharply [ˈʃɑːplɪ]	steil
peak [piːk]	Höhepunkt
fall [fɔːl]	Herbst
renewed [rɪˈnjuːd]	erneuert

climb [klaɪm] – Anstieg
dip [dɪp] – Abfall, Abnahme
former ['fɔ:mə] – erstere(r, s)
cordless ['kɔ:dləs] – schnurlos
latter ['lætə] – letztere(r, s)
practically ['præktɪkəlɪ] – fast
cellular phone [ˌseljələ'fəʊn] – Handy
clarify (v) ['klærɪfaɪ] – klar stellen
agenda [ə'dʒendə] – Tagesordnung
chairperson ['tʃeəˌpɜ:sn] – Vorsitzende(r)
make sure (v) [ˌmeɪk 'ʃɔ:] – sicherstellen
consensus [kən'sensəs] – Konsens
decision [dɪ'sɪʒn] – Entscheidung

Page 81

next to nothing [ˌnekst‿tə'nʌθɪŋ] – fast nichts
warranty ['wɒrəntɪ] – Garantie
plaster (v) ['plɑ:stə] – vollkleben
commit (v) [kə'mɪt] – sich verpflichten
submit to (v) [səb'mɪt‿tu:] – sich unterziehen
low-end [ˌləʊ'end] – einfach
pay up front [ˌpeɪ‿ʌp'frʌnt] – im Voraus zahlen
slide show ['slaɪdˌʃəʊ] – Diavorführung
animation [ˌænɪ'meɪʃn] – Animation, bewegte Bilder
right from the start [ˌraɪt‿frəmðə'stɑ:t] – von Anfang an
transparency [træn'spærənsɪ] – Folie

Page 82

background ['bækgraʊnd] – Hintergrund
consistency [kən'sɪstənsɪ] – Einheitlichkeit
semi-dark [ˌsemɪ'dɑ:k] – halbdunkel
attract (v) [ə'trækt] – anziehen
textured ['tekstʃəd] – strukturiert
stick to (v) ['stɪk tu:] – einhalten
backdrop ['bækdrɒp] – Kulisse, Hintergrund
in the middle of the act [ɪnðəˌmɪdləvðɪ'ækt] – mittendrin
align (v) [ə'laɪn] – angleichen, anpassen
bullet point ['bʊlɪtˌpɔɪnt] – Gliederungspunkt
focal point [ˌfəʊkl'pɔɪnt] – Fokus
caution ['kɔ:ʃn] – Vorsicht
for the sake of [fəðə'seɪkəv] – um einer Sache willen
well matched [ˌwel'mætʃt] – gut abgestimmt
not advised [ˌnɒtəd'vaɪzd] – nicht zu empfehlen
lead (v) [li:d] – führen
caps =capital letters [kæps] [ˌkæpɪtl‿'letəz] – Großbuchstaben
impression [ɪm'preʃn] – Eindruck
capitalize (v) ['kæpɪtəlaɪz] – groß schreiben
proper noun [ˌprɒpə'naʊn] – Eigenname

Page 83

straightforward [ˌstreɪt'fɔ:wəd] – geradlinig, einfach
legible ['ledʒəbl] – leserlich
sparingly ['speərɪŋlɪ] – sparsam
shade [ʃeɪd] – Abstufung
elaborate (v) [ɪ'læbəreɪt] – näher ausführen, ausarbeiten
concise [kən'saɪs] – kompakt
occur to (v) [ə'kɜ: tu:] – einfallen
conventional [kən'venʃənl] – herkömmlich

Page 84

redundancy [rɪ'dʌndənsɪ] – Redundanz, Überflüssigkeit
tedious ['ti:dɪəs] – ermüdend
retailer ['ri:teɪlə] – Einzelhändler(in)
turnover ['tɜ:nˌəʊvə] – (Gesamt)Umsatz
incur (v) [ɪn'kɜ:] – sich etw. zuziehen, etw. haben
furthermore [ˌfɜ:ðə'mɔ:] – außerdem, ferner
be entitled (v) [bɪ‿ɪn'taɪtld] – berechtigt sein
account balance [ə'kaʊnt‿ˌbæləns] – Kontostand
outstanding [ˌaʊt'stændɪŋ] – herausragend
replication [ˌreplɪ'keɪʃn] – Abgleich, Kopie
at any given moment [ətˌenɪˌgɪvn‿'məʊmənt] – zu jedem Zeitpunkt
go wrong (v) [ˌgəʊ'rɒŋ] – schief gehen
query ['kwɪərɪ] – Abfrage
declare (v) [dɪ'kleə] – vereinbaren, deklarieren
syntax ['sɪntæks] – Satzbau

Page 85

authorisation [ˌɔ:θəraɪ'zeɪʃn] – Berechtigung
regulate (v) ['regjəleɪt] – regulieren
mirror (v) ['mɪrə] – spiegeln
interference [ˌɪntə'fɪərəns] – Beeinträchtigung, Behinderung

Page 86

perspective [pə'spektɪv] – Perspektive
stock [stɒk] – Bestand
is supposed to [ɪz‿sə'pəʊzd‿tu:] – soll
browse through (v) [ˌbraʊz'θru:] – durchsuchen
warehouse ['weəhaʊs] – Lager
descending [dɪ'sendɪŋ] – absteigend

Page 87

unknown [ʌn'nəʊn] – unbekannt
valid ['vælɪd] – gültig
parameter [pə'ræmɪtə] – Parameter, Bestimmungsgröße
association [əˌsəʊʃɪ'eɪʃn] – Assoziierung, Zuordnung
path analysis ['pɑ:θəˌnæləsɪs] – Analyse des Weges
clustering ['klʌstərɪŋ] – Clustering, Clusterverfahren
document (v) ['dɒkjəment] – dokumentieren, belegen
reasonable ['ri:znəbl] – begründet, sinnvoll
discovery [dɪ'skʌvərɪ] – Entdeckung
deductive [dɪ'dʌktɪv] – deduktiv, folgernd
entail (v) [ɪnˌteɪl] – beinhalten
call for (v) ['kɔ:l fɔ:] – erfordern
prerequisite [ˌpri:'rekwɪzɪt] – Voraussetzung
formulation [ˌfɔ:mjə'leɪʃn] – Formulierung, Abfassung
growth [grəʊθ] – Zuwachs
neural network [ˌnjʊərəl'netwɜ:k] – neuronales Netz
decrease (v) [dɪ'kri:s] – abnehmen, fallen
sector ['sektə] – Bereich
insurance [ɪn'ʃɔ:rəns] – Versicherung
fraud [frɔ:d] – Betrug
assess (v) [ə'ses] – abschätzen

affinity [ə'fɪnəti]	Affinität, Neigung
preferred customer [prɪˌfɜːd'kʌstəmə]	bevorzugter Kunde/ bevorzugte Kundin

Page 88

in the wake of [ɪnðə'weɪkəv]	im Gefolge von
scope [skəʊp]	Umfang
means [miːnz]	Mittel
immigration [ˌɪmɪ'greɪʃn]	Einwanderung
records ['rekɔːdz]	Unterlagen
limitation [ˌlɪmɪ'teɪʃn]	Grenze
reveal (v) [rɪ'viːl]	aufdecken
significance [sɪg'nɪfɪkəns]	Signifikanz, Bedeutung
validity [və'lɪdəti]	Gültigkeit
dependent [dɪ'pendənt]	abhängig
circumstances ['sɜːkəmstɑːnsɪz]	Umstände
suspect ['sʌspekt]	Verdächtige(r)
behaviour [bɪ'heɪvjə]	Verhalten
conform to (v) [kən'fɔːm tuː]	entsprechen
causal ['kɔːzl]	kausal, ursächlich
propensity [prə'pensəti]	Hang, Neigung
depart (v) [dɪ'pɑːt]	abfliegen
income ['ɪnkʌm]	Einkommen
level of education [ˌlevləvˌedjʊ'keɪʃn]	Bildungsgrad
overriding [ˌəʊvə'raɪdɪŋ]	vorrangig, übergeordnet
concern (v) [kən'sɜːn]	betreffen
interoperability [ˌɪntərˌɒpərə'bɪləti]	Interoperabilität
mission creep ['mɪʃnˌkriːp]	schleichende Ausweitung eines Auftrags
privacy ['praɪvəsi]	Datenschutz
controversial [ˌkɒntrə'vɜːʃl]	umstritten, kontrovers
debate [dɪ'beɪt]	Debatte

Page 89

spotlight ['spɒtlaɪt]	Mittelpunkt des Interesses
agent ['eɪdʒənt]	Handelnde(r)
subject ['sʌbdʒekt]	Gegenstand
minor ['maɪnə]	klein
authorities [ɔː'θɒrətiz]	Behörde
merchandise ['mɜːtʃəndaɪs]	Güter, Waren
take care of (v) [teɪk‿'keər‿əv]	sich kümmern um
map [mæp]	Karte, Stadtplan

Page 90

retrieve (v) [rɪ'triːv]	abfragen
width [wɪtθ] [wɪdθ]	Breite
mail merging ['meɪlˌmɜːdʒɪŋ]	Serienbrieferstellung
directions [dɪ'rekʃnz] [daɪ'rekʃnz]	Wegbeschreibung
vocabulary [və'kæbjələri]	Wortschatz
coupled to ['kʌpld‿tuː]	gekoppelt mit
push back (v) [ˌpʊʃ'bæk]	nach hinten verschieben
proud [praʊd]	stolz
merger ['mɜːdʒə]	Fusion
ruthless ['ruːθləs]	rücksichtslos
per annum [pər'ænəm]	jährlich
sample ['sɑːmpl]	Muster

Unit 5 LANS, WANS and GANs

Page 91

LAN = local area network [læn] [ˌləʊklˌeərɪə'netwɜːk]	lokales Netz
WAN = wide area network [wæn] [ˌwaɪdˌeərɪə'netwɜːk]	Weitverkehrsnetz
GAN = global area network [gæn] [ˌgləʊblˌeərɪə'netwɜːk]	globales Netz
cover (v) ['kʌvə]	decken, abdecken
pool (v) [puːl]	gemeinsam benutzen, teilen
exchange (v) [ɪks'tʃeɪndʒ]	austauschen
junction ['dʒʌŋkʃn]	Kreuzung, Knotenpunkt
be composed of (v) [bɪ kəm'pəʊzd əv]	bestehen aus
interconnected [ˌɪntəkə'nektɪd]	untereinander verbunden
node [nəʊd]	Knoten

Page 92

interchangeably [ˌɪntə'tʃeɪndʒəbli]	austauschbar
protocol ['prəʊtəkɒl]	Protokol
connectivity [ˌkɒnek'tɪvɪti]	Verbindungsfähigkeit
topology [tɒp'ɒlədʒi]	Topologie
shape [ʃeɪp]	Form
route (v) [ruːt]	leiten
circular ['sɜːkjələ]	kreisförmig
loop [luːp]	Schleife

Page 93

mesh topology [ˌmeʃtɒp'ɒlədʒi]	Maschentopologie
reach [riːtʃ]	Reichweite
principal ['prɪnsəpl]	Haupt-
comparatively [kəm'pærətɪvli]	vergleichsweise, relativ
cost-effective [ˌkɒstɪ'fektɪv]	günstig, ökonomisch
jumbled ['dʒʌmbld]	durcheinander
token ['təʊkn]	Token, Wertmarke, Zeichen
act as (v) ['ækt‿əz]	fungieren als
gateway ['geɪtweɪ]	Gateway, Schnittstelle
transceiver [træn'siːvə]	Sende-Empfangsgerät
consequence ['kɒnsɪkwəns]	Konsequenz, Folge

Page 94

characterize (v) ['kærɪktəraɪz]	charakterisieren, kennzeichnen
peer-to-peer [ˌpɪətə'pɪə]	Peer to Peer-Netzwerk (mit gleichrangigen Arbeitsstationen)
client-server [ˌklaɪənt‿'sɜːvə]	Client/Server-System
equal ['iːkwəl]	gleich
host [həʊst]	Menge, Unzahl
grant (v) [grɑːnt]	gewähren

Page 95

wiring ['waɪərɪŋ]	Verkabelung
coax [ˌkəʊ'æks]	Koaxialkabel
wireless ['waɪələs]	drahtlos
powerline ['paʊəlaɪn]	Stromleitung

interference [ˌɪntə'fɪərəns]	Empfangsstörung
outlet ['aʊtlet]	Anschlussdose
insecure [ˌɪnsɪ'kjʊə]	unsicher
telephony [tə'lefənɪ]	Fernsprechtechnik
destination [ˌdestɪ'neɪʃn]	Endziel
packet ['pækɪt]	Datenpaket
reassemble (v) [ˌri:ə'sembl]	wieder zusammensetzen
pick up (v) [ˌpɪk 'ʌp]	aufnehmen
receiver [rɪ'si:və]	Hörer
originate (v) [ə'rɪdʒɪneɪt]	entstehen

Page 96

fibre-optic [ˌfaɪbər'ɒptɪk]	faseroptisch
permit (v) [pə'mɪt]	erlauben
aerial dish [ˌeərɪəl'dɪʃ]	Antennenschüssel
amplify (v) ['æmplɪfaɪ]	verstärken
subscriber [səb'skraɪbə]	Abonnent(in)
ordinary ['ɔ:dɪnrɪ]	gewöhnlich
take advantage of (v) [ˌteɪk əd'vɑ:ntɪdʒ əv]	sich etw. zu Nutze machen

Page 97

reproduce (v) [ˌri:prə'dju:s]	wiedergeben, reproduzieren
set-top box [ˌsettɒp'bɒks]	Digitalempfänger
emit (v) [ɪ'mɪt]	senden
incoming ['ɪnˌkʌmɪŋ]	eingehende(r, s)
smart card reader ['smɑ:tkɑ:dˌri:də]	Chipkartenleser
virtually ['vɜ:tʃʊəlɪ]	fast
touch screen ['tʌtʃˌskri:n]	Sensorbildschirm
rewind (v) [ˌri:'waɪnd]	zurückspülen

Page 98

increasingly [ɪn'kri:sɪŋlɪ]	zunehmend
Wi-Fi ['waɪfaɪ]	drahtlose Übertragung
proprietary (schemes) [prə'praɪətrɪ]	geschützte (Systeme)
wideband ['waɪdbænd]	Breitband
established [ɪ'stæblɪʃt]	etabliert

Page 99

order of magnitude [ˌɔ:dərəv'mægnɪtju:d]	Zehnerpotenz
footprint ['fʊtprɪnt]	Empfangsbereich
evolve (v) [ɪ'vɒlv]	entwickeln
high frequency [ˌhaɪ'fri:kwənsɪ]	Hochfrequenz
low-energy [ˌləʊ'enədʒɪ]	energiearm
pulse [pʌls]	Impuls
noise floor ['nɔɪzˌflɔ:]	Störpegel
scalable ['skeɪləbl]	skalierbar
beyond [bɪ'jɒnd]	jenseits, außerhalb
underneath [ˌʌndə'ni:θ]	unterhalb
undetectable [ˌʌndɪ'tektəbl]	nicht feststellbar

Page 100

residential [ˌrezɪ'denʃl]	Wohn-
facilitate (v) [fə'sɪlɪteɪt]	ermöglichen, erleichtern
prearrangement [ˌpri:ə'reɪndʒmənt]	Vorausbestimmung
thrust [θrʌst]	Hauptrichtung, Schub
engine ['endʒɪn]	Motor
twist [twɪst]	Drehung, Drall
alter (v) ['ɒltə] ['ɔ:ltə]	ändern
aid (v) [eɪd]	helfen
interfere (v) [ˌɪntə'fɪə]	stören
coexist (v) [ˌkəʊɪg'zɪst]	koexistieren, nebeneinander bestehen
transmission [trænz'mɪʃn]	Sendung, Übertragung

Page 101

conditional [kən'dɪʃənl]	Bedingungs-
speculative ['spekjələtɪv]	spekulativ
graduate (v) ['grædjʊeɪt]	den Abschluss machen
share [ʃeə]	Aktie
conjunction [kən'dʒʌŋkʃn]	Verbindungswort, Konjunktion
in case [ɪn'keɪs]	falls
provided [prə'vaɪdɪd]	sofern, vorausgesetzt
unless [ən'les]	außer wenn
on condition [ˌɒnkən'dɪʃn]	unter der Auflage, unter der Bedingung
emergency [ɪ'mɜ:dʒənsɪ]	Notfall
supply (v) [sə'plaɪ]	liefern, bereitstellen
joint venture [ˌdʒɔɪnt‿'ventʃə]	Joint Venture, Beteiligungsunternehmen
attachment [ə'tætʃmənt]	Anhang
miss (v) [mɪs]	verpassen

Unit 6 The Internet and globalization

Page 103

bidder ['bɪdə]	Anbieter(in)
unsolicited [ˌʌnsə'lɪsɪtɪd]	unaufgefordert
junk [dʒʌŋk]	Müll
like-minded [ˌlaɪk'maɪndɪd]	gleichgesinnt
engage in (v) [ɪn'geɪdʒ ɪn]	teilnehmen an
journal ['dʒɜ:nəl]	Tagebuch, Journal
search engine ['sɜ:tʃˌendʒɪn]	Suchmaschine
blog [blɒg]	Blog, Internet-Tagebuch
auction ['ɔ:kʃn]	Versteigerung
service provider ['sɜ:vɪsprəˌvaɪdə]	Dienstleistende(r), Internetdienstanbieter(in)
spam [spæm]	unerwünschte E-Mails

Page 104

hacker ['hækə]	Hacker(in)
blogroll ['blɒgˌrəʊl]	Blogroll (persönliche Linkliste zu weiteren Weblogs)
zero day ['zɪərəʊˌdeɪ]	sofortige Ausnutzung einer Internet-Sicherheitslücke
timeline ['taɪmlaɪn]	Zeitachse
Department of Defense [dɪˌpɑ:tməntəvdɪ'fens]	Verteidigungsministerium (USA)
Sputnik Scare ['spʌtnɪkˌskeə]	Sputnikschock
time-sharing ['taɪmˌʃeərɪŋ]	Mehrbenutzerbetriebsart
site [saɪt]	Aufstellungsort, Lage
domain [də'meɪn]	Domäne
worm [wɜ:m]	Wurm, Computervirus
host [həʊst]	Host
dial-up access [ˌdaɪəlʌp'ækses]	Verbindungsaufbau durch Einwahl (über das Telefonnetz)

emergence [ɪ'mɜ:dʒəns]	Aufkommen
emerge (v) [ɪ'mɜ:dʒ]	herauskommen, aufkommen
extended [ɪk'stendɪd]	erweitert
intrusion [ɪn'tru:ʒn]	Eindringen
benchmark ['bentʃmɑ:k]	Referenzpunkt
broadband ['brɔ:dbænd]	Breitband
former ['fɔ:mə]	ehemalig
paid [peɪd]	bezahlt
solution [sə'lu:ʃn]	Lösung
founder ['faʊndə]	Gründer(in)
backbone ['bækbəʊn]	Basisnetz
surfing the net [ˌsɜ:fɪŋðə'net]	im Internet surfen
coin (v) [kɔɪn]	prägen
reserve (v) [rɪ'zɜ:v]	reservieren, vorbehalten
assign (v) [ə'saɪn]	zuweisen
giant ['dʒaɪənt]	Riese

Page 105

slot [slɒt]	Einschnitt
chart (v) [tʃɑ:t]	eintragen
as a whole [əzə'həʊl]	gesamt

Page 106

refresh (v) [rɪ'freʃ]	auffrischen
navigation system [ˌnævɪ'geɪʃnˌsɪstəm]	Steuerungssystem
starting point ['stɑ:tɪŋˌpɔɪnt]	Ausgangspunkt
fairly ['feəlɪ]	ziemlich, einigermaßen
web crawler ['webˌkrɔ:lə]	Webcrawler, Suchmaschine
index (v) ['ɪndeks]	indexieren, katalogisieren
operator ['ɒpəreɪtə]	Betreiber(in)
hit [hɪt]	Treffer

Page 107

rating system ['reɪtɪŋˌsɪstəm]	Bewertungsverfahren
unimaginable [ˌʌnɪ'mædʒɪnəbl]	unvorstellbar
rate (v) [reɪt]	bewerten, einstufen
listing on the stock market [ˌlɪstɪŋ ɒnðə 'stɒkˌmɑ:kɪt]	Börsennotierung
solve (v) [sɒlv]	lösen
equation [ɪ'kweɪʒn]	Gleichung
rank [ræŋk]	Rang, Rangstelle
apt [æpt]	treffend
library ['laɪbrərɪ]	Bibliothek
paperback ['peɪpəbæk]	Taschenbuch
local paper [ˌləʊkl'peɪpə]	Lokalzeitung
webmaster ['webˌmɑ:stə]	Webmaster (Verantwortliche(r) für eine Website)
manipulate (v) [mə'nɪpjəleɪt]	manipulieren, beeinflussen

Page 108

technique [tek'ni:k]	Methode, Arbeitstechnik
crawling ['krɔ:lɪŋ]	Crawling (Internet-Suchmethode)
spidering ['spaɪdərɪŋ]	Spidering (Internet-Suchmethode)
gather (v) ['gæðə]	sammeln
crawl (v) [krɔ:l]	crawlen
extract (v) [ɪk'strækt]	extrahieren, herausnehmen
exclude (v) [ɪks'klu:d]	ausschließen, entfernen

Page 109

keyword ['ki:wɜ:d]	Schlüsselwort
relevance matching ['reləvənsˌmætʃɪŋ]	Übereinstimmung
recognize (v) ['rekəgnaɪz]	erkennen
trap [træp]	Falle
intervention [ˌɪntə'venʃn]	Eingreifen
entangle (v) [ɪn'tæŋgl]	verwickeln
fair [feə]	Messe

Page 110

mediation [ˌmi:dɪ'eɪʃn]	Vermittlung
mediate (v) ['mi:dɪeɪt]	vermitteln
rolling ['rəʊlɪŋ]	kontinuierlich
aircraft ['eəkrɑ:ft]	Flugzeug
seamless ['si:mləs]	makellos
blurry ['blɜ:rɪ]	verschwommen

Page 111

country code ['kʌntrɪˌkəʊd]	Ländercode
aviation industry [ˌeɪvɪ'eɪʃnˌɪndəstrɪ]	Luftfahrtindustrie
reasonably ['ri:znəblɪ]	vernünftigerweise, durchaus
distant ['dɪstənt]	entfernt

Page 112

crime [kraɪm]	Verbrechen
eclipse (v) [ɪ'klɪps]	etw. in den Schatten stellen, in den Hintergrund drängen
burglary ['bɜ:glərɪ]	Einbruch
perceive (v) [pə'si:v]	wahrnehmen
prevalent ['prevələnt]	verbreitet
mugging ['mʌgɪŋ]	Raubüberfall
criminal ['krɪmɪnəl]	Verbrecher(in)
conduct (v) [kən'dʌkt]	durchführen
awareness [ə'weənəs]	Bewusstsein
vulnerable ['vʌlnərəbl]	angreifbar
respondent [rɪ'spɒndənt]	Auskunftgebende(r)
expose (v) [ɪk'spəʊz]	aussetzen
phishing ['fɪʃɪŋ]	Phishing (mit Ködern nach Passwörtern angeln)
hoax [həʊks]	blinder Alarm, „Ente"
account [ə'kaʊnt]	Konto
scam [skæm]	Betrug
double (v) ['dʌbl]	sich verdoppeln
rogue [rəʊg]	Schurke/Schurkin
bully (v) ['bʊlɪ]	einschüchtern
roughly ['rʌflɪ]	ungefähr
community [kə'mju:nətɪ]	Gemeinde-, Gemeinschafts-

Page 113

groceries ['grəʊsərɪz]	Lebensmittel
fear [fɪə]	Angst
carry out (v) [ˌkærɪ‿'aʊt]	durch-, ausführen
be put off (v) [bɪ ˌpʊt'ɒf]	sich abschrecken lassen
deterred [dɪ'tɜ:d]	abgeschreckt
otherwise ['ʌðəwaɪz]	ansonsten
lose out on (v) [ˌlu:z‿'aʊt ɒn]	den Kürzeren ziehen bei

benefit ['benəfɪt]	Vorteil
sensible ['sensɪbl]	vernünftig
precautions [prɪ'kɔ:ʃnz]	Vorsichtsmaßnahmen
majority [mə'dʒɒrətɪ]	Mehrheit
safely ['seɪflɪ]	wohlbehalten
vital ['vaɪtl]	sehr wichtig, unerlässlich
be aware of (v) [bɪ‿ə'weər‿əv]	sich bewusst sein
confidently ['kɒnfɪdəntlɪ]	mit Zuversicht
be committed to (v) [bɪ kə'mɪtɪd‿tu:]	hinter etw. stehen, sich dafür einsetzen
long-term [ˌlɒŋ'tɜ:m]	langfristig
arm (v) [ɑ:m]	bewaffnen
knowledge ['nɒlɪdʒ]	Kenntnisse
commission (v) [kə'mɪʃn]	beauftragen
mark (v) [mɑ:k]	markieren
roadshow ['rəʊdʃəʊ]	Roadshow, Informationsveranstaltung
session ['seʃn]	Sitzung, Schulungseinheit
nationwide [ˌneɪʃn'waɪd]	landesweit
government agency [ˌgʌvənmənt'eɪdʒənsɪ]	Behörde
be concerned about (v) [bɪ kən'sɜ:nd əˌbaʊt]	besorgt sein um
abuse [ə'bju:s]	Missbrauch
population [ˌpɒpjə'leɪʃn]	Bevölkerung
bill [bɪl]	Rechnung
regard (v) [rɪ'gɑ:d]	betrachten
caution ['kɔ:ʃn]	Vorsichtsmaßnahme

Page 114

sham [ʃæm]	Betrug
worry ['wʌrɪ]	Sorge
consciousness ['kɒnʃəsnəs]	Bewusstsein
defenseless [dɪ'fensləs]	schutzlos
poll [pəʊl]	Umfrage
inhibit (v) [ɪn'hɪbɪt]	hindern, hemmen
spyware ['spaɪweə]	Spyware, Spionage-Software
secretly ['si:krətlɪ]	insgeheim
intent [ɪn'tent]	Absicht
spy out (v) [ˌspaɪ‿'aʊt]	ausspionieren
third party [ˌθɜ:d'pɑ:tɪ]	Dritte(r)
privacy ['praɪvəsɪ]	Privatsphäre
exploit (v) [ɪk'splɔɪt]	ausbeuten

Page 115

touch on sth (v) ['tʌtʃ ɒn ˌsʌmθɪŋ]	etw. erwähnen
be addictive (v) [bɪ‿ə'dɪktɪv]	süchtig machen
no doubt [ˌnəʊ'daʊt]	ohne Zweifel
overload ['əʊvələʊd]	Überlastung
tasteless ['teɪstləs]	geschmacklos
foolish ['fu:lɪʃ]	dumm
swap [swɒp]	austauschen
outweigh (v) [ˌaʊt'weɪ]	überwiegen
transient ['trænzɪənt]	kurzlebig
minority [maɪ'nɒrətɪ]	Minderheit
hit and miss [ˌhɪtən'mɪs]	auf gut Glück
principle ['prɪnsəpl]	Prinzip, Grundsatz

Page 116

sound (v) [saʊnd]	klingen
unstoppable [ʌn'stɒpəbl]	unaufhaltsam
interdependency [ˌɪntədɪ'pendənsɪ]	gegenseitige Abhängigkeit, Wechselwirkung
cheap [tʃi:p]	billig
remote [rɪ'məʊt]	entlegen
corner ['kɔ:nə]	Winkel
upgrowth ['ʌpgrəʊθ]	Zuwachs
in the course [ɪnðə'kɔ:s]	im Laufe
confront (v) [kən'frʌnt]	konfrontieren
native ['neɪtɪv]	heimisch, (hier) muttersprachlich
lingua franca [ˌlɪŋgwə'fræŋkə]	Verkehrssprache
desire [dɪ'zaɪə]	Wunsch
cultural context [ˌkʌltʃərəl'kɒntekst]	kultureller Zusammenhang
jump to a conclusion (v) [ˌdʒʌmp tʊ‿ə kən'klu:ʒn]	voreilig einen Schluss ziehen
sex [seks]	Geschlecht
just plain [ˌdʒʌst'pleɪn]	nur einfach
influence (v) ['ɪnflʊəns]	beeinflussen
core [kɔ:]	Kern
competence ['kɒmpɪtəns]	Kompetenz
open-mindedness [ˌəʊpn'maɪndɪdnəs]	Aufgeschlossenheit
specifically [spə'sɪfɪklɪ]	besonders
degree [dɪ'gri:]	Grad
style of addressing [ˌstaɪləvə'dresɪŋ]	Anredestil
counterpart ['kaʊntəpɑ:t]	Gegenüber, Kollege/Kollegin
time-management ['taɪmˌmænɪdʒmənt]	Zeitplanung

Page 117

import ['ɪmpɔ:t]	Wichtigkeit, Bedeutung
abroad [ə'brɔ:d]	im Ausland
frighten (v) ['fraɪtn]	erschrecken
de rigeur (French) [dərɪ'gɜ:]	obligat
notwithstanding [ˌnɒtwɪð'stændɪŋ]	trotz, ungeachtet
linguistic [lɪŋ'gwɪstɪk]	sprachlich
chauvinist ['ʃəʊvɪnɪst]	Chauvinist(in)
utility [ju:'tɪlətɪ]	Nützlichkeit
medium ['mi:dɪəm]	Medium
unfortunate [ʌn'fɔ:tʃənət]	bedauerlich, ungünstig
inevitability [ɪˌnevɪtə'bɪlətɪ]	Unabwendbarkeit
fierce [fɪəs]	leidenschaftlich, heftig
commitment [kə'mɪtmənt]	Engagement, Hingabe
preserve (v) [prɪ'zɜ:v]	bewahren
losing battle [ˌlu:zɪŋ'bætl]	verlorener Kampf
native speaker [ˌneɪtɪv'spi:kə]	Muttersprachler(in)
foreign language [ˌfɒrən'læŋgwɪdʒ]	Fremdsprache

Page 118

present perfect [ˌpreznt‿'pɜ:fekt]	Perfekt
clear-cut [ˌklɪə'kʌt]	eindeutig festehend, klar
ongoing ['ɒnˌgəʊɪŋ]	anhaltend
proceedings [prə'si:dɪŋz]	Vorgänge
emphasis ['emfəsɪs]	Betonung
intransitive [ɪn'trænsətɪv]	intransitiv
meantime ['mi:ntaɪm]	Zwischenzeit
misleading [mɪs'li:dɪŋ]	irreführend

a matter of [ə'mætərəv]	eine Sache/Frage der
state [steɪt]	Zustand
gain (v) [geɪn]	zunehmen
fire (v) [faɪə]	feuern

Unit 7 Programming

Page 120

process ['prəʊses]	Vorgang
icon ['aɪkɒn]	kleines Bild, Piktogramm
compile (v) [kəm'paɪl]	kompilieren
documentation [ˌdɒkjəmen'teɪʃn]	Dokumentation
feedback ['fi:dbæk]	Feedback, Rückmeldung
correct (v) [kə'rekt]	korrigieren
comment ['kɒment]	Kommentar, Anmerkung
code [kəʊd]	Code (in einer Programmiersprache abgefasster Text)
coding ['kəʊdɪŋ]	Programmierung (das Aufschreiben des Programms in einer Programmiersprache)
debugging [ˌdi:'bʌgɪŋ]	Fehlersuche und -behebung
structogram ['strʌktəgræm]	Struktogramm (grafische Darstelllung eines Programmablaufplans)
flowchart ['fləʊtʃa:t]	PAP (Programmablaufplan oder Datenflussplan)
serve (v) [sɜ:v]	dienen
memory address ['memrɪ‿əˌdres]	Speicheradresse
meaning ['mi:nɪŋ]	Bedeutung
agreed upon [[ə'gri:d‿əˌpɒn]	vereinbart

Page 121

iteration [ˌɪtər'eɪʃn]	Iteration, Wiederholung
necessarily [ˌnesə'serəlɪ]	zwingend
as long as [əz'lɒŋəz]	so lange wie
condition [kən'dɪʃn]	Bedingung
depending on [[dɪ'pendɪŋ‿ɒn]	abhängig von
dyadic [daɪ'ædɪk]	dyadisch
true branch ['tru:ˌbra:ntʃ]	Ja-Zweig
false branch ['fɒlsˌbra:ntʃ]	Nein-Zweig
foot controlled [ˌfʊtkən'trəʊld]	fußgesteuert
exit (condition) ['egzɪt] ['eksɪt] ['egzɪtkənˌdɪʃn]	Ausgang, Abbruch(bedingung)
cycle ['saɪkl]	Zyklus, Durchgang
interpret (v) [ɪn'tɜ:prɪt]	auslegen, deuten, interpretieren
associate (v) [ə'səʊʃɪeɪt]	verbinden, vereinigen
default (column) ['di:fɒltˌkɒləm]	Voreinstellung, („Sonstfall-Spalte“)
call [kɔ:l]	Abruf
procedure [prə'si:dʒə]	Verfahrensweise
call point ['kɔ:lˌpɔɪnt]	Aufrufstelle
block of instructions [ˌblɒkəvɪn'strʌkʃnz]	Anweisungsblock
unconditional jump [ˌʌnkəndɪʃənl'dʒʌmp]	unbedingter Sprungbefehl
continuous [kən'tɪnjʊəs]	ununterbrochen
monadic [mɒn'ædɪk]	monadisch, „einwegig“
head controlled [ˌhedkən'trəʊld]	kopfgesteuert

Page 122

advisable [əd'vaɪzəbl]	empfehlenswert
building society ['bɪldɪŋsəˌsaɪətɪ]	Bausparkasse
borrow (v) ['bɒrəʊ]	leihen
interest rate ['ɪntrəstˌreɪt]	Zinssatz
afford (v) [ə'fɔ:d]	sich leisten
take into consideration (v) ['teɪk ˌɪntə kənˌsɪdə'reɪʃn]	in Betracht ziehen, überlegen
instalment [ɪn'stɔ:lmənt]	Rate
debt [det]	Schulden
counter ['kaʊntə]	Zähler
loan [ləʊn]	Darlehen, Kredit
subtract (v) [səb'trækt]	abziehen, subtrahieren
remainder [rɪ'meɪndə]	Rest

Page 123

keep on top (v) [ˌki:p ɒn 'tɒp]	sich auf dem Laufenden halten
script [skrɪpt]	Skriptsprache
platform independent [ˌplætfɔ:mdɪ'pendənt]	plattformunabhängig
hybrid ['haɪbrɪd]	hybrid

Page 124

machine code [mə'ʃi:nˌkəʊd]	Maschinencode, Binärcode
assembly language [ə'semblɪˌlæŋgwɪdʒ]	Assembliersprache
assembler [ə'semblə]	Assembler (Übersetzungsprogramm für Assembliersprachen)
mnemonic [nɪ'mɒnɪk]	mnemotechnisch, das Gedächtnis stützend
so-called [ˌsəʊ'kɔ:ld]	so genannt
high-level language [ˌhaɪlevl‿'læŋgwɪdʒ]	höhere Programmiersprache
low-level language [ˌləʊlevl‿'læŋgwɪdʒ]	maschinenorientierte Programmiersprache
source program ['sɔ:sˌprəʊgræm]	Quellenprogramm, Primärprogramm
object program ['ɒbdʒektˌprəʊgræm]	ausführbares Programm, lauffähiges Maschinenprogramm
scientific [ˌsaɪən'tɪfɪk]	wissenschaftlich
walk-on [ˌwɔ:k'ɒn]	Statistenrolle
center stage [ˌsentə'steɪdʒ]	Mittelpunkt
object oriented ['ɒbdʒektˌɔ:rɪentɪd]	objektorientiert
introduce (v) [ˌɪntrə'dju:s]	einführen
enter the scene (v) [ˌentə ðə 'si:n]	Einzug halten
stand-alone ['stændəˌləʊn]	eigenständig, unabhängig
applet ['æplət]	kleine Anwendung
incorporate (v) [ɪn'kɔ:pəreɪt]	einbauen, berücksichtigen
predefine (v) [ˌpri:dɪ'faɪn]	vordefinieren
toolbox ['tu:lbɒks]	Werkzeugkasten
derive from (v) [dɪ'raɪv frɒm]	ableiten von
construct (v) [kən'strʌkt]	bauen

artifact ['ɑ:tɪfækt]	Artefakt
business modeling ['bɪznɪs,mɒdlɪŋ]	Geschäftsprozess-modellierung
engineering [ˌendʒɪ'nɪərɪŋ]	technisch
practice ['præktɪs]	Verfahren, Praktik

Page 125

characteristic [ˌkærɪktə'rɪstɪk]	Eigenschaft
unify (v) ['ju:nɪfaɪ]	vereinen
standardize (v) ['stændədaɪz]	standardisieren, normieren
differ from (v) ['dɪfə frəm]	sich unterscheiden von
apt [æpt]	angemessen

Page 126

automate (v) ['ɔ:təmeɪt]	automatisieren
accounting program [ə'kaʊntɪŋ ˌprəʊgræm]	Abrechnungsprogramm
alert [ə'lɜ:t]	Alarm
tactic ['tæktɪk]	Taktik, Maßnahme
run-time error ['rʌntaɪm,erə]	Laufzeitfehler
syntax error ['sɪntæks,erə]	Syntaxfehler
dot your i's (v) [ˌdɒtjər'aɪz]	penibel sein
contradictory [ˌkɒntrə'dɪktərɪ]	widersprüchlich
dead-end [ˌded'end]	Sackgasse, nicht weiterführend
trace (v) [treɪs]	aufspüren
availability [əˌveɪlə'bɪlətɪ]	Vorhandensein
missing ['mɪsɪŋ]	fehlend
segmentation fault [ˌsegmen'teɪʃnˌfɒlt]	Speicherzugriffsfehler

Page 127

illogical [ɪ'lɒdʒɪkl]	nicht logisch
repair (v) [rɪ'peə]	reparieren, richten
in points of [ɪn'pɔɪntsəv]	betreffend
rectify (v) ['rektɪfaɪ]	berichtigen, korrigieren
tricky ['trɪkɪ]	kniffelig
source of the trouble [ˌsɔ:səvðə'trʌbl]	Problemursache

Page 128

outer ['aʊtə]	äußere

Page 129

senior ['si:nɪə]	Chef-
dissatisfied [ˌdɪs'sætɪsfaɪd]	unzufrieden
be annoyed (v) [bɪ‿ə'nɔɪd]	verärgert sein
eager ['i:gə]	eifrig

Page 130

rough plan [ˌrʌf'plæn]	grober Entwurf
encode (v) [ɪn'kəʊd]	kodieren
clip-art ['klɪpɑ:t]	ClipArt (für Computerbearbeitung erstellte Bilder, Grafiken)
upload (v) ['ʌpləʊd] [ʌp'ləʊd]	hochladen
set objectives (v) [ˌset əb'dʒektɪvz]	Ziele setzen
advertise ['ædvətaɪz]	werben, bekannt machen

Page 131

rating ['reɪtɪŋ]	Beurteilung
high-impact [ˌhaɪ'ɪmpækt]	wirkungsvoll
remarkable [rɪ'mɑ:kəbl]	bemerkenswert
top-selling [ˌtɒp'selɪŋ]	meistverkauft
packed with ['pækt wɪð]	vollgepackt mit
hands-on [ˌhændz'ɒn]	praktisch
tutorial [tju:'tɔ:rɪəl]	Anleitung, Selbstlerneinheit
basics ['beɪsɪks]	Grundkenntnisse
in no time [ɪn‿'nəʊˌtaɪm]	im Nu, im Handumdrehen
prototyping ['prəʊtəʊtaɪpɪŋ]	Bau eines Prototyps, Muster
coverage ['kʌvərɪdʒ]	Anwendungsbereich
style sheet ['staɪlˌʃi:t]	Formatvorlage, Musterblatt
punch up (v) [ˌpʌntʃ'ʌp]	beleben
client-side ['klaɪənt‿saɪd]	klientbezogen
template ['templəɪt]	Template, Dokumentvorlage
custom ['kʌstəm]	kundenspezifisch, maßgeschneidert
tag [tæg]	Tag
oral report [ˌɔ:rəlrɪ'pɔ:t]	mündlicher Bericht
cause [kɔ:z]	Sache
convey (v) [kən'veɪ]	vermitteln
clutter (v) ['klʌtə]	vollstopfen

Page 132

mess [mes]	Durcheinander
retrospect ['retrəspekt]	Rückblick
trade off sth for sth (v) ['treɪd ɒf ˌsʌmθɪŋ fə 'sʌmθɪŋ]	abwägen, tauschen, verzichten auf
reliability [rɪˌlaɪə'bɪlətɪ]	Zuverlässigkeit
fundamental [ˌfʌndə'mentl]	elementar
vitiate (v) ['vɪʃɪeɪt]	beeinträchtigen
account for (v) [ə'kaʊnt‿fɔ:]	erklären, begründen
resent (v) [rɪ'zent]	verübeln
broadly ['brɔ:dlɪ]	allgemein
dumb down (v) [ˌdʌm 'daʊn]	vereinfachen
second-guess (v) [ˌsekənd‿'ges]	etw. im Nachhinein anzweifeln
vintage ['vɪntɪdʒ]	Jahrgang
be proud of (v) [bɪ 'praʊd əv]	stolz sein auf

Page 133

appalling [ə'pɔ:lɪŋ]	entsetzlich
maintainability [meɪnˌteɪnə'bɪlətɪ]	Wartungsfreundlichkeit
state of emergency [ˌsteɪtəvɪ'mɜ:dʒənsɪ]	Ausnahmezustand
grasp at straws (v) [ˌgrɑ:spət'strɔ:z]	nach einem Strohhalm greifen
minor miracle [ˌmaɪnə'mɪrəkl]	kleines Wunder
through trial and error [θru:ˌtraɪlən'erə]	durch Ausprobieren
brute force [ˌbru:t'fɔ:s]	Brachialgewalt
educate (v) ['edʒʊkeɪt]	ausbilden
reward (v) [rɪ'wɔ:d]	belohnen
punish (v) ['pʌnɪʃ]	bestrafen
sloppiness ['slɒpɪnəs]	Schlampigkeit
buggy ['bʌgɪ]	verwanzt, voller Fehler
fancy ['fænsɪ]	ausgefallen
gadget ['gædʒɪt]	Gerät, technische Spielerei
glib [glɪb]	unbedacht
aesthetics [es'θetɪks]	Ästhetik
matter (v) ['mætə]	von Bedeutung sein
first and foremost [ˌfɜ:stən'fɔ:məʊst]	zuallererst

succinctly [sək'sɪŋktlɪ]	kurz und bündig
affordably [ə'fɔ:dəblɪ]	erschwinglich
meet (v) [mi:t]	erfüllen
generality [ˌdʒenə'rælətɪ]	Allgemeingültigkeit
trade-off ['treɪdɒf]	Kompromiss
dichotomy [daɪ'kɒtəmɪ]	Zwiespalt
bogus ['bəʊgəs]	falsch
view [vju:]	Ansicht
stuff [stʌf]	Sachen
libraries ['laɪbrərɪz]	Sammlungen
abstraction [æb'strækʃn]	Abstraktion

Page 134

compromise (v) ['kɒmprəmaɪz]	einen Kompromiss eingehen
underlying [ˌʌndə'laɪɪŋ]	grundlegend, eigentlich
comprise (v) [kəm'praɪz]	beinhalten, enthalten
achievement [ə'tʃi:vmənt]	Leistung
colloquial [kə'ləʊkwɪəl]	umgangsprachlich
long haul [ˌlɒŋ'hɔ:l]	langfristig

Page 135

steady job [ˌstedɪ'dʒɒb]	feste Stelle
out for lunch [ˌaʊtfə'lʌntʃ]	zum Mittagessen gegangen
sign (v) [saɪn]	unterschreiben
confusing [kən'fju:zɪŋ]	verwirrend
admittedly [əd'mɪtədlɪ]	zugegebenermaßen
abound (v) [ə'baʊnd]	reichlich vorhanden sein

Unit 8 System administration and security

Page 136

sysadmin (system administrator) [ˌsɪstəməd'mɪnɪstreɪtə] [ˌsɪs'ædmɪn]	Systemverwalter(in)
supervise (v) ['su:pəvaɪz]	überwachen, kontrollieren
well-founded [ˌwel'faʊndɪd]	fundiert
know-how ['nəʊhaʊ]	Kenntnisse
soft skills ['sɒft‿skɪlz]	Sozialkompetenz
day-to-day [ˌdeɪtə'deɪ]	täglich
be called on (v) [bɪ 'kɔ:ld ɒn]	aufgefordert sein
protection [prə'tekʃn]	Schutz

Page 137

consultant [kən'sʌltənt]	Berater(in)
thorough ['θʌrə]	gründlich
reset (v) [ˌri:'set]	zurücksetzen
rights [raɪts]	Rechte
guest [gest]	Gast
priviledge ['prɪvəlɪdʒ]	Privileg, Bevorzugung
lowest ['ləʊɪst]	niedrigste(r, s)
file replication ['faɪlreplɪˌkeɪʃn]	Dateikopie
ordinary ['ɔ:dɪnrɪ]	normal, üblich
obviously ['ɒbvɪəslɪ]	offensichtlich
as detailed [əz'di:teɪld]	wie aufgeführt

Page 138

hire (v) [haɪə]	anstellen, einstellen
more or less [ˌmɔ:rə'les]	mehr oder weniger
from scratch [frəm'skrætʃ]	von Grund auf
routine [ru:'ti:n]	Routine, Gewohnheit
payroll ['peɪrəʊl]	Gehaltsabrechnung

Page 139

be familar with (v) [bɪ fə'mɪljə wɪð]	vertraut sein mit
case study ['keɪs‿stʌdɪ]	Fallstudie
proposal [prə'pəʊzl]	Vorschlag
near future [ˌnɪə'fju:tʃə]	nahe Zukunft
coordinate (v) [kəʊ'ɔ:dɪneɪt]	koordinieren, leiten
take notes (v) [ˌteɪk 'nəʊts]	sich Notizen machen
outline (v) ['aʊtlaɪn]	entwerfen
specified time [ˌspesɪfaɪd‿'taɪm]	bestimmte Zeit
opposite number [ˌɒpəzɪt'nʌmbə]	Gegenspieler(in)
final draft [ˌfaɪnl'drɑ:ft]	endgültiger Entwurf
plan of action [ˌplænəv'ækʃn]	Schlachtplan

Page 140

acquisition [ˌækwɪ'zɪʃn]	Firmenübernahme
practice ['præktɪs]	Praxis, Tätigkeit
part-time [ˌpɑ:t‿'taɪm]	Teilzeit
overworked [ˌəʊvə'wɜ:kt]	überarbeitet
temp agency ['tempˌeɪdʒənsɪ]	Zeitarbeitsfirma
worth the while [ˌwɜ:θ‿ðə'waɪl]	die Mühe wert sein, sich lohnen
reduction [rɪ'dʌkʃn]	Reduzierung
workload ['wɜ:kləʊd]	Arbeitsbelastung
proposed [prə'pəʊzd]	vorgeschlagen
cope with (v) ['kəʊp wɪð]	fertig werden mit
senior partner [ˌsi:nɪə'pɑ:tnə]	Seniorpartner
scepticism ['skeptɪsɪzm]	Skepsis, Zweifel
cost-efficiency [ˌkɒstɪ'fɪʃənsɪ]	Kosteneffizienz
conversion [kən'vɜ:ʃn]	Umstellung
town house ['taʊnˌhaʊs]	Stadthaus
panelling ['pænəlɪŋ]	Holzverkleidung
wooden floor [ˌwʊdn'flɔ:]	Parkettboden
winding staircase [ˌwaɪndɪŋ'steəkeɪs]	gewundene Treppe
pertaining to [pə'teɪnɪŋ‿tu:]	betreffend
compliance [kəm'plaɪəns]	Einhaltung
workplace safety ['wɜ:kpleɪs‿seɪftɪ]	Arbeitsplatzsicherheit
health regulations ['helθregjəˌleɪʃnz]	Gesundheitsvorschriften
crowded ['kraʊdɪd]	überfüllt
integral ['ɪntɪgrəl]	wesentlich
luckily ['lʌkɪlɪ]	glücklicherweise
reasonably priced [ˌri:znəblɪ'praɪst]	günstig, preiswert
cubicle ['kju:bɪkl]	Arbeitsplatz im Großraumbüro, Arbeitsnische
speech therapist [ˌspi:tʃ'θerəpɪst]	Logopäde/Logopädin
physiotherapist [ˌfɪzɪəʊ'θerəpɪst]	Krankengymnast(in)
occupational therapist [ˌɒkjʊ'peɪʃənl'θerəpɪst]	Beschäftigungstherapeut(in), Ergotherapeut(in)
registered nurse [ˌredʒɪstəd'nɜ:s]	examinierte(r) Krankenpfleger(in)

nurse's aid [ˌnɜ:sɪz'eɪd]	Hilfskrankenpfleger(in)
social worker ['səʊʃl,wɜ:kə]	Sozialarbeiter(in)
stroke [strəʊk]	Schlaganfall
brain-damaged ['breɪn,dæmɪdʒd]	gehirngeschädigt
victim ['vɪktɪm]	Opfer, Betroffene(r)
scale [skeɪl]	Rahmen
recreation room [ˌrekrɪ'eɪʃn,ru:m]	Gemeinschaftsraum
funding ['fʌndɪŋ]	Finanzierung
accommodate (v) [ə'kɒmədeɪt]	aufnehmen
live-in [ˌlɪv'ɪn]	stationär

Page 141

kernel ['kɜ:nəl]	Kernel, „Kern"
effort ['efət]	Bemühung
dump [dʌmp]	Hauptspeicherauszug, „Müllhalde"
hop [hɒp]	Sprung von einem Knotenrechner zum nächsten
tune (v) [tju:n]	abstimmen, einstellen
handshaking ['hænd,ʃeɪkɪŋ]	Austausch von Steuerungsinformation
allocation [ˌælə'keɪʃn]	Zuweisung
memory content ['memrɪ,kɒntent]	Speicherinhalt
prearranged [ˌpri:ə'reɪndʒd]	vorbestimmt
agreement [ə'gri:mənt]	Vereinbarung

Page 142

error message ['erə,mesɪdʒ]	Fehlermeldung
unreadable [ʌn'ri:dəbl]	unleserlich
retry (v) [ˌri:'traɪ]	wieder versuchen
fail (v) [feɪl]	fehlschlagen
abort (v) [ə'bɔ:t]	abbrechen
reconstruct (v) [ˌri:kən'strʌkt]	wieder aufbauen
referenced ['refrənst]	angesprochen, auf das verwiesen wird
rename (v) [ˌri:'neɪm]	neu bennen
stack [stæk]	Stack, Stapelspeicher (speziell behandelter Speicherbereich zur Datenablage)
invalid [ɪn'vælɪd]	ungültig
incorrectly [ˌɪnkər'ektlɪ]	falsch
remember (v) [rɪ'membə]	daran denken, nicht vergessen
backslash ['bækslæʃ]	Backslash, umgekehrter Schrägstrich
unavailable [ˌʌnə'veɪləbl]	nicht zur Verfügung stehend
cancel (v) ['kænsl]	stornieren
memory parity error [ˌmemrɪ'pærətɪ,erə]	Paritätsfehler im RAM
record (v) [rɪ'kɔ:d]	aufnehmen

Page 144

analogous [ə'næləgəs]	analog, vergleichbar mit
infect (v) [ɪn'fekt]	infizieren, anstecken
mind-boggling ['maɪnd,bɒglɪŋ]	verblüffend
on the rise [ˌɒnðə'raɪz]	im Zunehmen
up to ['ʌptə]	bis zu
flame up (v) [ˌfleɪm 'ʌp]	aufflammen
annual ['ænjʊəl]	jährlich
growth rate ['grəʊθ,reɪt]	Wachstumsrate
infection [ɪn'fekʃn]	Ansteckung
affected [ə'fektɪd]	betroffen
headache ['hedeɪk]	(hier) Problem
sharp [ʃɑ:p]	steil
in other words [ɪn'ʌðə,wɜ:dz]	anders gesagt
corrupt (v) [kə'rʌpt]	verfälschen (Daten)
take advantage of (v) [ˌteɪk əd'vɑ:ntɪdʒ əv]	ausnutzen

Page 145

vulnerability [ˌvʌlnərə'bɪlətɪ]	Schwachstelle
hole [həʊl]	Loch
benign [bɪ'naɪn]	harmlos
unexpectedly [ˌʌnɪk'spektɪdlɪ]	unerwartet
waste (v) [weɪst]	verschwenden
countless ['kaʊntləs]	zahllos
manpower ['mæn,paʊə]	Arbeitskraft, Personal
malignant [mə'lɪgnənt]	bösartig
consume (v) [kən'sju:m]	aufbrauchen
lethal ['li:θl]	tödlich
on the loose [ˌɒnðə'lu:s]	frei im Umlauf
jam (v) [dʒæm]	verstopfen
downtime ['daʊntaɪm]	Ausfallzeit
understandably [ˌʌndə'stændəblɪ]	verständlicherweise
react (v) [rɪ'ækt]	reagieren
run counter to (v) [ˌrʌn 'kaʊntə tu:]	im Widerspruch stehen zu
myth building ['mɪθ,bɪldɪŋ]	Mythenbildung
media sensation [ˌmi:dɪəsen'seɪʃn]	Medienaufsehen
surround (v) [sə'raʊnd]	umgeben, umringen
flash memory ['flæʃ,memrɪ]	Flash-Speicher
countermeasure ['kaʊntə,meʒə]	Gegenmaßnahme
peddle (v) ['pedl]	hausieren, (auf der Straße) verkaufen
lucrative ['lu:krətɪv]	einträglich
payload ['peɪləʊd]	Payload, Ladung, „Sprengladung"
retro ['retrəʊ]	rückwirkend, rückwärtsgerichtet
latch onto (v) [ˌlætʃ 'ɒntu:]	sich einklinken in
wipe out (v) [ˌwaɪp 'aʊt]	zerstören
nasty ['næstɪ] ['nɑ:stɪ]	unangenehm, böse
in contrast to [ɪn 'kɒntrɑ:st‿tu:]	im Gegensatz zu
reboot (v) [ˌri:'bu:t]	neu starten
bootable ['bu:təbl]	automatisch ladend
human ['hju:mən]	Mensch
dangerous ['deɪndʒərəs]	gefährlich
trigger (v) ['trɪgə]	auslösen

Page 146

landmark ['lændmɑ:k]	einen Meilenstein bedeutend, historisch
media coverage [ˌmi:dɪə'kʌvərɪdʒ]	Medienberichterstattung

hit (v) [hɪt]	erreichen
turn out (v) [ˌtɜːn 'aʊt]	sich erweisen
anticipate (v) [æn'tɪsɪpeɪt]	erwarten
struggle (v) ['strʌgl]	kämpfen, sich abmühen
hold the record (v) [ˌhəʊld ðə 'rekɔːd]	den Rekord halten
malicious [mə'lɪʃəs]	bösartig
disguise (v) [dɪs'gaɪz]	tarnen
destructive [dɪ'strʌktɪv]	zerstörerisch
dismantle (v) [dɪ'smæntl]	deinstallieren
observe (v) [əb'zɜːv]	beachten
crack down on (v) [ˌkræk 'daʊn ɒn]	hart durchgreifen bei
arrest [ə'rest]	Verhaftung
infamous ['ɪnfəməs]	berüchtigt
bother (v) ['bɒðə]	sich die Mühe machen
stupidly ['stjuːpɪdlɪ]	dummerweise
gullible ['gʌləbl]	leichtgläubig

Page 147

cryptography [krɪp'tɒgrəfɪ]	Kryptographie, Verschlüsselung
decryption [ˌdiː'krɪpʃn]	Entschlüsselung
ciphertext ['saɪfətekst]	Chiffretext
secrecy ['siːkrəsɪ]	Geheimhaltung
supposed [sə'pəʊzd]	vermutet, angenommen
feasible ['fiːzəbl]	durchführbar
approach [ə'prəʊtʃ]	Vorgehensweise, Ansatz
random ['rændəm]	zufällig, beliebig
withstand (v) [wɪð'stænd]	sich widersetzen
reformulate (v) [ˌriː'fɔːmjəleɪt]	neu formulieren
small case [ˌsmɔːl'keɪs]	klein (Buchstaben)
space [speɪs]	Abstand
jot down (v) [ˌdʒɒt 'daʊn]	kurz notieren
reissue (v) [ˌriː'ɪʃuː]	neu ausgeben

Page 148

firewall ['faɪəwɔːl]	Firewall (Zugangsschutzsystem)
user-defined [ˌjuːzədɪ'faɪnd]	benutzerdefiniert
transparent [træn'spærənt]	transparent
susceptible [sə'septəbl]	anfällig
spoofing ['spuːfɪŋ]	Manipulation
gateway ['geɪtweɪ]	Schnittstelle
impose (v) [ɪm'pəʊz]	auferlegen
degradation [ˌdegrə'deɪʃn]	Verschlechterung
proxy server ['prɒksɪˌsɜːvə]	Proxy-Server
intercept (v) [ˌɪntə'sept]	auffangen, abfangen
in concert [ɪn'kɒnsət]	zusammen
first line of defense [ˌfɜːstlaɪnəvdɪ'fens]	erste Verteidigungslinie/Art der Verteidigung
intruder [ɪn'truːdə]	Eindringling
trusted ['trʌstɪd]	vertraut
engage in (v) [ɪn'geɪdʒ ɪn]	betreiben

Page 149

downsize (v) ['daʊnsaɪz]	verringern
cut back on (v) [ˌkʌt 'bæk ɒn]	einschränken
idiom ['ɪdɪəm]	Idiom, Redewendung
give up (v) [ˌgɪv 'ʌp]	aufgeben
give away (v) [ˌgɪv ə'weɪ]	verschenken
give back (v) [ˌgɪv 'bæk]	zurückgeben
give in (v) [ˌgɪv 'ɪn]	nachgeben
give out (v) [ˌgɪv 'aʊt]	verteilen, ausfallen
whim [wɪm]	Laune
raise (v) [reɪz]	aufziehen
venture ['ventʃə]	Unternehmen, Projekt
get discouraged (v) [ˌget dɪ'skʌrɪdʒd]	sich entmutigen lassen
issue ['ɪʃuː]	Ausgabe
cross your fingers [ˌkrɒsjə'fɪŋgəz]	drück die Daumen

Unit 9 Projects, meetings and presentations

Page 151

closure ['kləʊʒə]	Abschluss
initiation [ɪˌnɪʃɪ'eɪʃn]	Initiierung
roll-out ['rəʊlaʊt]	Vorstellung
mitigate (v) ['mɪtɪgeɪt]	entschärfen, mildern
outing ['aʊtɪŋ]	Ausflug
vocational [vəʊ'keɪʃənl]	Berufs-

Page 152

quotation [kwəʊ'teɪʃn]	Zitat
call a meeting to order (v) [ˌkɔːl ə ˌmiːtɪŋ tʊ'ɔːdə]	eine Besprechung offiziell eröffnen
resolution [ˌrezə'luːʃn]	Beschluss
unanimous [juː'nænɪməs]	einstimmig
out of order [ˌaʊtəv'ɔːdə]	(hier) "nicht an der Reihe", außer Betrieb
motion ['məʊʃn]	Antrag
minutes (of a meeting) ['mɪnɪts (əvə ˌmiːtɪŋ)]	Protokoll
show of hands [ˌʃəʊəv'hændz]	Handzeichen, Handheben
move (v) [muːv]	vorschlagen
amend (v) [ə'mend]	ergänzen, abändern
adjourn (v) [ə'dʒɜːn]	vertagen (Sitzung)
vote (n) (v) [vəʊt]	Stimme, Wahl; wählen
amendment [ə'mendmənt]	Ergänzung, Änderung
abstention [æb'stenʃn]	Enthaltung
break [breɪk]	Pause
yield the floor (v) [ˌjiːld ðə 'flɔː]	das Wort (Rederecht) übergeben
as read [əz'red]	als bekannt voraussetzen
go around in circles (v) [ˌgəʊ əˌraʊnd ɪn 'sɜːklz]	sich im Kreis drehen
appoint (v) [ə'pɔɪnt]	benennen
second (v) ['sekənd]	unterstützen
investigation [ɪnˌvestɪ'geɪʃn]	Untersuchung

Page 153

chair (v) [tʃeə]	den Vorsitz haben

Page 154

refocus (v) [ˌriː'fəʊkəs]	neu fokussieren
outline (v) ['aʊtlaɪn]	skizzieren, kurz darstellen
move on (v) [ˌmuːv 'ɒn]	weitergehen
sum up (v) [ˌsʌm 'ʌp]	zusammenfassen, resümieren
be in favo(u)r (v) [bɪ ɪn'feɪvə]	für etw. sein, dafür sein

resolve (v) (a problem) [rɪ'zɒlv] [rɪˌzɒlv ə 'prɒbləm]	(ein Problem) lösen
wrap sth up (v) [ˌræp ˌsʌmθɪŋ 'ʌp]	etw. unter Dach und Fach bringen
close (v) [kləʊz]	beenden
matter in hand [ˌmætərɪn'hænd]	vorliegende Angelegenheit
participant [pɑː'tɪsɪpənt]	Teilnehmer(in)
monopolize (v) [mə'nɒpəlaɪz]	an sich reißen, alleine bestreiten
drag on (v) [ˌdræg 'ɒn]	in die Länge ziehen
stick to (v) ['stɪk tuː]	sich halten an
reading ['riːdɪŋ]	Lesen

Page 155

hold a meeting (v) [ˌhəʊld‿ə 'miːtɪŋ]	ein Meeting/eine Besprechung abhalten
call (a meeting) (v) [ˌkɔːl‿ə 'miːtɪŋ]	(ein Meeting) einberufen
pharmaceutical [ˌfɑːmə'sjuːtɪkl]	Pharma-
wholesaler ['həʊlˌseɪlə]	Großhändler(in)
logistics [lə'dʒɪstɪks]	Logistik
acclimatise (v) [ə'klaɪmətaɪz]	sich akklimatisieren, eingewöhnen
populace ['pɒpjələs]	Bevölkerung, Volk

Page 156

speech [spiːtʃ]	Rede
dos and don'ts [ˌduːzən'dəʊnts]	was man tun und nicht tun sollte
accomplish (v) [ə'kʌmplɪʃ]	erreichen
convince (v) [kən'vɪns]	überzeugen
motivate (v) ['məʊtɪveɪt]	motivieren, anregen
goal [gəʊl]	Ziel
customize (v) ['kʌstəmaɪz]	anpassen, maßschneidern
line up (v) [ˌlaɪn 'ʌp]	(hier) organisieren
portray (v) [pɔː'treɪ]	porträtieren, darstellen
ramble (v) ['ræmbl]	schwafeln, vom Hundertsten ins Tausendste kommen
rule of thumb [ˌruːləv'θʌm]	Faustregel

Page 157

signpost (v) ['saɪnpəʊst]	(hier) mit Signalwörtern versehen, „ausschildern"
rehearse (v) [rɪ'hɜːs]	proben
be an absolute must (v) [bɪ‿ənˌæbsəluːt‿'mʌst]	unabdingbar sein
mirror ['mɪrə]	Spiegel
body language ['bɒdɪˌlæŋgwɪdʒ]	Körpersprache
equipment [ɪ'kwɪpmənt]	Geräte
posture ['pɒstʃə]	Körperhaltung
gesture ['dʒestʃə]	Geste
volume ['vɒljuːm]	Lautstärke
fidget (v) ['fɪdʒɪt]	herumzappeln
lean (v) [liːn]	lehnen
flashy ['flæʃɪ]	aufdringlich, grell
ornament ['ɔːnəmənt]	Schmuck
allotted [ə'lɒtɪd]	zugeteilt
rapport [ræ'pɔː]	Rapport, Beziehung
pronounceable [prə'naʊnsəbl]	aussprechbar

Page 158

rhetorical question [rɪˌtɒrɪkl'kwəstʃn]	rhetorische Frage
realize (v) ['rɪəlaɪz]	wahrnehmen, implementieren
joke [dʒəʊk]	Witz
talk [tɔːk]	(hier) Rede, Vortrag
challenge ['tʃælɪndʒ]	Herausforderung
outcome ['aʊtkʌm]	Ergebnis
preliminary [prɪ'lɪmɪnərɪ]	vorläufig
in conclusion [ɪn kən'kluːʒn]	zum Schluss, abschließend
attention [ə'tenʃn]	Aufmerksamkeit
framework ['freɪmwɜːk]	Grundgerüst

Page 159

drop [drɒp]	Abnahme
constant ['kɒnstənt]	konstant
slightly ['slaɪtlɪ]	etwas, leicht
hardly ['hɑːdlɪ]	kaum
load [ləʊd]	Belastung, Auslastung
dark blue [ˌdɑːk'bluː]	dunkelblau
light blue [ˌlaɪt‿'bluː]	hellblau
start off (v) [ˌstɑːt 'ɒf]	anfangen
dip [dɪp]	Abfall
stock market index [ˌstɒkmɑːkɪt'ɪndeks]	Aktienindex

Page 160

entrepreneur [ˌɒntrəprə'nɜː]	Unternehmer(in)
embody (v) [ɪm'bɒdɪ]	verkörpern
enterprise ['entəpraɪz]	Unternehmen
attitude ['ætɪtjuːd]	Einstellung
willingness ['wɪlɪŋnəs]	Bereitschaft
uncertainty [ʌn'sɜːtəntɪ]	Ungewissheit, Unsicherheit
self-confidence [ˌself'kɒnfɪdəns]	Selbstbewusstsein
work ethic ['wɜːkˌeθɪk]	Arbeitsethos
root (v) [ruːt]	(hier) anbinden
educator ['edʒʊkeɪtə]	Pädagoge/Pädagogin
profitable ['prɒfɪtəbl]	einträglich
build on the back of (v) [ˌbɪldɒnðə'bækəv]	Folgeprodukt entwickeln
buy into (v) [ˌbaɪ‿'ɪntuː]	sich in eine Firma einkaufen
franchise ['fræntʃaɪz]	Franchise, Lizenz
budding ['bʌdɪŋ]	neu, am Anfang stehend
work out (v) [ˌwɜːk 'aʊt]	ausarbeiten
break down into (v) [ˌbreɪk 'daʊn ˌɪntuː]	aufschlüsseln in
swot analysis ['swɒtəˌnæləsɪs]	Swot-Analyse (Analyse der Stärken und Schwächen)
come up with (v) [ˌkʌm 'ʌp wɪð]	sich etw. einfallen lassen/ausdenken
swap shop ['swɒpˌʃɒp]	Tauschladen, Tauschgeschäft
discounted [dɪ'skaʊntɪd]	reduziert
start-up costs [ˌstɑːtʌp'kɒsts]	Gründungs-, Anlaufkosten
running cost [ˌrʌnɪŋ'kɒst]	laufende Kosten
continued [kən'tɪnjuːd]	kontinuierlich

Page 161

overhead costs [ˌəʊvəhed'kɒsts]	Fixkosten
cashflow ['kæʃˌfləʊ]	Cashflow

receipts [rɪ'si:ts]	Einnahmen, Einkünfte
payments ['peɪmənts]	Ausgaben, Zahlungen
owner ['əʊnə]	Besitzer(in)
funds [fʌndz]	Finanzmittel
savings ['seɪvɪŋz]	Ersparnisse
overdraft ['əʊvədrɑ:ft]	Kontoüberziehung
venture capital [ˌventʃə'kæpɪtl]	Risikokapital
speculator ['spekjəleɪtə]	Spekulant(in)
trade credit ['treɪd,kredɪt]	Handelskredit
ordered ['ɔ:dəd]	bestellt
curriculum [kə'rɪkjələm]	Lehrplan
beyond [bɪ'jɒnd]	darüber hinaus
stage [steɪdʒ]	Stadium

Page 162

pick up (v) [ˌpɪk 'ʌp]	abholen
break off (v) [ˌbreɪk 'ɒf]	abbrechen
discontinue (v) [ˌdɪskən'tɪnju:]	aufhören
wristband ['rɪstbænd]	Armband
donator [dəʊ'neɪtə]	Spender(in)
excuse (v) [ɪk'skju:z]	entschuldigen
pretend [prɪ'tend]	vorgeben
imagine (v) [ɪ'mædʒɪn]	sich vorstellen
on an off chance [ˌɒnən'ɒftʃɑ:ns]	aufs Geratewohl

Unit 10 Jobs in computing

Page 163

job chances ['dʒɒb,tʃɑ:nsɪz]	Aussichten auf eine Stelle, Berufsaussichten
employment [ɪm'plɔɪmənt]	Beschäftigung
U.S. Bureau of Labor Statistics [ˌju:es ˌbju:rəʊ_əv 'leɪbəstəˌtɪstɪks]	Amt für Arbeitsmarktstatistik in den USA
project (v) [prə'dʒekt]	vorhersagen, hochrechnen
output growth rate [ˌaʊtpʊt_'grəʊθ,reɪt]	Produktionszuwachsrate
demand [dɪ'mɑ:nd]	Nachfrage
advance [əd'vɑ:ns]	Fortschritt
outside [ˌaʊt'saɪd]	außerhalb
complementary [ˌkɒmplɪ'mentərɪ]	ergänzend
transferable [træns'fɜ:rəbl]	übertragbar
adaptability [əˌdæptə'bɪlətɪ]	Anwendbarkeit
in its own right [ɪnɪts,əʊn'raɪt]	selber
suffer from (v) ['sʌfə frɒm]	leiden, zu schaffen machen
shortage ['ʃɔ:tɪdʒ]	Mangel

Page 164

job advertisement ['dʒɒb ədˌvɜ:tɪsmənt] ['dʒɒb ædvəˌtaɪzmənt]	Stellenangebot
personal quality [ˌpɜ:sənl'kwɒlɪtɪ]	persönliche Eigenschaft, Soft Skills
professional ability [prəˌfeʃənlə'bɪlətɪ]	berufliche Qualifikation
job duties ['dʒɒb,dju:tɪz]	berufliche Aufgaben
benefits ['benəfɪts]	Leistungen, Zuwendungen
team-oriented ['ti:m,ɔ:rɪentɪd]	teamorientiert
fluent ['flu:ənt]	fließend
sales force ['seɪlz,fɔ:s]	Verkaufsstab, Außendienst
bonus ['bəʊnəs]	Bonus, Gehaltszuschlag, von Vorteil
commensurate [kə'mensjərət]	entsprechend
retail branch ['ri:teɪl,brɑ:ntʃ]	Einzelhandelsfiliale
mainframe computer [ˌmeɪnfreɪmkəm'pju:tə]	Großrechner
in-house training [ˌɪnhaʊs'treɪnɪŋ]	innerbetriebliche Weiterbildung
benefit from (v) ['benəfɪt frɒm]	Vorteil ziehen aus
proficiency [prə'fɪʃənsɪ]	Kenntnisse
certification [ˌsɜ:tɪfɪ'keɪʃn]	Zertifizierung, Bescheinigung
CS degree [ˌsi:'es dɪˌgri:]	Informatikabschluss mit dem "Bachelor's Degree".
self-starter [ˌself'stɑ:tə]	hoch motivierte Person mit viel Eigeninitiative
strong sense of [ˌstrɒŋ'sensəv]	starkes Gespür/Gefühl für etw.
team spirit [ˌti:m'spɪrɪt]	Teamgeist
fascinating ['fæsɪneɪtɪŋ]	faszinierend
wide scope [ˌwaɪd'skəʊp]	großer Spielraum
creative potential [krɪˌeɪtɪvpə'tenʃl]	kreatives Potential
career [kə'rɪə]	Berufs

Page 165

demonstrate (v) ['demənstreɪt]	aufweisen, zeigen
make offers (v) [ˌmeɪk 'ɒfəz]	Angebote machen
follow-up ['fɒləʊʌp]	Anschluss-
solving faults [ˌsɒlvɪŋ 'fɒlts]	Fehlerbehebung
maximising ['mæksɪmaɪzɪŋ]	Maximierung
along with [ə'lɒŋ wɪð]	zusammen mit
enthusiasm [ɪn'θju:zɪæzm]	Begeisterung
courtesy ['kɜ:təsɪ]	Höflichkeit
customer management [ˌkʌstəmə'mænɪdʒmənt]	Kundenmanagement
base salary [ˌbeɪs'sælərɪ]	Grundgehalt
commission [kə'mɪʃn]	Provision
opportunity for advancement [ˌɒpə'tju:nətɪ fər_əd'vɑ:nsmənt]	Aufstiegschance
profit sharing ['prɒfɪt,ʃeərɪŋ]	Gewinnbeteiligung
cover letter ['kʌvə,letə]	Anschreiben, Begleitschreiben
CV= curriculum vitae [ˌsi:'vi:] [kəˌrɪkjələm'vi:taɪ]	Lebenslauf
leading ['li:dɪŋ]	führend
high speed [ˌhaɪ'spi:d]	schnell
oscillator ['ɒsɪleɪtə]	Oszillator, Schwinger
voltage ['vɒltɪdʒ]	Spannung
candidate ['kændɪdət]	Kandidat(in), Bewerber(in)
CMOS = complementary metal oxide semiconductor [ˌsi:eməʊ'es] [ˌkɒmplɪmentrɪ ˌmetl'ɒksaɪd ˌsemɪkən'dʌktə]	komplementärer Metall-Oxid-Halbleiter

BSEE= bachelor of science in electrical engineering [ˌbi:esi:ˈi:] [ˌbætʃələrəvˈsaɪəns ɪn ɪˌlektrɪklˌendʒɪˈnɪərɪŋ]	Bachelor-Abschluss in Elektrotechnik
MSEE= master of science in electrical engineering [ˌemesi:ˈi:] [ˌmɑ:stərəvˈsaɪəns ɪn ɪˌlektrɪklˌendʒɪˈnɪərɪŋ]	MA-Abschluss in Elektrotechnik
PHD=Doctor of Philosophy [ˌpi:eɪtʃˈdi:] [ˌdɒktərəv‿fɪˈlɒsəfɪ]	Doktor/Doktorin der Philosophie
analog circuit design [ˌænəlɒg ˈsɜ:kɪt‿dɪˌzaɪn]	Analogschaltungsaufbau
CAD= Computer Aided Design [ˌsi:eɪˈdi:] [kəmˌpju:tərˌeɪdɪd‿dɪˈzaɪn]	computerunterstütztes Design
CAE= Computer Aided Engineering [ˌsi:eɪˈi:] [kəmˌpju:tərˌeɪdɪd ˌendʒɪˈnɪərɪŋ]	computerunterstützter Maschinenbau
fabulous [ˈfæbjələs]	fabelhaft
maternity/parental leave [məˌtɜ:nətɪ/pəˌrentl‿ˈli:v]	Mutterschutz/Elternzeit

Page 166

undergo (v) [ˌʌndəˈgəʊ]	durchleben
revision [rɪˈvɪʒn]	Änderung
entail (v) [ɪnˈteɪl]	mit sich bringen
expertise [ˌekspɜ:ˈti:z]	Expertise, Fachkenntnis
key account manager [ˌki:‿əˈkaʊnt ˌmænɪdʒə]	Key-Account-Manager(in), Kundenberater(in) für Hauptkunden
front desk manager [ˈfrʌnt‿desk ˌmænɪdʒə]	Empfangsmitarbeiter(in)
customer service [ˌkʌstəməˈsɜ:vɪs]	Kundendienst
pricing [ˈpraɪsɪŋ]	Preisgestaltung, Preiskalkulation
relocation counselor [ˌri:ləʊˈkeɪʃnˌkaʊnsələ]	Berater(in) beim Standortwechsel
office head [ˌɒfɪsˈhed]	Büroleiter(in)
DTP=Desktop Publishing [ˌdi:ti:ˈpi:] [ˌdesktɒp‿ˈpʌblɪʃɪŋ]	Desktop-Publishing
all-rounder [ˌɔ:lˈraʊndə]	Alleskönner(in)
helpdesk [ˈhelpdesk]	Beratung, Beratungsstelle
carrier liaison [ˌkærɪəlɪˈeɪzɒn]	Logistikkoordinator(in)
art director [ˈɑ:t‿daɪˌrektə]	künstlerischer Leiter/ künstlerische Leiterin
admanager [ˈædˌmænɪdʒə]	Werbeleiter(in)

Page 167

technical institute [ˌteknɪkl ˈɪnstɪtju:t]	Fachhochschule
university (polytechnic) [ˌju:nɪˈvɜ:sətɪ] [ˌpɒlɪˈteknɪk]	Fachhochschule
junior high school diploma [ˌdʒu:nɪə ˌhaɪsku:l dɪˈpləʊmə]	Hauptschulabschluss
school leaving certificate [ˌsku:lˈli:vɪŋsəˌtɪfɪkət]	Hauptschulabschluss
junior high school [ˌdʒu:nɪə ˈhaɪˌsku:l]	Hauptschule
secondary modern school [ˌsekəndrɪˈmɒdən ˌsku:l]	Hauptschule
high school diploma, non-academic orientation [ˌhaɪsku:l dɪˈpləʊmə ˌnɒnækəˈdemɪk ɔ:rɪenˌteɪʃn]	mittlere Reife
high school diploma with college entrance qualification [ˌhaɪsku:l dɪˈpləʊmə wɪð ˌkɒlɪdʒˈentrəns kwɒlɪfɪˌkeɪʃn]	Abitur
O (= ordinary)-level [ˈəʊˌlevl]	mittlere Reife
A (= advanced)-level [ˈeɪˌləvl]	Abitur
Bachelor of Arts/Science [ˌbætʃələrəvˈɑ:ts] [ˌbætʃələrəvˈsaɪəns]	BA-Hochschulabschluss
Master of Arts [ˌmɑ:stərəvˈɑ:ts]	MA-Abschluss
MBA (= Master of Business Administration) [ˌemˌbi:ˈeɪ] [ˌmɑ:stərəv ˈbɪznɪs ədmɪnɪˌstreɪʃn]	Aufbaustudium Betriebswirtschaft

Page 168

encourage (v) [ɪnˈkʌrɪdʒ]	ermutigen
mobility [məʊˈbɪlətɪ]	Beweglichkeit
lifelong [ˌlaɪfˈlɒŋ]	lebenslang
transparency [trænˈspærənsɪ]	Transparenz
citizen [ˈsɪtɪzn]	Bürger(in)
occupational [ˌɒkjəˈpeɪʃənl]	beruflich
complete (v) [kəmˈpli:t]	ausfüllen
visible [ˈvɪzəbl]	sichtbar
overview [ˈəʊvəvju:]	Überblick
work experience [ˈwɜ:kɪkˌspɪərɪəns]	Arbeitserfahrung, Praxiserfahrung
training scheme [ˈtreɪnɪŋˌski:m]	Ausbildungssystem
remote connectivity [rɪˌməʊt‿ˌkɒnekˈtɪvətɪ]	Fernverbindung
male [meɪl]	männlich

Page 169

surname [ˈsɜ:neɪm]	Vorname
gender [ˈdʒendə]	Geschlecht
desired employment [dɪˌzaɪəd ɪmˈplɔɪmənt]	gewünschte Anstellung/ Arbeit
occupation [ˌɒkjəˈpeɪʃn]	Beruf
employer [ɪmˈplɔɪə]	Arbeitgeber(in)
mother tongue [ˌmʌðəˈtʌŋ]	Muttersprache
self-assessment [ˌselfəˈsesmənt]	Selbsteinschätzung
hand out (v) [ˌhænd ˈaʊt]	austeilen

Page 170

marital status [ˌmærɪtlˈsteɪtəs]	Familienstand
anonymously [əˈnɒnɪməslɪ]	anonym
post (v) [pəʊst]	ausschreiben
appealing [əˈpi:lɪŋ]	ansprechend

Page 171

colleague ['kɒli:g]	Kollege/Kollegin
unpleasant [ʌn'plezənt]	unangenehm
brainstorm (v) ['breɪnstɔ:m]	ein Brainstorming machen

Page 172

weakness ['wi:knəs]	Schwäche
asset ['æset]	Vorzug, Pluspunkt
extract ['ekstrækt]	Auszug
letter of application [ˌletərəvˌæplɪ'keɪʃn]	Bewerbungsanschreiben
homework ['həʊmwɜ:k]	Hausaufgabe
further training [ˌfɜ:ðə'treɪnɪŋ]	Weiterbildung
round [raʊnd]	Runde

Page 173

fill each other in on (v) [ˌfɪl ˌi:tʃʌðər‿'ɪn ɒn]	sich gegenseitig informieren über
job applicant ['dʒɒbˌæplɪkənt]	Bewerber(in)
intimidate (v) [ɪn'tɪmɪdeɪt]	einschüchtern
simulation [ˌsɪmjə'leɪʃn]	Simulation
essay ['eseɪ]	Aufsatz
invest (v) [ɪn'vest]	investieren

Page 174

relocate (v) [ˌri:ləʊ'keɪt]	umziehen

Page 175

vastly ['vɑ:stlɪ]	gewaltig, erheblich
distinct [dɪ'stɪŋkt]	ausgeprägt
critical ['krɪtɪkl]	sehr wichtig, entscheidend
internship ['ɪntɜ:nʃɪp]	Praktikum
well-educated [ˌwel'edʒʊkeɪtɪd]	gebildet
young professional [ˌjʌŋprə'feʃənl]	Berufseinsteiger(in)
hospitality [ˌhɒspɪ'tæləti]	Gastfreundschaft
stipend ['staɪpend]	Stipendium
State Department ['steɪtdɪˌpɑ:tmənt]	Außenministerium

Page 176

in keeping with [ɪn 'ki:pɪŋ wɪð]	im Einklang mit
crucial ['kru:ʃl]	ausschlaggebend, entscheidend
allowance [ə'laʊəns]	finanzielle Unterstützung
zealous ['zeləs]	eifrig
collocation [ˌkɒləʊ'keɪʃn]	Kollokation

Page 177

ambitious [æm'bɪʃəs]	ehrgeizig
to date [tə'deɪt]	bis jetzt
regardless [rɪ'gɑ:dləs]	ungeachtet
tight deadline [ˌtaɪt'dedlaɪn]	enge Abgabefrist, enger Termin

Alphabetical vocabulary

Die Zahlen hinter den Einträgen geben mit der Seitenzahl die Fundstelle an.

A

3-D graphics 3-D-Bild 28
A (= advanced)-level Abitur 167
a matter of eine Sache/Frage der 118
abbreviation Abkürzung 35
ability Fähigkeit 42
abort abbrechen 142
abound (v) reichlich vorhanden sein 135
above all vor allem 22
abroad im Ausland 117
abstention Enthaltung 152
abstraction Abstraktion 133
abuse Missbrauch 113
acceptable annehmbar 22
access Zugang 9
accidental unbeabsichtigt 53
acclimatise (v) sich akklimatisieren, eingewöhnen 155
accommodate (v) aufnehmen 140
accommodating entgegenkommend, kulant 66
accomplish (v) erreichen 156
according to laut, nach, gemäß 31
account Konto 112
account balance Kontostand 84
account for (v) erklären, begründen 132
accounting program Abrechnungsprogramm 126
accounts Buchhaltung 21
accumulator Akkumulator, Speicher 30
achieve (v) erreichen 49
achievement Leistung 134
acquisition Firmenübernahme 140
acronym Akronym, Abkürzungswort 46
act as (v) fungieren als 93
actually tatsächlich 20
adaptability Anwendbarkeit 163
addition Zusatz, Bereicherung 33
additional zusätzlich 28
adequate ausreichend 55
adjourn (v) vertagen (Sitzung) 152
adjust (v) anpassen 76
admanager Werbeleiter(in) 166
administrate (v) verwalten; Verwaltungs- 8
admittedly zugegebenermaßen 135
adopt (v) übernehmen 11
advance Fortschritt 163
advanced (technology) hochmoderne, fortgeschrittene (Technologie) 33
advancement Fortschritt, Verbesserung 59
advantage Vorteil 11
advantageous vorteilhaft 32
adventure Abenteuer 24
advertise werben, bekannt machen 130
advertisement Inserat, Werbung 22
advisable empfehlenswert 122
advise (v) beraten 56
aerial dish Antennenschüssel 96
aesthetics Ästhetik 133
affect (v) beeinflussen 79
affected betroffen 144
affinity Affinität, Neigung 87
afford (v) sich leisten 122
affordably erschwinglich 133
agenda Tagesordnung 80
agent Handelnde(r) 89
agree (v) einverstanden sein 22
agreed upon vereinbart 120
agreement Vereinbarung 141
aid (v) helfen 100
aim (n) (v) Ziel; zielen 11
air pressure Luftdruck 8
aircraft Flugzeug 110
alert Alarm 126
algorithm Algorithmus, Befehlsfolge zur Lösung eines Problems 64
align (v) angleichen, anpassen 82
alignment Ausrichtung, Anordnung 76
allocation Zuweisung 141
allotted zugeteilt 157
allow (v) erlauben 11
allowance finanzielle Unterstützung 176
all-rounder Alleskönner(in) 166
along with zusammen mit 165
alongside neben 70
alter (v) ändern 100
although obwohl 25
ambitious ehrgeizig 177
amend (v) ergänzen, abändern 152
amendment (Gesetzes)Änderung, Ergänzung 39
amount Menge 8
amplify (v) verstärken 96
analog circuit design Analogschaltungsaufbau 165
analogous analog, vergleichbar mit 144
animation Animation, bewegte Bilder 81
announce (v) bekannt geben 71
annual jährlich 144
anonymously anonym 170
anticipate (v) erwarten 146
antimony Antimon 38
apart auseinander, voneinander entfernt 51
appalled entsetzt 26
appalling entsetzlich 133
appealing ansprechend 170
appear (v) erscheinen 31
appearance Aussehen 74
applet kleine Anwendung 124
application Anwendung 33
application suite Anwendungspaket 73
apply to (v) anwenden auf 29
appoint (v) benennen 152
appointment Termin 14
approach Vorgehensweise, Ansatz 147
appropriate passend, angebracht 22
approximately ungefähr 49
apt treffend, angemessen 107
areal density Flächendichte 53
arm (v) bewaffnen 113
arrange (v) zusammensetzen, arrangieren 35
array Palette, Array 36
arrest Verhaftung 146
arrow Pfeil 69
art director künstlerischer Leiter/ künstlerische Leiterin 166
artifact Artefakt 124
as a whole gesamt 105
as agreed wie vereinbart 22
as detailed wie aufgeführt 137
as long as so lange wie 121
as opposed to im Gegensatz/Vergleich zu 10
as read als bekannt voraussetzen 152
asap = as soon as possible so bald wie möglich 23
aside Nebenbemerkung 26
aside from abgesehen von 12
assembler Assembler (Übersetzungsprogramm für Assembliersprachen) 124
assembly language Assembliersprache 124
assess (v) abschätzen 87
asset Vorzug, Pluspunkt 172
assign (v) zuweisen 104
associate (v) verbinden, vereinigen 121
association Assoziierung, Zuordnung 87
assume (v) annehmen, vermuten 23
assurance Zusicherung 31
at any given moment zu jedem Zeitpunkt 84
at face value für bare Münze 31
at large insgesamt, im Allgemeinen 22
at present zurzeit 39
attach (v) anbringen, anbinden 27
attachment Anhang 101
attend (v) teilnehmen 22
attention Aufmerksamkeit 158
attitude Einstellung 160
attract (v) anziehen 82
attribute Attribut, Eigenschaft 67
auction Versteigerung 103
authentically authentisch, echt 62
authorisation Berechtigung 85
authorities Behörde 89
automate (v) automatisieren 126
availability Vorhandensein 126
available verfügbar 25
average durchschnittlich 34
average seek time durchschnittliche Suchzeit 53
aviation industry Luftfahrtindustrie 111
avoid (v) (ver)meiden 26
award Auszeichnung 55
awareness Bewusstsein 112

B

Bachelor of Arts/Science BA-Hochschulabschluss 167
backbone Basisnetz 104
backdrop Kulisse, Hintergrund 82

background Hintergrund 82
backslash Backslash, umgekehrter Schrägstrich 142
back-up Sicherungs- 50
backup program Sicherungsprogramm 61
backwards rückwärts 43
ban (v) verbieten 39
bankers draft Überweisung 22
bar chart Balkendiagramm 79
bare bones Grundgerüst, Grundausstattung 27
barely kaum 38
barrel Fass 39
barrier Hindernis 11
base salary Grundgehalt 165
basically hauptsächlich, im Großen und Ganzen 10
basics Grundkenntnisse 131
be addictive (v) süchtig machen 115
be an absolute must (v) unabdingbar sein 157
be annoyed (v) verärgert sein 129
be aware of (v) sich bewusst sein 113
be called on (v) aufgefordert sein 136
be committed to (v) hinter etw. stehen, sich dafür einsetzen 113
be composed of (v) zusammengesetzt sein aus, bestehen aus 57
be concerned about (v) besorgt sein um 113
be cut off (v) abgeschnitten sein 12
be entitled (v) berechtigt sein 84
be familar with (v) vertraut sein mit 139
be in a hurry (v) es eilig haben 49
be in charge of (v) verantwortlich sein, leiten 8
be in favo(u)r (v) für etw. sein, dafür sein 154
be of service (v) helfen 20
be on a low budget (v) sparen müssen 46
be prone to (v) anfällig sein für 62
be proud of (v) stolz sein auf 132
be put off (v) sich abschrecken lassen 113
be readily available (v) leicht verfügbar sein 12
be satisfied (v) zufrieden sein 24
be used to (v) gewohnt sein 59
behaviour Verhalten 88
belong to (v) gehören zu 58
benchmark Referenzpunkt 104
benefit Vorteil 113
benefit from (v) Vorteil ziehen aus 164
benefits Leistungen, Zuwendungen 164
benign harmlos 145
beryllium Beryllium 38
beyond jenseits, außerhalb, darüber hinaus 99
bidder Anbieter(in) 103
bill (n) (v) Rechnung; berechnen 25
bit Bit 27
blank space Leerstelle 76
block of instructions Anweisungsblock 121
blog (n) (v) Blog, Internet-Tagebuch (hiermit können Internet-Tagebucheinträge gemacht werden) 70
blogroll Blogroll (persönliche Linkliste zu weiteren Weblogs) 104
blurry verschwommen 110
boast sich rühmen 33
body Gremium, Organ 35
body language Körpersprache 157
bogus falsch 133
bold fett 75
bond (v) verbinden, verkleben 52
bonus Bonus, Gehaltszuschlag, von Vorteil 164
boom Aufschwung 38
boot (v) starten (Computer), laden 63
bootable automatisch ladend 145
booth Stand 22
bootstrap Bootstrap, Ladeprogramm 63
boring langweilig 32
borrow (v) leihen 122
bother to (v) sich die Mühe machen 22
bottom unteres Ende 69
bracelet Armband 19
bracket Klammer 78
brain-damaged gehirngeschädigt 140
brainstorm (v) ein Brainstorming machen 171
branch Zweig 21
break Pause 152
break down into (v) aufschlüsseln in 160
break off (v) abbrechen 162
breakthrough Durchbruch 47
bridge Brücke 28
brief kurz 10
bright hell 33
broad breit 11
broadband Breitband 104
broadcast Rundfunk, Sendung 54
broadly allgemein 132
browse through (v) durchsuchen 86
brute force Brachialgewalt 133
BSEE= bachelor of science in electrical engineering Bachelor-Abschluss in Elektrotechnik 165
budding neu, am Anfang stehend 160
buffer Puffer 29
buggy verwanzt, voller Fehler 133
bug-laden verseucht 26
build on the back of (v) Folgeprodukt entwickeln 160
building society Bausparkasse 122
bullet point Gliederungspunkt 82
bully (v) einschüchtern 112
bundle (v) bündeln 73
burglary Einbruch 112
burn brennen 33
burst data transfer rate Datenübertragungsrate, Burst-Data-Rate 53
business modeling Geschäftsprozess-modellierung 124
busy besetzt 15
button Taste, Knopf 29
buy into (v) sich in eine Firma einkaufen 160
by any chance möglicherweise 20
by heart auswendig 61
bypass (v) überspringen 49

C

CAD= Computer Aided Design computerunterstütztes Design 165
cadmium Kadmium 38
CAE= Computer Aided Engineering computerunterstützter Maschinenbau 165
calculator Rechner 10
call Abruf 121
call (a meeting) (v) (ein Meeting) einberufen 155
call a meeting to order (v) eine Besprechung offiziell eröffnen 152
call for (v) erfordern 87
call point Aufrufstelle 121
campaign Aktion 41
cancel (v) stornieren 142
candidate Kandidat(in), Bewerber(in) 165
capable fähig 62
capacitive kapazitiv 44
capacitor Kondensator 39
capital letter Großbuchstabe 78
capitalize (v) groß schreiben 82
caps =capital letters Großbuchstaben 82
capture (v) erfassen 48
carbon copy Durchschlag, Kopie 49
care (v) sich kümmern 22
career Berufs- 164
careless sorglos 72
carriage Wagen 49
carrier liaison Logistikkoordinator(in) 166
carry out (v) durch-, ausführen 113
case Fall, Gehäuse 25
case study Fallstudie 139
cash machine Geldautomat 8
cashflow Cashflow 161
catch (n) (v) Haken; verstehen, mitbekommen 15
causal kausal, ursächlich 88
cause (n) (v) Sache; verursachen 29
caution Vorsicht(smaßnahme) 82
cellular phone Handy 80
center stage Mittelpunkt 124
century Jahrhundert 71
certain gewisse(r, s) 45
certification Zertifizierung, Bescheinigung 164
chair (v) den Vorsitz haben 153
chairperson Vorsitzende(r) 80
challenge (n) (v) Herausforderung; herausfordern 66
championship Meisterschaft 18
channel Kanal 11
character Zeichen 29
characteristic Eigenschaft 125
characterize (v) charakterisieren, kennzeichnen 94
charcoal Holzkohle 39
charge Kosten 54
chart (v) eintragen 105
chauvinist Chauvinist(in) 117
cheap billig 116
check (v) (nach-/über)prüfen, kontrollieren 13
chief executive officer (CEO) Geschäftsführer(in) 18
choose (v) wählen 38
chromium Chrom 38
churn out (v) (in großen Mengen) ausstoßen, schnell herstellen 48
ciphertext Chiffretext 147
circuit Schaltkreis 10
circular kreisförmig 92
circulation Kreislauf 57
circumlocution Umschreibung 26
circumstances Umstände 88
citizen Bürger(in) 168
claim (v) behaupten 25
clarify (v) klar stellen 80
clean up (v) aufräumen 65
clear-cut eindeutig feststehend, klar 118
clearly eindeutig, offensichtlich 59
client-server Client/Server-System 94
client-side klientbezogen 131
climb Anstieg 80
clip-art ClipArt (für Computerbearbeitung erstellte Bilder, Grafiken) 130

clock rate Taktfrequenz 27
close (v) beenden 154
closure Abschluss 151
clue Hinweis 69
clustering Clustering, Clusterverfahren 87
clutter (n) (v) Unordnung; vollstopfen 26
CMOS= complementary metal oxide semiconductor komplementärer Metall-Oxid-Halbleiter 165
coat (v) auftragen 57
coax Koaxialkabel 95
code Code (in einer Programmiersprache abgefasster Text) 120
coding Programmierung (das Aufsschreiben des Programms in einer Programmiersprache) 120
coexist (v) koexistieren, nebeneinander bestehen 100
coin (v) prägen 104
colleague Kollege/Kollegin 171
collection Sammlung 35
collocation Kollokation 176
colloquial umgangsprachlich 134
colo(u)rful farbenfroh, bunt 65
column Spalte 79
combine (v) kombinieren, verbinden 33
come up with (v) sich ausdenken, sich etw. einfallen lassen 42
command Befehl 41
commensurate entsprechend 164
comment Kommentar, Anmerkung 120
commission (n) (v) Provision; beauftragen 113
commit (v) sich verpflichten 81
commitment Engagement, Hingabe 117
common gemeinsam, weitverbreitet 41
community Gemeinde, Gemeinschafts- 39
comparable vergleichbar 52
comparatively vergleichsweise, relativ 93
comparison Vergleich 30
compete (v) wetteifern 12
competence Kompetenz 116
competition Konkurrenz 55
competitive konkurrenzfähig 54
compile (v) kompilieren 120
complain (v) sich beschweren 20
complementary ergänzend 163
complete (v) ausfüllen, vervollständigen 17
completely völlig 25
compliance Einhaltung 140
complimentary close Schlussformel 24
comprehensive umfangreich 74
compress (v) komprimieren 64
comprise (v) beinhalten, enthalten 134
compromise (v) Kompromisse machen, einen Kompromiss eingehen 33
computer science Informatik 31
computing Rechen-; EDV- 28
conceive (v) anlegen, konzipieren 62
concern (v) betreffen 88
concerning betreffend 32
concerns Bedenken 70
concise kompakt 83
condition Bedingung 121
conditional Bedingungs- 101
conduct (v) durchführen 40
confidently mit Zuversicht 113
confirm (v) bestätigen 24
conform to (v) entsprechen 88
confront (v) konfrontieren 116
confuse with (v) verwechseln mit 59
confusing verwirrend 135
conjunction Verbindungswort, Konjunktion 101
connectivity Verbindungsfähigkeit 92
connector Anschlussstecker 27
consciousness Bewusstsein 114
consensus Konsens 80
consequence Konsequenz, Folge 93
consider (v) bedenken 39
considerable beachtlich 25
consideration Rücksichtnahme 20
considered angesehen 22
consist of (v) bestehen aus 21
consistency Einheitlichkeit 82
consistent beständig 53
constant konstant 159
constantly dauernd 74
construct (v) bauen 124
construction Bau 49
consultant Berater(in) 137
consume (v) aufbrauchen 145
consumer Verbraucher(in) 12
contain (v) beinhalten 27
contemporary zeitgemäß 33
continue (v) weitermachen 35
continued kontinuierlich 160
continuous ununterbrochen 121
contradictory widersprüchlich 126
contribution Beitrag 31
control stick Steuerknüppel 43
controversial umstritten, kontrovers 88
convenient passend 14
conventional herkömmlich 83
conversion Umstellung 140
convert (v) umwandeln 37
convey (v) vermitteln 131
convince (v) überzeugen 156
cookie Cookie, Profildatei (kleine Datei, die den Besuch einer Website anzeigt) 65
coordinate (v) koordinieren, leiten 139
cope with (v) fertig werden mit 140
copper Kupfer 39
cord Kabel 39
cordially herzlich 22
cordless schnurlos 80
core Kern 116
corner Winkel 116
correct (v) korrigieren 120
correspond to (v) entsprechen 37
corrupt (v) verfälschen (Daten) 144
corruption Verfälschung 36
cost-effective günstig, ökonomisch 93
cost-efficiency Kosteneffizienz 140
cottage Ferienhaus 58
count (v) zählen, von Bedeutung sein 22
counter Zähler 122
counteract (v) entgegenwirken 63
countermeasure Gegenmaßnahme 145
counterpart Gegenüber, Kollege/Kollegin 116
countless zahllos 145
country code Ländercode 111
coupled to gekoppelt mit 90
courtesy Höflichkeit 26
cover (v) decken, abdecken 91
cover letter Anschreiben, Begleitschreiben 165
coverage Anwendungsbereich 131
crack down on (v) hart durchgreifen bei 146
crawl (v); crawling crawlen; Crawling (Internet-Suchmethode) 108
creative potential kreatives Potential 164
crime Verbrechen 112
criminal Verbrecher(in) 112
critical sehr wichtig, entscheidend 175
cross reference Querverweis 75
cross your fingers drück die Daumen 149
crowded überfüllt 140
crucial ausschlaggebend, entscheidend 176
crude grob 52
cryptography Kryptographie, Verschlüsselung 147
CS (Computer science) degree Bachelor-Abschluss in Informatik 164
cubicle Arbeitsplatz im Großraumbüro, Arbeitsnische 140
cultural context kultureller Zusammenhang 116
current aktuell 10
curriculum Lehrplan 161
cursor Cursor, Positionsanzeiger 43
cushion Kissen 57
custom Gewohnheit, Geschäft; kundenspezifisch, maßgeschneidert 11
customer Kunde/Kundin 8
customer management Kundenmanagement 165
customer service Kundendienst 166
customize (v) anpassen, maßschneidern 156
cut and paste (v) ausschneiden und einfügen 74
cut back on (v) einschränken 149
cutting edge innovativ 33
CV= curriculum vitae Lebenslauf 165
cycle Zyklus, Durchgang 121

D

daily täglich 8
damage Schaden 57
dangerous gefährlich 145
dark blue dunkelblau 159
data Daten 8
data loss Datenverlust 53
database Datenbank 8
day trading Day Trading, Tagesspekulationsgeschäft 31
day-to-day täglich 136
dazzling strahlend, umwerfend 47
de rigeur (French) obligat 117
dead-end Sackgasse, nicht weiterführend 126
deadline Frist, Fertigstellungstermin 26
deafening betäubend 26
dealings Geschäfte 25
debate Debatte, Wortstreit 88
debt Schulden 122
debugging Fehlersuche und -behebung 120
decent anständig, ordentlich 48
decide (v) entscheiden 8
decision Entscheidung 80
declare (v) vereinbaren, deklarieren 84
decrease (v) abnehmen, fallen 87
decryption Entschlüsselung 147
dedicate (v) widmen, vormerken 67
deductive deduktiv, folgernd 87
default (column) Voreinstellung, („Sonstfall-Spalte") 121
default document properties Standardeinstellungen für das Dokument 54
defenseless schutzlos 114
degradation Verschlechterung 148
degree Grad 116
delayed verzögert 79

delete (v) löschen, entfernen 45
delivery Lieferung 22
demand Anforderung, Nachfrage 28
demonstrate (v) aufweisen, zeigen 165
density Dichte 50
deny (v) verweigern, versagen, verleugnen 33
depart (v) abfliegen 88
department Abteilung 21
Department of Defense Verteidigungsministerium (USA) 104
depend (v) darauf ankommen 13
dependable zuverlässig 32
dependent abhängig 88
depending on abhängig von 121
depict (v) darstellen 36
deplorable bedauernswert 25
depth Tiefe 52
derive from (v) ableiten von 124
descending absteigend 86
description Beschreibung 24
designed konzipiert 28
desire Wunsch 116
desired employment gewünschte Anstellung/Arbeit 169
despite trotz 35
destination Endziel 95
destructive zerstörerisch 146
detect (v) aufspüren 57
detection Erkennung 52
determine (v) festlegen 37
deterred abgeschreckt 113
develop (v) entwickeln 12
device Gerät 10
dial (v) wählen 25
dial-up access Verbindungsaufbau durch Einwahl (über das Telefonnetz) 104
diary Terminkalender 14
dichotomy Zwiespalt 133
dictionary Wörterbuch 74
differ from (v) sich unterscheiden von 125
difficulty Schwierigkeit 59
digit Zahl, Ziffer 36
digitized digitalisiert 44
dip Abfall, Abnahme 80
directions Wegbeschreibung 90
directory Verzeichnis 67
disadvantage Nachteil 36
disconnect (v) unterbrechen 25
discontinue (v) aufhören 162
discount Nachlass 22
discounted reduziert 160
discovery Entdeckung 87
disguise (v) tarnen 146
disjointed unzusammenhängend 64
dismantle (v) deinstallieren 146
dispense with (v) verzichten auf 49
display (v) zeigen 37
disposal Entsorgung 39
dissatisfactory unzufriedenstellend 22
dissatisfied unzufrieden 129
distant entfernt 111
distinct ausgeprägt 175
distinguish (v) unterscheiden 49
distortion Verkrümmung, Verformung 51
distribute (v) verteilen 50
divide (v) aufteilen 80
document (v) dokumentieren, belegen 87
documentation Dokumentation 120
domain Domäne 104
donator Spender(in) 162
donor Spender(in) 39

dos and don'ts was man tun und nicht tun sollte 156
dot Punkt 37
dot your i's (v) penibel sein 126
dot-matrix (printer) Nadeldrucker 48
double (v) sich verdoppeln 112
download (v) herunterladen 66
downright ausgesprochen 25
downside Nachteil 63
downsize verringern 149
downtime Ausfallzeit 145
drag on (v) in die Länge ziehen 154
drawback Nachteil 49
drawing Zeichnung 8
driver Treiber 48
driving force Antriebskraft 31
drop (n) (v) Abnahme; fallen lassen 40
drop a line (v) kurz schreiben 23
droplet Tröpfchen 49
DTP=Desktop Publishing Desktop-Publishing 166
due to aufgrund, wegen 25
dumb down (v) vereinfachen 132
dump (n) (v) Hauptspeicherauszug, Müllhalde; wegwerfen 38
duplexing beidseitig 47
duplicate Doppel-, doppelte(r, s) 65
dust Staub 57
duty Aufgabe 21
dyadic dyadisch 121
dynamic dynamisch, beweglich 48

E

eager eifrig 129
earn (v) verdienen 39
earnings Einnahmen 79
ease Leichtigkeit 44
echo (v) sich wiederholen 33
eclipse (v) etw. in den Schatten stellen, in den Hintergrund drängen 112
ecology-minded umweltbewusst 38
edge Rand, Überlegenheit 12
edit (v) editieren, bearbeiten 33
educate (v) ausbilden 133
educational Lern-, Bildungs- 73
educator Pädagoge/Pädagogin 160
effect Wirkung 12
effort Bemühung 141
effortless mühelos 33
elaborate (v) näher ausführen, ausarbeiten 83
eliminate (v) beseitigen, entfernen 64
embed (v) einbetten 52
embody (v) verkörpern 160
emerge (v) herauskommen, aufkommen 104
emergence Aufkommen 104
emergency Notfall 101
emit (v) ausstoßen, senden 39
emphasis Betonung 118
emphasize (v) betonen 59
employ (v) beschäftigen, verwenden 21
employer Arbeitgeber(in) 169
employment Beschäftigung 163
empower (v) ermächtigen 11
emulation Emulation, Nachahmung 47
enable (v) ermöglichen 36
enclose (v) beifügen, beilegen 22
encode (v) kodieren 130
encoding Kodierung 36
encompass (v) umfassen 12
encourage (v) ermutigen 168

encryption Ent-/Verschlüsselung 64
engage in (v) teilnehmen an, sich an etw. beteiligen, betreiben 103
engine Motor 100
engineering technisch 124
enhanced verbessert 33
enjoy (v) genießen 67
enlarge (v) vergrößern, erweitern 69
enquire (v) anfragen 13
ensure (v) sicherstellen 30
entail (v) beinhalten, mit sich bringen 87
entangle (v) verwickeln 109
enter the scene (v) Einzug halten 124
enterprise Unternehmen 160
enthusiasm Begeisterung 165
entire ganz 39
entrepreneur Unternehmer(in) 160
envelope Briefumschlag 47
environmental ökologisch, umweltpolitisch 12
equal (v) ergeben (Mathematik); gleich 36
equally genauso 25
equation Gleichung 107
equipment Geräte 157
equipped with ausgestattet mit 38
equivalent Entsprechung 19
erasable löschbar 63
ergonomically ergonomisch 43
ergonomics Ergonomie, körpergerechte Gestaltung 49
error Fehler 25
error message Fehlermeldung 142
especially insbesondere 28
essay Aufsatz 173
essential notwendig, erforderlich 22
establish (v) einführen, etablieren 12
established etabliert 98
estimate (v) (ein)schätzen 39
evenly gleichmäßig 74
eventually schließlich, endlich 55
ever increasing ständig steigend 29
everyday speech Alltagssprache 40
evolve (v) entwickeln 99
e-waste Elektroschrott 38
examination Untersuchung 43
examine (v) untersuchen 29
example Beispiel 37
exasperating ärgerlich 66
exceed (v) übersteigen 79
exception Ausnahme 58
exchange (v) austauschen 91
exciting aufregend 32
exclude (v) ausschließen, entfernen 108
excuse (v) entschuldigen 162
executable ausführbar 28
execute (v) durchführen 8
execution Ausführung 29
executive Topmanager(in), Führungskraft 55
exhibit (v) zeigen, darstellen 80
exit (condition) Ausgang, Abbruch(bedingung) 121
expand (v) erweitern 42
expandable erweiterbar 47
expansion Erweiterung 49
expenditures Ausgaben 79
expenses Ausgaben, Auslagen 78
expensive teuer 32
experience Erfahrung 33
expertise Expertise, Fachkenntnis 166
explain (v) erklären 11
explanation Erklärung 59

exploit (v) ausbeuten 114
expose (v) bloßlegen, freilegen, aussetzen 39
express (v) ausdrücken 58
extend to (v) sich erstrecken bis 33
extended erweitert 104
extension Durchwahl 25
extensive weitreichend, beträchtlich 71
extract (n) (v) Auszug; gewinnen, entnehmen, extrahieren, herausnehmen 39

F

fabulous fabelhaft 165
facilitate (v) ermöglichen, erleichtern 100
fade (v) schwächer werden 55
fail (v) fehlschlagen 142
failure Ausfall 64
fair Messe 109
fairly ziemlich, einigermaßen 106
fall Herbst 80
fall for (v) es jmdm. angetan haben 55
false branch Nein-Zweig 121
fancy ausgefallen 133
fascinating faszinierend 164
faulty fehlerhaft 26
favo(u)rite Lieblings-, bevorzugt 65
fear Angst 113
feasible durchführbar 147
feature Funktion, Eigenschaft 33
fee Gebühren, Honorar 78
feed (v) füttern, zuführen 10
feed in (v) eingeben 77
feedback Feedback, Rückmeldung 120
feeder Dokumentenzuführung 47
ferrous eisenhaltig 38
fibre-optic faseroptisch 96
fidget (v) herumzappeln 157
fierce leidenschaftlich, heftig 117
figure on (v) damit rechnen 23
figures Zahlen 80
file Datei 10
file replication Dateikopie 137
file search Dateisuche 61
fill (position) (v) besetzen 20
fill each other in on (v) sich gegenseitig informieren über 173
final (step) letzter (Schritt) 10
final draft endgültiger Entwurf 139
finally schließlich 29
findings Ergebnisse 39
fire (v) feuern 118
firewall Firewall (Zugangsschutzsystem) 148
first and foremost zuallererst 133
first line of defense erste Verteidigungslinie/ Art der Verteidigung 148
fit in (v) einen Termin geben 14
flagship Flaggschiff, Hauptprodukt 70
flame up (v) aufflammen 144
flame-retardant Flammschutzmittel 38
flash memory Flash-Speicher 145
flashy aufdringlich, grell 157
flat flach 52
flexi-time Gleitzeit 58
flight Flug 8
flip down runterklappen 41
flow Fluss 12
flowchart PAP (Programmablaufplan oder Datenflussplan) 120
flowery blumig 26
fluctuation Schwankung 79
fluent fließend 164
flush bündig 74
flyer Flyer 46
focal point Fokus 82
folder Ordner 69
follow-up Nachfolger, Anschluss- 62
font Schriftart 75
foolish dumm 115
foot controlled fußgesteuert 121
footer Fußzeile 75
footnote Fußnote 75
footprint Empfangsbereich 99
for the sake of um einer Sache willen 82
force (n) (v) Kraft, Macht; zwingen 12
forecast (v) vorhersagen 8
foreign language Fremdsprache 117
formatting Formatierung 48
former erstere(r, s), ehemalig 80
formula Formel 79
formulation Formulierung, Abfassung 87
fortune Vermögen 48
forward (v) weiterleiten 25
foundation Basis 70
founder Gründer(in) 104
framework Grundgerüst 158
franchise Franchise, Lizenz 160
fraud Betrug 87
freelance freiberuflich 13
frequently oft, häufig 10
frighten (v) erschrecken 117
from scratch von Grund auf 138
front desk manager Empfangsmitarbeiter(in) 166
front side Vorderseite 33
fulfill (v) erfüllen 41
full-featured voll ausgestattet 74
full-scale umfassend, in Originalgröße 34
fundamental elementar 132
funding Finanzierung 140
funds Finanzmittel 161
funky flippig 33
further weiter 63
further training Weiterbildung 172
furthermore außerdem, ferner 84
futile nutzlos 25

G

gadget Gerät, technische Spielerei 133
gain (v) zunehmen 118
gaming device Spielegerät 43
GAN = global area network globales Netz 91
gap Kluft 35
gate Gate, Gatter 30
gateway Gateway, Schnittstelle 93
gather (v) sammeln 108
gender Geschlecht 169
generality Allgemeingültigkeit 133
generate (v) erzeugen 44
generic allgemein 71
gesture Geste 157
get back to (v) zurückmelden 19
get discouraged sich entmutigen lassen 149
get the hang of sth. den Dreh bei etw. heraushaben 77
get together (v) treffen, zusammenkommen 14
giant Riese 104
gist das Wesentliche 8
give away (v) verschenken 149
give back (v) zurückgeben 149
give in (v) nachgeben 149
give out (v) verteilen, ausfallen 149
give up (v) aufgeben 149
glib unbedacht 133
glossary Glossar, Worterklärungsliste 49
glyph Bildzeichen 36
go around in circles (v) sich im Kreis drehen 152
go wrong (v) schief gehen 84
goal Ziel 156
goods Waren 8
govern (v) steuern 61
government agency Behörde 113
GPS weltumspannendes Ortungssystem, Navigationssystem 10
gradually allmählich 29
graduate (v) Abschluss machen 101
grain Korn 57
grant (v) gewähren 94
grasp at straws (v) nach einem Strohhalm greifen 133
grid Gitternetz 79
groceries Lebensmittel 113
growth Zuwachs 87
growth rate Wachstumsrate 144
guarantee (n) (v) Garantie; garantieren 49
guest Gast 137
guide Führer 33
guideline Richtlinie 26
gullible leichtgläubig 146

H

habit Gewohnheit 8
hacker Hacker(in) 104
hand out (v) austeilen 169
handheld tragbar 43
handicapped behindert 44
handle (v) handhaben, umgehen mit 8
handshaking Austausch von Steuerungsinformation 141
hands-on praktisch 131
handy praktisch, handlich 32
happen (v) passieren 29
hard disk Festplatte 10
hardly kaum 159
hassle-free problemlos 47
hazardous gefährlich 39
head (hier) Leiter 8
head controlled kopfgesteuert 121
headache (hier) Problem 144
header Kopf, Kopfzeile 23
heading Kopfzeile, Überschrift 26
headquarters Hauptsitz 21
health Gesundheit 65
health regulations Gesundheitsvorschriften 140
heavy metal Schwermetall 39
heavy-duty Hochleistungs- 52
helpdesk Beratung, Beratungsstelle 166
hidden versteckt 64
high frequency Hochfrequenz 99
high ranking hochgestellt 26
high school diploma with college entrance qualification Abitur 167
high school diploma, non-academic orientation mittlere Reife 167
high speed schnell 165
high volume große Anzahl 46
high-end hochwertig, Spitzen- 33
high-impact wirkungsvoll 131
high-level language höhere Programmiersprache 124
highlight (v) hervorheben 74
high-performance Hochleistungs- 33

hint (n) (v) Hinweis; hinweisen, andeuten 26
hire (v) anstellen, einstellen 138
hit (n) (v) Treffer; erreichen 106
hit and miss auf gut Glück 115
hoax blinder Alarm, „Ente" 112
hold (v) halten 28
hold a meeting (v) ein Meeting/eine Besprechung abhalten 155
hold the line (v) am Apparat bleiben 14
hold the record (v) den Rekord halten 146
hole Loch 145
home appliance Haushaltsgerät 10
homework Hausaufgabe 172
hop Sprung von einem Knotenrechner zum nächsten 141
hospitality Gastfreundschaft 175
host (n) (v) Menge, Unzahl, Host; veranstalten 71
host computer Hauptrechner, Hostcomputer 42
hot plug Einbau bei laufendem Betrieb 63
hub Wickelkern, Mittelpunkt 51
huge sehr groß 34
human Mensch 145
human resources Personalwesen 21
hunt down (v) Jagd machen auf 63
hybrid hybrid 123
hyphenation Silbentrennung 74

I

icon kleines Bild, Piktogramm 120
idiom Idiom, Redewendung 149
ignore (v) nicht beachten 25
illogical nicht logisch 127
illustration Abbildung 44
image Bild 10
imagine (v) sich vorstellen 162
immediate sofortig 22
immigration Einwanderung 88
impact Wirkung 11
impart verleihen, geben 12
implement (v) einführen 39
imply (v) andeuten, implizieren 29
import Wichtigkeit, Bedeutung 117
impose (v) auferlegen 148
impossible unmöglich 12
impression Eindruck 82
impressive eindrucksvoll 33
improperly unsachgemäß 63
improve (v) verbessern 51
in advance im Voraus 26
in case falls 101
in concert zusammen 148
in conclusion zum Schluss, abschließend 158
in contrast to im Gegensatz zu 145
in its own right selber 163
in keeping with im Einklang mit 176
in no time im Nu, im Handumdrehen 131
in operation in Betrieb 45
in order in Ordnung 63
in order to um (zu) 42
in other words anders gesagt 144
in points of betreffend 127
in reference to Bezug nehmend auf 24
in stock auf Lager 25
in the course im Laufe 116
in the making in Bearbeitung 70
in the middle of the act mittendrin 82
in the wake of im Gefolge von 88
incentive Anreiz 11
include (v) beinhalten 11
income Einkommen 88
incoming eingehende(r, s) 97
incompatible inkompatibel, unvereinbar 36
inconvenience (v) Umstände machen 15
incorporate (v) einbauen, berücksichtigen 124
incorporated (company) eingetragene Aktiengesellschaft 17
incorrectly falsch 142
increase (n) (v) Anstieg; anheben 31
increasingly zunehmend 98
incur (v) sich etw. zuziehen, etw. haben 84
indentation Einrückung, Einzug 75
independent selbstständig 44
index (n) (v) Inhalts-/Stichwortverzeichnis; indexieren, katalogisieren 49
index finger Zeigefinger 43
indicate (v) andeuten 40
indicator Hinweis 48
indispensable unverzichtbar 10
inevitability Unabwendbarkeit 117
inexpensive preisgünstig 50
infamous berüchtigt 146
infect (v) infizieren, anstecken 144
infection Ansteckung 144
infinitesimal unendlich klein 34
influence (v) beeinflussen 116
infrared infrarot 51
inhibit (v) hindern, hemmen 114
in-house training innerbetriebliche Weiterbildung 164
initial anfänglich 63
initiate (v) einleiten 29
initiation Initiierung 151
ink Tinte 47
ink powder Tintenpulver 49
ink-jet Tintenstrahl- 48
input (n) (v) Eingabe; eingeben 10
insecure unsicher 95
insert (v) einfügen 45
insertion point Einfügestrich 76
insist on (v) bestehen auf 59
inspect (v) untersuchen 63
instalment Rate 122
instant Moment 51
instead stattdessen 15
instruct (v) anweisen 45
instruction Anweisung 10
instruction decoder Befehlsdecoder 30
insufficient unzureichend 70
insurance Versicherung 87
intangible nicht greifbar 10
integral wesentlich 140
intend (v) vorhaben 72
intended beabsichtigt 39
intent Absicht 114
intercept (v) auffangen, abfangen 148
interchangeably austauschbar 92
interconnected untereinander verbunden 91
interdependency gegenseitige Abhängigkeit, Wechselwirkung 116
interest Zins 78
interest rate Zinssatz 122
interface (n) (v) Schnittstelle; verbinden 10
interfere (v) stören 100
interference Beeinträchtigung, Behinderung, Empfangsstörung 85
interim vorläufig 30
intermediate Zwischen- 34
internship Praktikum 175
interoperability Interoperabilität 88
interplay Zusammenspiel 63
interpret (v) auslegen, interpretieren, deuten, auswerten 29
interrupt (n) (v) Unterbrechung; unterbrechen 27
intersection Schnittpunkt 79
interval Abstand, Interval 64
intervention Eingreifen 109
intimidate (v) einschüchtern 173
intransitive intransitiv 118
introduce (v) einführen 124
introduction Einführung, Vorstellung 11
intruder Eindringling 148
intrusion Eindringen 104
invalid ungültig 142
invent (v) erfinden 38
invest (v) investieren 173
investigation Untersuchung 152
invitation Einladung 22
invoice Rechnung 22
involve (v) mit sich bringen 38
involve (v) in mit etw. zu tun haben 10
is supposed to soll 86
issue (n) (v) Ausgabe, Punkt; erteilen 41
italics kursiv 75
iteration Iteration, Wiederholung 121

J

jam (v) verstopfen 145
job advertisement Stellenangebot 164
job applicant Bewerber(in) 173
job chances Aussichten auf eine Stelle, Berufsaussichten 163
job duties berufliche Aufgaben 164
join (v) sich jmdm./etw. anschließen 71
joint venture Joint Venture, Beteiligungsunternehmen 101
joke Witz 158
jot down (v) kurz notieren 147
journal Tagebuch, Journal 103
jumbled durcheinander 93
jump to a conclusion (v) voreilig einen Schluss ziehen 116
jumper Jumper, Steckbrücke 27
junction Kreuzung, Knotenpunkt 91
junior high school Hauptschule 167
junior high school diploma Hauptschulabschluss 167
junk Müll 103
just about any kind fast jede Art 54
just as genauso 54
just plain nur einfach 116
justification Blocksatz 74

K

keep (sth) running (v) etwas am Laufen halten 61
keep free of (v) freihalten von 57
keep in mind (v) beachten 48
keep in touch (v) in Kontakt bleiben 31
keep on top (v) sich auf dem Laufenden halten 123
kernel Kernel, „Kern" 141
key entscheidend 31
key account manager Key-Account-Manager(in), Kundenberater(in) für Hauptkunden 166
keyboard Tastatur 10
keystroke Anschlag einer Taste, Tastendruck 75
keyword Schlüsselwort 109
kick in (v) aktiviert werden 74

knock off (v) abziehen 23
know-how Kenntnisse 136
knowledge Kenntnisse 113

L

labelling Etikettierung 33
lack Mangel 35
LAN = local area network lokales Netz 91
landfill Deponie, Geländeauffüllung 39
landmark einen Meilenstein bedeutend, historisch 146
language Sprache 36
lap Schoß 55
latch onto (v) sich einklinken in 145
latest neueste(r, s) 22
latter letztere(r, s) 80
launch (v) starten 41
layering technology Schichttechnologie 47
layout Layout, Design, Anordnung 75
lead Blei 38
lead (v) führen 82
leader Führer(in) 31
leading führend 165
leading edge Spitzen- 33
lean (v) lehnen 157
leave off (v) aufhören 30
legacy Vorläufer, Alt- 36
legible leserlich 83
lend (v) leihen 20
lens Linse 51
lethal tödlich 145
letter Buchstabe 36
letter of application Bewerbungsanschreiben 172
level Ebene 63
level of education Bildungsgrad 88
libraries Sammlungen 133
library Bibliothek 107
license (v) lizenzieren, berechtigen 66
lifelong lebenslang 168
lifespan Lebensdauer 38
light blue hellblau 159
light wave Lichtwelle 44
like-minded gleichgesinnt 103
limb Glied 44
limit (v) begrenzen 12
limitation Grenze 88
line Produktpalette 55
line graph Kurvendiagramm 79
line up (v) (hier) organisieren 156
line-spacing Zeilenabstand 76
lingua franca Verkehrssprache 116
linguistic sprachlich 117
link (n) (v) Verbindung; verbinden 10
listing on the stock market Börsennotierung 107
live-in stationär 140
livelihood Lebensunterhalt 39
load (n) (v) Belastung, Auslastung; laden 63
loading mechanism Lademechanismus 53
loan Darlehen, Kredit 122
local paper Lokalzeitung 107
lock (v) sperren 69
log (v) anmelden 63
log out (v) abmelden 69
logistics Logistik 155
long haul langfristig 134
long-awaited lang erwartet 70
long-term langfristig 113
look forward (v) sich freuen auf 13
looks Aussehen 51
loop Schleife 92
lose out (v) schlecht wegkommen 12
lose out on (v) den Kürzeren ziehen bei 113
losing battle verlorener Kampf 117
lounge (v) entspannen, es sich bequem machen 55
low-end einfach 81
low-energy energiearm 99
lowest niedrigste(r, s) 137
low-level language maschinenorientierte Programmiersprache 124
luckily glücklicherweise 140
lucrative einträglich 145

M

machine code Maschinencode, Binärcode 124
macros Makros 75
maddening ärgerlich, unerträglich 32
magazine article Zeitschriftenartikel 44
magnetize (v) magnetisieren 57
mail client Mail-Client (Programm zur Inanspruchnahme von E-Mail-Diensten) 68
mail merging Serienbrieferstellung 90
main memory Hauptspeicher 29
mainframe computer Großrechner 164
mainly hauptsächlich 9
mainstream etabliert 55
maintainability Wartungsfreundlichkeit 133
maintenance Wartung 48
major größere(r, s) 64
majority Mehrheit 113
make a jump (v) überspringen 69
make a typo (v) sich verschreiben 74
make offers (v) Angebote machen 165
make or break (v) entscheidend sein (für) 61
make sure (v) sicherstellen 80
make up (v) bilden, erfinden 10
male männlich 168
malicious bösartig 146
malignant bösartig 145
mammal Säugetier 43
manage (v) einrichten, etw. schaffen 14
manipulate (v) (Daten) bearbeiten, manipulieren, beeinflussen 10
manner Art und Weise 71
manpower Arbeitskraft, Personal 145
manual Handbuch 66
manually mit der Hand 67
map Karte, Stadtplan 89
margin Rand 74
marital status Familienstand 170
mark (v) markieren 113
market share Marktanteil 80
mass storage device Massenspeicher 28
Master of Arts MA-Abschluss 167
maternity/parental leave Mutterschutz/Elternzeit 165
matter (n) (v) Angelegenheit, Frage; von Bedeutung sein 63
matter in hand vorliegende Angelegenheit 154
maximising Maximierung 165
MBA (= Master of Business Administration) Aufbaustudium Betriebswirtschaft 167
mean (n) (v) Mittelwert; durchschnittlich; meinen, bedeuten 10
meaning Bedeutung 120
means Mittel 88
meantime Zwischenzeit 118
measure (v) messen 35
measurement Messung 35
media coverage Medienberichterstattung 146
media sensation Medienaufsehen 145
mediate (v) vermitteln 110
mediation Vermittlung 110
mediator Vermittler(in) 28
medium Medium 117
meet (v) erfüllen 133
melt down (v) schmelzen 39
member Mitglied 32
memory Speicher 10
memory address Speicheradresse 120
memory content Speicherinhalt 141
memory parity error Paritätsfehler im RAM 142
mention (v) erwähnen 54
merchandise Güter, Waren 89
mercury Quecksilber 38
merge (v) zusammenfügen, mischen 75
merger Fusion 90
mesh topology Maschentopologie 93
mess Durcheinander 132
message Nachricht 14
middle-sized mittelgroß, von mittlerer Größe 34
mind-boggling verblüffend 144
minimize (v) minimieren, verkleinern 69
minor klein 89
minor miracle kleines Wunder 133
minority Minderheit 115
minute winzig 34
minutes (of a meeting) Protokoll 152
mirror (n) (v) Spiegel; spiegeln 85
misc./miscellaneous Diverses, Verschiedenes 78
misleading irreführend 118
miss (v) verpassen 101
missing fehlend 126
mission creep schleichende Ausweitung eines Auftrags 88
misspell (v) falsch buchstabieren 75
mistake Fehler 26
mitigate (v) entschärfen, mildern 151
mixed vermischt 54
mnemonic mnemotechnisch, mnemonisch, das Gedächtnis stützend 124
mobility Beweglichkeit 168
modification Änderung 66
modify (v) ändern 57
monadic monadisch, „einwegig" 121
monitor (n) (v) Bildschirm; steuern 8
monochrome einfarbig 37
monopolize (v) an sich reißen, alleine bestreiten 154
more or less mehr oder weniger 138
mortgage Hypothek 78
mother tongue Muttersprache 169
motion Bewegung, Antrag 44
motivate (v) motivieren, anregen 156
motor-impaired motorisch beeinträchtigt 44
mount (v) anbringen, installieren 42
mouth (v) nachplappern, deutlich artikulieren 20
move (v) bewegen, vorschlagen 43
move on (v) weitergehen 154
movement Bewegung 11
moving parts bewegliche Teile 53
MSEE= master of science in electrical engineering MA-Abschluss in Elektrotechnik 165
mugging Raubüberfall 112
multiple Mehrfach- 35

multi-purpose Mehrzweck- 43
multi-segmented buffer mehrfach segmentierter Puffer 53
multi-tiered mehrstufig 36
my pleasure gern geschehen 77
myth building Mythenbildung 145

N

nasty unangenehm, böse 145
nationwide landesweit 113
native heimisch, (hier) muttersprachlich 116
native speaker Muttersprachler(in) 117
navigation system Steuerungssystem 106
near future nahe Zukunft 139
neat ordentlich 74
necessarily zwingend 121
need Bedürfnis 33
neural network neuronales Netz 87
next to nothing fast, nichts 81
no doubt ohne Zweifel 115
no way keineswegs 20
node Knoten 91
noise Lärm 49
noise floor Störpegel 99
nonprofit gemeinnützig 12
nonrecyclable nicht wiederverwertbar 38
not advised nicht zu empfehlen 82
notation Bezeichnung 35
note (n) (v) Merkzettel; beachten 24
notify (v) benachrichtigen 65
notwithstanding trotz, ungeachtet 117
number of Anzahl von, mehrere 54
numbering Nummerierung 75
numerous zahlreich 57
nurse's aid Hilfskrankenpfleger(in) 140

O

O (= ordinary)-level mittlere Reife 167
object oriented objektorientiert 124
object program ausführbares Programm, lauffähiges Maschinenprogramm 124
observe (v) beachten 146
obsolete überholt, obsolet 38
obvious(ly) offensichtlich 48
occasion Gelegenheit 25
occasionally gelegentlich 40
occupation Beruf 169
occupational beruflich 168
occupational therapist Beschäftigungstherapeut(in), Ergotherapeut(in) 140
occur (v) stattfinden 11
occur to (v) einfallen 83
of late in der letzten Zeit 22
offer (v) anbieten 8
office head Büroleiter(in) 166
offshoot Ableger 62
old-fashioned altmodisch 32
on an off chance aufs Geratewohl 162
on condition unter der Auflage, unter der Bedingung 101
on the loose frei im Umlauf 145
on the rise im Zunehmen 144
once sobald 67
ongoing anhaltend 118
opening salutation Grußformel 24
open-mindedness Aufgeschlossenheit 116
operate as (v) fungieren als 49
operating system Betriebssystem 10
operation Arbeit 29
operator Betreiber(in) 106
opinion Meinung 10
opportunity Chance 12
opportunity for advancement Aufstiegschance 165
opposite Gegenteil 32
opposite number Gegenspieler(in) 139
optical pickup optischer Lesekopf 51
oral report mündlicher Bericht 131
order (n) (v) Reihenfolge; bestellen 8
order of magnitude Zehnerpotenz 99
ordered bestellt 161
ordinary gewöhnlich, normal, üblich 96
originally ursprünglich 35
originate (v) entstehen 95
ornament Schmuck 157
oscillator Oszillator, Schwinger 165
otherwise ansonsten 113
out for lunch zum Mittagessen gegangen 135
out of order außer Betrieb, hier: nicht an der Reihe 152
outcome Ergebnis 158
outer äußere 128
outfitted with ausgestattet mit 43
outing Ausflug 151
outlet Anschlussdose 95
outline (n) (v) Abriss; entwerfen, skizzieren, kurz darstellen 23
output (v) (n) ausgeben; Ausgabe 10
output growth rate Produktionszuwachsrate 163
outside außerhalb 163
outstanding herausragend 84
outweigh (v) überwiegen 115
over time im Zeitablauf 80
overcharge (v) zu viel berechnen 25
overdraft Kontoüberziehung 161
overhead costs Fixkosten 161
overlap (v) überschneiden 11
overload Überlastung 115
overlook (v) übersehen, vergessen 48
overriding vorrangig, übergeordnet 88
oversee (v) überblicken 10
oversized überdimensional 47
overtime Überstunden 21
overview Überblick 168
overwhelming überwältigend 12
overworked überarbeitet 140
own right eigenständig 62
owner Besitzer(in) 161
ownership Besitz 40

P

pace Tempo 11
packaging Verpackung 24
packed with vollgepackt mit 131
packet Datenpaket 95
paid bezahlt 104
palladium Palladium 38
panelling Holzverkleidung 140
paperback Taschenbuch 107
paragraph Absatz 26
parameter Parameter, Bestimmungsgröße 87
parenthesis Klammern, Parenthese 78
participant Teilnehmer(in) 154
participate (v) teilnehmen 12
partition (v) aufteilen 57
part-time Teilzeit 140
pass on (v) weitergeben, -leiten 22
pass over (v) übergehen 63
pass through (v) passieren, durchlaufen 29
paste (v) einfügen 74
path Pfad 29
path analysis Analyse des Weges 87
pattern Muster 44
pay up front im Voraus zahlen 81
payload Payload, Ladung, „Sprengladung" 145
payment Bezahlung 22
payments Ausgaben, Zahlungen 161
payroll Gehaltsabrechnung 138
peak Höhepunkt 80
peddle (v) hausieren, (auf der Straße) verkaufen 145
peer-to-peer Peer-to-Peer-Netzwerk (mit gleichrangigen Arbeitsstationen) 94
pending anstehend 39
pen-like stiftähnlich 43
per annum jährlich 90
perceive (v) wahrnehmen 112
percentage Prozentsatz 80
perform (v) aus-, durchführen 29
performance Leistung 27
peripheral device Peripheriegerät, Anschlussgerät 9
permanent fest, dauerhaft 13
permission Erlaubnis 22
permit (v) erlauben 96
persist (v) anhalten 25
personal quality persönliche Eigenschaft, Soft Skills 164
personnel Personal, Personalwesen 8
perspective Perspektive 86
pertaining to betreffend 140
pharmaceutical Pharma- 155
PHD=Doctor of Philosophy Doktor/Doktorin der Philosophie 165
phenomenon Erscheinung 11
phishing Phishing (mit Ködern nach Passwörtern angeln) 112
phrase Formulierung 14
physiotherapist Krankengymnast(in) 140
pick up (v) aufnehmen, abholen 95
pie chart Tortendiagramm 38
piece back together (v) wieder zusammensetzen 64
pin Nadel 49
pit Vertiefung, Rille, Pit 51
pixel Pixel, Bildelement 36
placard Plakat 46
place the ball in their court den anderen die Schuld geben/den Schwarzen Peter zuspielen 26
plain einfach, schlicht 78
plan of action Schlachtplan 139
plaster (v) vollkleben 81
plastic Kunststoff 38
platform Plattform, Programm 36
platform independent plattformunabhängig 123
platinum Platin 38
platter Platte 57
plug in (v) einstecken 28
pocket Tasche 31
point out (v) hinweisen (auf) 25
poison Gift 38
politeness Höflichkeit 14
poll Umfrage 114
pool (n) (v) Zusammenlegung; zusammenlegen, gemeinsam benutzen, teilen 11
pop up (v) plötzlich erscheinen 65
populace Bevölkerung, Volk 155
population Bevölkerung 113

port Port, Anschluss 28
portable tragbar 28
portray (v) porträtieren, darstellen 156
positioning reference Positionsbezug 44
possess (v) besitzen 52
post (v) ausschreiben 170
posture Körperhaltung 157
poverty Armut 38
power cut-off Stromausfall 53
power supply Energieversorgung 27
powerful leistungsstark, -fähig 33
powerline Stromleitung 95
practically fast 80
practice (n) (v) Verfahren, Praktik, Praxis, Tätigkeit; üben 14
prearranged vorbestimmt 141
prearrangement Vorausbestimmung 100
precautions Vorsichtsmaßnahmen 113
precision Genauigkeit 51
precision equipment Feinmesszeug 46
predecessor Vorgänger 62
predefine (v) vordefinieren 124
predict (v) vorhersagen 70
predominant vorherrschend 49
prefer (v) bevorzugen 45
preferred customer bevorzugter Kunde/ bevorzugte Kundin 87
prefix Vorsilbe 34
preliminary vorläufig 158
prepare (v) vorbereiten 15
preposition Verhältniswort, Präposition 41
prerequisite Voraussetzung 87
present (v) zeigen 80
present perfect Perfekt 118
preserve (v) bewahren 117
press (v) drücken 41
pretend vorgeben 162
prevalent verbreitet 112
prevent (v) verhindern 53
preview Vorschau 43
previously vormals 12
pricing Preisgestaltung, Preiskalkulation 166
primary Grund- 37
principal Haupt- 93
principle Prinzip, Grundsatz 115
print (v) drucken 27
printout Ausdruck 29
priority Priorität, wichtigste Sache 49
prison labour Arbeit von Strafgefangenen 39
privacy Datenschutz, Privatsphäre 88
priviledge Privileg, Bevorzugung 137
probably wahrscheinlich 61
procedure Verfahrensweise 121
proceed (v) fortfahren 63
proceedings Vorgänge 118
process (n) (v) Vorgang; verarbeiten 10
professional ability berufliche Qualifikation 164
proficiency Kenntnisse 164
profiler Profilkorrektureinrichtung 64
profit sharing Gewinnbeteiligung 165
profitable einträglich 160
program counter Programmzähler, Befehlszähler 29
progress Fortschritt 31
progressive fortschrittlich 32
project (v) spritzen, schleudern, vorhersagen, hochrechnen 49
promise (v) versprechen 70
prompt Eingabeaufforderung 67
pronounce (v) aussprechen 36
pronounceable aussprechbar 157
pronunciation mark Betonungszeichen 36
propensity Hang, Neigung 88
proper richtig 22
proper noun Eigenname 82
property Besitz 66
proposal Vorschlag 139
propose (v) vorschlagen 39
proposed vorgeschlagen 140
proprietary (schemes) geschützte (Systeme) 98
prosper (v) gedeihen, Erfolg haben 12
protect (v) schützen 65
protection Schutz 136
protocol Protokol 92
prototyping Bau eines Prototyps, Muster 131
proud stolz 90
provide (v) zur Verfügung stellen 8
provided sofern, vorausgesetzt 101
proxy server Proxy-Server 148
publish (v) veröffentlichen 36
pull down (v) herunterziehen 69
pulse Impuls 99
punch up (v) beleben 131
punctuate (v) Satzzeichen setzen 23
punish (v) bestrafen 133
puny kümmerlich, winzig 55
purchasing Einkauf 18
purpose Zweck 8
push back (v) nach hinten verschieben 90
put off (v) vertrösten, verschieben 19
put on hold (v) zurückstellen 19

Q

quadrant Quadrant 80
quarterly quartalsweise, vierteljährlich 79
query Abfrage 84
queue Warteschlange 25
quiz (v) ausfragen 67
quotation Zitat 152
quotation mark Anführungszeichen 78
quote (v) anbieten 22

R

race Rennen 54
raise (v) aufziehen 149
raise money (v) Geld sammeln 12
ramble (v) schwafeln, vom Hundertsten ins Tausendste kommen 156
random zufällig, beliebig 147
random access wahlfreier Zugriff 10
range Spektrum 11
rank Rang, Rangstelle 107
rapport Rapport, Beziehung 157
rate (v) bewerten, einstufen 107
rating Beurteilung 131
rating system Bewertungsverfahren 107
razor sharp messerscharf 48
reach (n) (v) Reichweite; erreichen 23
react (v) reagieren 145
reading Lesen 154
ready (v) bereitstellen 30
real tatsächlich 35
realize (v) wahrnehmen, implementieren 158
real-time Echtzeit 27
reason Grund 8
reasonable begründet, sinnvoll 87
reasonably vernünftigerweise, durchaus 111
reasonably priced günstig, preiswert 140
reassemble (v) wieder zusammensetzen 95
reboot (v) neu starten 145
receipt Empfang 22
receipts Einnahmen, Einkünfte 161
receive (v) empfangen 8
receiver Hörer 95
recipient Empfänger(in) 23
recognition Erkennung 44
recognize (v) erkennen 109
recommend (v) empfehlen 67
reconstruct (v) wieder aufbauen 142
record (v) aufnehmen 142
recording Aufnahme 41
records Unterlagen 88
recover (v) wiederherstellen 65
recreation room Gemeinschaftsraum 140
recruit (v) anwerben, einstellen 12
rectify (v) berichtigen, korrigieren 127
recycling Wiederverwertung 38
redo (v) neu anfangen 76
reduce (v) reduzieren 51
reduction Reduzierung 140
redundancy Redundanz, Überflüssigkeit 84
re-engineer (v) umarbeiten 36
refer to (v) sich beziehen auf 10
referenced angesprochen, auf das verwiesen wird 142
references Quellenangaben, Referenzen, Empfehlungen 75
reflective layer reflektierende Schicht 51
refocus (v) neu fokussieren 154
reformulate (v) neu formulieren 147
refresh (v) auffrischen 106
refuse (n) (v) Abfall; ablehnen 12
regard (v) betrachten 113
regardless ungeachtet 177
region Bereich 57
register (v) anmelden, erfassen 29
registered nurse examinierte(r) Krankenpfleger(in) 140
regret (v) bedauern 72
regulate (v) regulieren 85
rehearse (v) proben 157
reimbursement Rückerstattung 22
reinforce (v) verstärken 11
reissue (v) neu ausgeben 147
reject (v) ablehnen 20
related verwandt 8
relationship Verhältnis 11
relay (v) leiten, weiterleiten 43
release (v) freigeben, veröffentlichen 70
relevance matching Übereinstimmung 109
reliability Zuverlässigkeit 132
reliable zuverlässig 32
relocate (v) neu zuordnen, umziehen 51
relocation counselor Berater(in) beim Standortwechsel 166
rely on (v) sich verlassen auf 51
remain (v) bleiben 52
remainder Rest 122
remaining übrig, restlich 39
remarkable bemerkenswert 131
remember (v) daran denken, nicht vergessen 142
remind of (v) erinnern an 20
reminder Erinnerung 65
remote entlegen 116
remote connectivity Fernverbindung 168
removable entfernbar, herausnehmbar 50
removal Entfernung, Entnahme 53

rename (v) neu bennen 42
renewed erneuert 80
renowned berühmt 53
rent Miete 78
repair (n) (v) Reparatur; reparieren, richten 49
repeat (v) wiederholen 15
repeatedly wiederholt 55
replace (v) ersetzen 22
replacement Ersatz 55
replication Abgleich, Kopie 84
report back (v) berichten 32
report to (v) unterstehen, unterstellt sein 21
represent (v) darstellen 35
representation Darstellung 36
reproduce (v) wiedergeben, reproduzieren 97
reputation Ruf 66
request (n) (v) Bitte, Anfrage; bitten 18
require (v) benötigen 24
requirement Anforderung 33
research and development Forschung und Entwicklung 21
resent (v) verübeln 132
reserve (v) reservieren, vorbehalten 104
reset (v) zurücksetzen 137
residential Wohn- 100
resize (v) in der Größe anpassen 67
resolution Auflösung, Beschluss 43
resolve (a problem) (v) (ein Problem) lösen 154
respective jeweilige(r, s) 80
respectively beziehungsweise 36
respondent Auskunftgebende(r) 112
response Antwort, Reaktion 14
responsibility Verantwortung 21
restrict (v) einschränken 66
result Ergebnis 30
résumé Lebenslauf 47
retail branch Einzelhandelsfiliale 164
retail price Verkaufs-, Ladenpreis 24
retailer Einzelhändler(in) 84
retrieve (v) abfragen 90
retro rückwirkend, rückwärtsgerichtet 145
retrospect Rückblick 132
retry (v) wieder versuchen 142
return (v) zurückkehren 30
reunification Wiedervereinigung 71
reveal (v) aufdecken 88
revenue Einnahmen 78
review Besprechung, Rezension 54
reviewer Rezensent(in) 54
revision Änderung 166
reward (v) belohnen 133
rewind (v) zurückspülen 97
re-writable wieder beschreibbar 50
rhetorical question rhetorische Frage 158
ribbon cable Bandkabel 27
right away sofort 67
right from the start von Anfang an 81
rights Rechte 137
rise Zuwachs 12
roadshow Roadshow, Informationsveranstaltung 113
rock bottom allerunterste(r,s) 55
rodent Nagetier 43
rogue Schurke/Schurkin 112
roll up one's sleeves die Ärmel hochkrempeln 66
rolling kontinuierlich 110
roll-out Vorstellung 151
root (v) (hier) anbinden 160
rotation Rotation, Umdrehung 53
rough plan grober Entwurf 130
roughly grob, ungefähr 57
round Runde 172
route (n) (v) Route, Weg; leiten 8
routine Routine, Gewohnheit 138
row Reihe 74
rudeness Unhöflichkeit 25
rule of thumb Faustregel 156
run counter to (v) im Widerspruch stehen zu 145
run into (v) zufällig treffen 18
run out of the home innerhalb der eigenen vier Wände geführt 46
running cost laufende Kosten 160
run-time error Laufzeitfehler 126
rushed unter Zeitdruck 17
ruthless rücksichtslos 90

S

safely wohlbehalten 113
salary Gehalt 78
sales force Verkaufsteam, Außendienst 46
sales representative Vertreter(in) 18
sample Muster 90
saving Einsparung 36
savings Ersparnisse 161
scalable in der Größe veränderbar 80
scale Rahmen 140
scam Betrug 112
scavenge (v) ergattern 39
scepticism Skepsis, Zweifel 140
schedule Terminplan 23
school leaving certificate Hauptschulabschluss 167
scientific wissenschaftlich 124
scope Umfang 88
scrap heap Müllhalde 39
screen Bildschirm 31
script Skriptsprache 123
scrolling Scrollen 76
seal (v) versiegeln 57
seamless nahtlos, makellos 51
search and replace (v) suchen und ersetzen 74
search engine Suchmaschine 103
search for (v) suchen nach 67
seasonal saisonabhängig 79
second (v) unterstützen 152
secondary modern school Hauptschule 167
second-guess (v) etw. im Nachhinein anzweifeln 132
secrecy Geheimhaltung 147
secretly insgeheim 114
section Abschnitt 74
sector Bereich 87
security Sicherheit 33
segment Segment, Abschnitt 80
segmentation fault Speicherzugriffsfehler 126
select (v) auswählen 33
selection Auswahl 24
self-assessment Selbsteinschätzung 169
self-confidence Selbstbewusstsein 160
self-starter hoch motivierte Person mit viel Eigeninitiative 164
semi-dark halbdunkel 82
senior Chef- 129
senior partner Seniorpartner 140
sensible vernünftig 113
sensitive empfindlich 50
sequence Ablauf 30
series Reihe, Serie 80
serve (v) dienen 120
service provider Dienstleistende(r), Internetdienstanbieter(in) 103
session Sitzung, Schulungseinheit 113
set Satz 45
set objectives (v) Ziele setzen 130
set theory Mengenlehre 31
set up (v) vereinbaren 14
settings Einstellungen 28
settle for (v) sich für etw. entscheiden 67
set-top box Digitalempfänger 97
several einige 25
severely schwerwiegend 25
sex Geschlecht 116
shade Abstufung 83
shake (v) erschüttern 25
sham Betrug 114
shape Form 92
share (n) (v) Aktie; gemeinsam benutzen, teilen 66
sharp(ly) steil 80
sheet Blatt 42
shipbreaking Schiffsverschrottung 38
shipping Versand 24
shortage Mangel 163
show of hands Handzeichen, Handheben 152
sign (v) unterschreiben 135
significance Signifikanz, Bedeutung 88
signpost (v) (hier) mit Signalwörtern versehen, „ausschildern" 157
similar ähnlich 32
simplify (v) vereinfachen 35
simply einfach 35
simulation Simulation 173
simultaneously simultan, gleichzeitig 43
site Aufstellungsort, Lage 104
sizeable beträchtlich, ziemlich groß 34
sketch Skizze 44
skill Fertigkeit 13
skim (v) überfliegen (Text) 39
skip (v) überspringen 63
sleep mode Schlafmodus 47
slide show Diavorführung 81
slightly etwas, leicht 159
slip in (v) gleiten lassen in 33
sloppiness Schlampigkeit 133
slot Schlitz, Einschnitt 27
slow down (v) verlangsamen 48
small case klein (Buchstaben) 147
smart card reader Chipkartenleser 97
smooth problemlos 71
snail mail "Schneckenpost" (normaler Postweg) 46
snoop (v) ausspähen 65
so-called so genannt 124
social worker Sozialarbeiter(in) 140
society Gesellschaft 11
socket Anschlussdose 27
soft skills Sozialkompetenz 136
softening besänftigend 20
sole einzig 55
solution Lösung 104
solve (v) lösen 107
solving faults Fehlerbehebung 165
sound (v) klingen 116
sound control Ton- und Musikeinstellung 68
sound wave Schallwelle 43
source Quelle 28
source of the trouble Problemursache 127

source program Quellenprogramm, Primärprogramm 124
space (n) (v) Platz, Abstand; platzieren 43
space hogging viel Platz einnehmend 64
spam unerwünschte E-Mails 103
sparingly sparsam 83
speak up (v) lauter sprechen 15
specific bestimmt, spezifisch 36
specifically besonders 116
specified time bestimmte Zeit 139
specify (v) spezifizieren 35
speculative spekulativ 101
speculator Spekulant(in) 161
speech Rede 156
speech therapist Logopäde/Logopädin 140
speed up (v) beschleunigen 11
spell (v) buchstabieren 15
spell checker Rechtschreibprüfprogramm 75
spend (v) verbringen, ausgeben 9
spidering Spidering (Internet-Suchmethode) 108
spin (v) drehen 57
spindle Drehspindel 57
spiral track spiralförmige Spur 51
split (v) trennen 74
spoofing Manipulation 148
spot (v) ausfindig machen, entdecken 64
spotlight Mittelpunkt des Interesses 89
spread Verbreitung 11
spreadsheet Tabellenkalkulation 8
Sputnik Scare Sputnikschock 104
spy out (v) ausspionieren 114
spyware Spyware, Spionage-Software 114
stack Stack, Stapelspeicher (speziell behandelter Speicherbereich zur Datenablage) 142
stack pointer Stapelzeiger 30
staff Belegschaft, Mitarbeiterstab 25
stage Stadium, Bühne, Stadium 67
stance Haltung 26
stand for (v) stehen für 46
stand-alone eigenständig, unabhängig 124
standardize (v) standardisieren, normieren 125
start off (v) anfangen 159
starting point Ausgangspunkt 106
start-up costs Gründungs-, Anlaufkosten 160
state Zustand 118
State Department Außenministerium 175
state of affairs Zustand 25
state of emergency Ausnahmezustand 133
statement Aussage 8
state-of-the-art auf dem neuesten Stand der Technik, hochmodern 33
steady job feste Stelle 135
steep learning curve großer Lernaufwand 66
step Schritt 29
stick to (v) einhalten, sich halten an 82
stipend Stipendium 175
stipulation Bedingung 66
stock Bestand 86
stock market index Aktienindex 159
stocks Aktien 78
store (v) speichern 10
straightforward geradlinig, einfach 83
stream Datenkette 64
streamline (v) optimieren 65
strictly speaking streng genommen 36
string Kette 35
stroke Schlaganfall 140
strong sense of starkes Gespür/Gefühl für etw. 164
structogram Struktogramm (grafische Darstelllung eines Programmablaufplans) 120
struggle (v) kämpfen, sich abmühen 146
stuff Sachen 133
stupidly dummerweise 146
style of addressing Anredestil 116
style sheet Formatvorlage, Musterblatt 131
sub-category Unterklasse, Untergruppe 73
subject Fach, Thema, Gegenstand 8
subject line Betreff 24
subject to abhängig von 50
submit to (v) sich unterziehen 81
sub-program Unterprogramm 30
subscriber Abonnent(in) 96
subsidiary Tochtergesellschaft 21
subtract (v) abziehen, subtrahieren 122
succeed (v) Erfolg haben 59
successful erfolgreich 32
succinctly kurz und bündig 133
suffer from (v) leiden, zu schaffen machen 163
suggestion Vorschlag 20
suitable passend 17
sum up (v) zusammenfassen, resümieren 154
summary Zusammenfassung 36
superfluous überflüssig 64
superior überdurchschnittlich 33
superlative Superlativ, 2. Steigerungsform 59
supervise (v) überwachen, kontrollieren 136
supplant (v) ersetzen 29
supplier Lieferant(in) 18
supply (v) liefern, bereitstellen 101
support Unterstützung 33
supposed vermutet, angenommen 147
surface Oberfläche 44
surfing the net im Internet surfen 104
surname Vorname 169
surround (v) umgeben 145
survey Umfrage 40
susceptible anfällig 148
suspect Verdächtige(r) 88
swap austauschen 115
swap shop Tauschladen, Tauschgeschäft 160
switch (n) (v) Switch, Schalter; umschalten 30
switch off (v) ausschalten 28
swot analysis Swot-Analyse (Analyse der Stärken und Schwächen) 160
synch (v) synchroniesieren, abstimmen 65
synchronize (v) synchronisieren 27
synonym Synonym, alternative Bezeichnung 75
syntax Satzbau 84
syntax error Syntaxfehler 126
sysadmin (system administrator) Systemverwalter(in) 136
system utility Hilfsprogramm 61

T

tab Tabulator 76
table of contents Inhaltsverzeichnis 75
tactic Taktik, Maßnahme 126
tag Tag 131
tailor (v) maßschneidern, auf etw./jmdn. zuschneiden 75
tailor-made maßgeschneidert 33
take a pass (v) darauf verzichten 55
take advantage of (v) sich etw. zu Nutze machen 96
take care of (v) sich kümmern um 89
take into consideration (v) in Betracht ziehen, überlegen 122
take notes (v) sich Notizen machen 139
take over (v) übernehmen 63
talk (hier) Rede, Vortrag 158
talking/speaking of da gerade die Rede von ... ist 20
target (v) abzielen, erreichen 36
task Aufgabe 40
tasteless geschmacklos 115
team spirit Teamgeist 164
team-oriented teamorientiert 164
technical institute Fachhochschule 167
technique Methode, Arbeitstechnik 108
tedious ermüdend 84
telephony Fernsprechtechnik 95
temp agency Zeitarbeitsfirma 140
template Template, Dokumentvorlage 131
temporarily vorübergehend 10
tend to (v) neigen zu 54
tense Zeitform, Tempus 13
term Begriff 10
terminate (v) beenden 63
terms of Bedingungen 22
text editor Texteditor (Programm zur Bearbeitung von Textdateien) 68
textured strukturiert 82
theft Diebstahl 70
thereby dabei 29
thesaurus Synonymwörterbuch 75
thick dick 51
third party Dritte(r) 114
thorough gründlich 137
thought Gedanke 32
threat Bedrohung 26
threaten (v) bedrohen 12
through durch 14
through trial and error durch Ausprobieren 133
throughput Datendurchlauflauf, Durchsatz(rate) 28
thrust Hauptrichtung, Schub 100
tight deadline enge Abgabefrist, enger Termin 177
tighter enger 51
timeless zeitlos 32
timeline Zeitachse 104
time-management Zeitplanung 116
time-saving zeitsparend 32
time-sharing Mehrbenutzerbetriebsart 104
tiny winzig 34
to date bis jetzt 177
to no avail erfolglos 26
token Token 93
toner cartridge Toner-Kartusche, Patrone 49
tool Werkzeug 10
toolbar Werkzeugleiste 54
toolbox Werkzeugkasten 124
topic Thema 26
top-of-the-line anspruchsvoll, auf dem neuesten Stand 48
topology Topologie 92
top-selling meistverkauft 131
touch on sth (v) etw. erwähnen 115
touch pad Cursor-Steuerungsfeld 44
touch screen Sensorbildschirm 97
town house Stadthaus 140
toxic giftig 39
toxicity Giftigkeit 38
trace (v) aufspüren 126

track pitch Spurabstand 51
trade Handel 11
trade credit Handelskredit 161
trade off sth for sth (v) abwägen, tauschen, verzichten auf 132
trade-off Kompromiss 133
traffic Verkehr 8
training scheme Ausbildungssystem 168
transceiver Sende-Empfangsgerät 93
transfer (n) (v) Übertragung; übertragen 11
transferable übertragbar 163
transform (v) verändern, wandeln 11
transient kurzlebig 115
transition Übergang 51
translate (v) übersetzen 19
transmission Sendung, Übertragung 100
transparency Folie, Transparenz 81
transparent transparent 148
trap Falle 109
travel through (v) durchbohren 52
tray Ablage 47
treat (v) behandeln 25
tricky kniffelig 127
tricky business schwierige Sache 14
trigger (v) auslösen 145
triplet Drilling 51
trouble Schwierigkeit 72
troubleshoot (v) Fehler suchen 21
true branch Ja-Zweig 121
trusted vertraut 148
tune (v) abstimmen, einstellen 141
tuner Empfänger 33
tuning Einstellung 51
turn out (v) sich erweisen 146
turnover (Gesamt)Umsatz 84
tutorial Anleitung, Selbstlerneinheit 131
twin doppelt 12
twist Drehung, Drall 100
two tone zweifarbig 33

U

U.S. Bureau of Labor Statistics Amt für Arbeitsmarktstatistik in den USA 163
ultimately letzlich, letzten Endes 11
unalterable unveränderbar 63
unambiguous eindeutig 35
unanimous einstimmig 152
unauthorized unbefugt, unerlaubt 32
unavailable nicht zur Verfügung stehend 142
uncertainty Ungewissheit, Unsicherheit 160
unconditional jump unbedingter Sprungbefehl 121
undergo (v) durchleben 166
underline (v) unterstreichen 78
underlying grundlegend, eigentlich 134
undermine (v) untergraben 12
underneath unterhalb 99
understandably verständlicherweise 145
undertake (v) unternehmen 26
undetectable nicht feststellbar 99
unexpectedly unerwartet 145
unfamiliar nicht vertraut 44
unfortunate bedauerlich, ungünstig 117
unfortunately leider 55
unify (v) vereinen 125
unimaginable unvorstellbar 107
unique einmalig, einzigartig 36
unit Einheit 29
university (polytechnic) Fachhochschule 167
unknown unbekannt 87
unless außer wenn 101
unnecessary unnötig 26
unpleasant unangenehm 171
unprecedented noch nie da gewesen, beispiellos 12
unreadable unleserlich 142
unsolicited unaufgefordert 103
unstoppable unaufhaltsam 116
unusable nicht verwendbar, unbrauchbar 63
unveil (v) enthüllen 70
up to bis zu 144
upcoming bevorstehend 65
update (v) erneuern, aktualisieren 36
upgrade (v) verbessern, aufrüsten 64
upgrowth Zuwachs 116
upkeep Wartung 49
upload (v) hochladen 130
upper obere(r, s) 45
upside down verkehrt herum 44
up-to-date modern, zeitgemäß 32
user-defined benutzerdefiniert 148
user-friendly benutzerfreundlich 32
utilities Nebenkosten 78
utility Nützlichkeit 117

V

vacation Urlaub 58
valid gültig 87
validity Gültigkeit 88
valuable wertvoll 32
value Wert 11
variable Variable 80
variety Vielfalt 8
various verschiedene 29
vary (v) variieren, sich unterscheiden 61
vast umfangreich 50
vastly gewaltig, erheblich 175
VAT = value added tax Mehrwertsteuer 47
vendor Verkäufer(in), Lieferant(in) 55
venture Unternehmen, Projekt 149
venture capital Risikokapital 161
venue Veranstaltungsort 71
versus verglichen mit 29
via mittels 10
victim Opfer, Betroffene(r) 140
view (n) (v) Ansicht; betrachten 12
vintage Jahrgang 132
virtual touch screen Sensorbildschirm 44
virtually fast 97
visible sichtbar 168
vital sehr wichtig, unerlässlich 113
vitiate (v) beeinträchtigen 132
vocabulary Wortschatz 90
vocational Berufs- 151
vocational training school Berufsschule 21
voice (n) (v) Stimme; äußern 44
voltage Spannung 165
volume Menge, Umfang, Lautstärke 39
volunteer Freiwillige(r) 12
vote (n) (v) Stimme, Wahl; wählen 152
vulnerability Schwachstelle 145
vulnerable angreifbar 112

W

wait (v) warten 29
walk you through (v) Schritt für Schritt durchführen 67
walk-on Statistenrolle 124
WAN = wide area network Weitverkehrsnetz 91
warehouse Lager 86
warranty Garantie 81
waste (v) verschwenden 145
wavelength Wellenlänge 51
weakness Schwäche 172
wealth Reichtum 33
web crawler Webcrawler, Suchmaschine 106
webmaster Webmaster (Verantwortliche(r) für eine Website) 107
weed out (v) aussondern 65
weigh wiegen 54
well matched gut abgestimmt 82
well-educated gebildet 175
well-founded fundiert 136
whether ob 13
whim Laune 149
wholesaler Großhändler(in) 155
wide scope großer Spielraum 164
wideband Breitband 98
widely weitgehend 35
widen (v) ausweiten 35
widespread weitverbreitet 36
width Breite 90
Wi-Fi drahtlose Übertragung 98
willingness Bereitschaft 160
winding staircase gewundene Treppe 140
wipe out (v) zerstören 145
wire Draht 35
wireless drahtlos 95
wiring Verkabelung 95
with regard to bezüglich 71
withstand (v) standhalten, sich widersetzen 52
wooden floor Parkettboden 140
word completion Wortvervollständigung 75
word wrap Zeilenumbruch 74
work ethic Arbeitsethos 160
work experience Arbeitserfahrung, Praxiserfahrung 168
work out (v) ausarbeiten 160
working knowledge of Grundkenntnisse in 12
workload Arbeitsbelastung 140
workplace safety Arbeitsplatzsicherheit 140
worm Wurm, Computervirus 104
worry Sorge 114
worth wert 26
worth the while die Mühe wert sein, sich lohnen 140
wrap sth up (v) etw. unter Dach und Fach bringen 154
wrist Handgelenk 43
wristband Armband 162

Y

yield (v) ergeben 39
yield the floor (v) das Wort (Rederecht) übergeben 152
young professional Berufseinsteiger(in) 175

Z

zealous eifrig 176
zero day sofortige Ausnutzung einer Internet-Sicherheitslücke 104

Abbildungsverzeichnis

Titel: Avenue Images GmbH(Comstock),Hamburg; STOCK4B(Stefanie Sudek),München; Getty Images(iconica),München; S.7: stocktogo.com(Yuri Arcurs),New York, NY • S.8: Fotolia LLC(Laurent Vella),New York; iStockphoto(Buretsu),Calgary, Alberta; • Avenue Images GmbH(CorbisRF),Hamburg; JupiterImages(photos.com),Tucson, AZ; • iStockphoto(Nick Schlax),Calgary, Alberta • S.10: JupiterImages,Tucson, AZ • S.11: stocktogo.com(Lance Bellers),New York, NY • S.13: JupiterImages,Tucson, AZ; Fotosearch RF(Banana Stock),Waukesha, WI • S.14: JupiterImages,Tucson, AZ • S.16: Avenue Images GmbH(Image Source),Hamburg • S.17: iS tockphoto(marmion),Calgary, Alberta • S.27: JupiterImages(RF/photos.com),Tucson, AZ • S.28: Klett-Archiv,Stuttgart • S.29: Fotolia LLC(RF /Svetlov),New York • S.31: Corbis(Bettmann),Düsseldorf • S.37: JupiterImages(RF/photos.com),Tucson, AZ • S.38: Fotolia LLC(RF/Bandmann),New York • S.42: TDK Electronics Europe GmbH,Ratingen; stocktogo.com(Feng Yu),New York, NY; • Fotolia LLC(RF /Van Deursen),New York; Getty Images RF(Photo Disc),München • S.43: iStockphoto(Jeffrey Schmieg),Calgary, Alberta; iStockphoto(Kenneth Cheung),Calgary, Alberta; iStockphoto(RF/webking),Calgary, Alberta; iStockphoto(Rafa Irusta),Calgary, Alberta; iStockphoto(Asian),Calgary, Alberta; • S.45: stocktogo.com(RF/Black Ink Designers, Corp),New York, NY • S.46: stocktogo.com(pixelman),New York, NY • S.47: iStockphoto(Donald Gruener),Calgary, Alberta; stocktogo.com(Benjamin Howell),New York, NY • S.48: Alamy Images RM(Kim Karpeles),Abingdon, Oxon • S.51: TDK Electronics Europe GmbH,Ratingen; TDK Electronics Europe GmbH,Ratingen • S.52: Wikimedia Foundation Inc.,St. Petersburg FL • S.53: iStockphoto(RF),Calgary, Alberta; MEV,Augsburg; iStockphoto(Clayton Hansen),Calgary, Alberta • S.55: JupiterImages(RF/Photos.com),Tucson, AZ • S.56: iStockphoto(RF/Sascha Reiterer),Calgary, Alberta • S.57: stocktogo.com(Zhiltsov Alexandr),New York, NY • S.60: AP(PAUL SAKUMA),Frankfurt • S.61: JupiterImages,Tucson, AZ • S.65: Internet/Screenshot(http: //migosoftware.com/),xxx; • Internet/ Screenshot(http: //migosoftware.com/),xxx; • Internet/Screenshot(http: //www.tuneup.de),xxx • S.66: Linux; Wikimedia Foundation Inc.,St. Petersburg FL • S.68: Klett-Archiv,Stuttgart • S.70: Getty Images(Stringer/AFP),München • S.73: Avenue Images GmbH,Hamburg • S.74: Alamy Images RF(RF),Abingdon, Oxon • S.77: Avenue Images GmbH(Stock4B),Hamburg • S.80: Symantec; iStockphoto(RF/Izabela Habur),Calgary, Alberta; • JupiterImages(RF/Photos.com),Tucson, AZ • S.82: iStockphoto(RF/ vm),Calgary, Alberta • S.87: Picture-Alliance(Thomas Lehmann),Frankfurt • S.91: iStockphoto(scot spencer),Calgary, Alberta • S.97: Fotosearch RF(Photodisc),Waukesha, WI • S.98: iStockphoto(Ed Hidden),Calgary, Alberta • S.103: JupiterImages,Tucson, AZ • S.106: Comet Photoshopping(L. Chapchal),Zürich; JupiterImages,Tucson, AZ • S.110: Internet/Screenshot,xxx • S.112: iStockphoto(doodlemachine),Calgary, Alberta • S.114: Fotolia LLC(Kerry Werry),New York • S.116: JupiterImages,Tucson, AZ • S.119: iStockphoto(Krzysztof Zmij),Calgary, Alberta • S.124: JupiterImages,Tucson, AZ • S.127: JupiterImages,Tucson, AZ • S.129: iStockphoto(Steven Miric),Calgary, Alberta • S.132: FOCUS(xxpool/Louis Psihoyos),Hamburg • S.136: iStockphoto(Tyler Stalman),Calgary, Alberta • S.140: iStockphoto(Jeffrey Smith),Calgary, Alberta; iStockphoto(Justin Horrocks),Calgary, Alberta; iStockphoto(Nathan Maxfield),Calgary, Alberta • S.142: JupiterImages,Tucson, AZ • S.144: iStockphoto(Sami Suni),Calgary, Alberta • S.147: stocktogo.com(Alexander Fediachov),New York, NY • S.148: stocktogo.com(Hans-Joachim Roy),New York, NY • S.150: JupiterImages,Tucson, AZ • S.152: iStockphoto(aldra),Calgary, Alberta • S.153: iStockphoto(Diane Diederich),Calgary, Alberta • S.155: iStockphoto(lijlexmom),Calgary, Alberta • S.156: iStockphoto(vm),Calgary, Alberta • S.157: iStockphoto(Tom Gufler),Calgary, Alberta • S.160: JupiterImages,Tucson, AZ • S.163: iStockphoto(Joris van Caspel),Calgary, Alberta; BigStockPhoto. com(kiankhoon),Davis, CA; Fotolia LLC(Laurent Vella),New York; • Corbis(Najlah Feanny),Düsseldorf • S.167: Getty Images RF(Photodisc),München; Comstock,Luxemburg • S.169: Nationale Agentur Bildung für Europ,Bonn • S.170: JupiterImages(photos. com),Tucson, AZ • S.171: JupiterImages,Tucson, AZ • S.174: iStockphoto(Lucas Cornwell),Calgary, Alberta; iStockphoto(Pascal Genest),Calgary, Alberta; Fotolia LLC(Laurent Vella),New York; Hans-Werner Thunig,Winterbach; Avenue Images GmbH(StockDisc),Hamburg • S.175: Bananastock RF,Watlington/Oxon